BIRDS
of
PREY

BIRDS
of
PREY

BOEING VS. AIRBUS:
A BATTLE FOR THE SKIES

By Matthew Lynn

Four Walls Eight Windows
New York

© 1995, 1997 Matthew Lynn

Published in the United States by:
Four Walls Eight Windows
39 West 14th Street, room 503
New York, N.Y. 10011

A revised edition of "Birds of Prey," first published in 1995 by Reed
International Books Ltd., London.

First printing April 1997.

Library of Congress Cataloging-in-Publication Data:
Birds of prey: Boeing vs. Airbus: A Battle for the Skies/by Matthew Lynn.
— Rev. ed.
p.   cm.
ISBN 1-56858-086-X
1. Boeing Company. 2. Airbus Industrie. 3. Aircraft industry—United States. 4.
Aircraft industry—France. 5. Competition, International. I. Title.
HD9711.U63B634 1997
338.8'872913334349'0973—dc21
96-47592
CIP

 10 9 8 7 6 5 4 3 2 1

Text design by Acme Art, Inc.
Printed in the United States

A day will come when you, France; you Russia; you Italy; you Britain; and you Germany — all of you, all nations of the Continent will merge tightly, without losing your remarkable originality. . . . A day will come when markets, open to trade, and minds, open to ideas, will become the sole battlefields.

—Victor Hugo

More than any other sphere of activity, aerospace is a test of strength between states, in which each participant deploys his technical and political forces.

—Report of the French Parliament, 1977

INTRODUCTION

A WAR IN THE
GULF

If a single thought was uppermost in the mind of President Clinton as he put a phone call through from the Oval Office on the afternoon of August 17, 1993, it was this: time for some payback. Still a relative novice, only seven months into his presidency, Clinton had campaigned on a ticket of restoring American living standards after a decade during which the U.S. economy had suffered from the harshness of international competition. Around him were theorists and advisers who believed that it was time to start turning the military and political might of the United States into harder coinage: money, trade, jobs. Now was the moment to make theory reality.

Clinton was put through to King Faud of Saudi Arabia. The two men could not have had more different origins: Clinton came from a poor family and had risen to the leadership of the most powerful Western country; Faud was the secretive hereditary monarch of one of the world's most repressive and autocratic regimes. But Clinton made the call eagerly; there was business to be done, money to be made and an economy to be protected.

Clinton thanked Faud for his recent letter, a response from the Saudi king to an earlier communication from Clinton. The President had been made aware that the national Saudi Arabian airline, Saudia, was in the market for some new planes, thirty new planes to be precise, worth some $6 billion. Clinton had wanted Faud to know that he would be grateful if the order were placed with the two major American aerospace companies, Boeing and McDonnell Douglas. Faud had noted Clinton's views, thanked him for his advice, and said that he would bear it in mind. That was an encouraging start for the White House, but not enough; they wanted that $6 billion wrapped up and in the bag. After all, the Saudis owed them at least a simple airplane order: the U.S. had mobilized its military might in 1990 to evict the Iraqis from Kuwait, an operation designed to protect Saudi Arabia and its oilfields at least as much as to liberate the Kuwaitis. Favors were owed, payback.

Clinton came away from the phone call with the impression that the order was clinched, that Boeing and McDonnell Douglas would share the $6 billion between them. But across the Atlantic — in Toulouse, Paris, Brussels, Berlin and London — there were other ideas and other ambitions. So confident was Clinton of success that the story of the commercial triumph and the President's role were carefully leaked. Two days after the phone conversation, Senator Patty Murray popped up on the national news to declare that the order was secure for the Americans, and that Clinton had secured it. The senator may indeed have believed this, but in Europe the declaration was simply a signal that the battle for the Saudia order had begun, that the Americans were prepared to play seriously rough, and that the European retaliation would have to be coordinated, massive and deadly.

For the Airbus consortium, the grouping of European manufacturers which had risen like a phoenix from the debris of the continent's individual domestic industries, the Gulf was almost home territory. Over nearly a quarter of a century during which the consortium had mounted its challenge to the traditional dominance of the aerospace industry by American manufacturers, they had scored some of their greatest successes in that region. They looked at it as part of their territory, and believed that, all things being equal, the order would go to them. This time, however, all things were not equal. The Americans were hauling out their biggest guns.

In many instances, an aircraft sales campaign will be left to the professionals. Both Airbus and Boeing maintain teams of salesmen, and every major manufacturer has one salesperson dedicated to a specific account. Building contacts, keeping track of fleet requirements and monitoring shifts of executive power within an airline take years of work, all preparation for the once or twice in a decade when the airline is ready to place a major order. Then every fact, however small, about the operational requirements of the airline is scrutinized and twisted to suit the planes offered. Mock-ups of interiors and seating designs are put on show and senior executives ingratiate themselves with the man identified as the key decision-maker.

But all that is just preliminary background work; the stakes for major orders are too high for commercial rules to apply. With only a hundred or so significant customers around the world, each order is too important to be left to the dry calculations of dollars-per-seatmile used by the mathematicians of the trade. After the presentations have been made, and the sums done, aircraft sales campaigns move into the darker territory of geo-industrial politics, a vicious mercantile struggle between economic power blocs jousting for a share of the world's riches.

As soon as Senator Murray spoke, the Saudia order slipped its moorings; the economic and commercial mechanisms of competition were dumped, replaced by a primitive struggle in which all the tactics, devices and deceptions of statecraft would be wheeled out. Over the next six months, the scale and scope of the war between Boeing and Airbus became dangerously clear. And the subterranean theme of that war — its role as a proxy contest for the economic war between Europe and the United States — would be exposed in the dessert.

From the White House, the action moved to the Elysée Palace in Paris, via the headquarters of Airbus Industrie in Toulouse. A gleaming white, low-slung, modernist building on the tarmac of Toulouse airport, the Airbus headquarters is a center of aeronautical intrigue. Picking up on the involvement of President Clinton in the campaign, the Airbus team, led by Jean Pierson, rumbustious and combative, lost little time in flying their heavyweights into the Gulf. Airbus had always been a skilful player of the strings connecting industry and government; this time it would have to tune its instruments particularly well.

Airbus is closest to the French government; its headquarters is in France, the planes are assembled in France, and the French — or so they like to claim — were the driving force in creating the consortium. For their salesmen, the Elysée is always the first port of call.

The active intervention by Clinton in the aircraft sale was reinforced by the U.S. Transportation Secretary, Frederico Peña. The overt pitch by Clinton was that his country had saved the Saudis from Saddam, but additional sweeteners were available. Peña arrived in Saudi Arabia on September 30. It was the first time a U.S. Department of Transport official had visited the country — the Gulf is not usually a high priority for the department — and the apparent reason for his trip was to negotiate a new bilateral air agreement between the two countries. Over two days he met Prince Sultan, Saudi Minister of Defense and Aviation, and Husayn Ibrahim Mansouri, Minister of Communications. Their gatherings were fruitful: by the end of the visit, Peña had signed the first civil aviation accord between the U.S. and Saudi Arabia, allowing Saudia to fly to New York, Washington and Florida, while American airlines could fly to three destinations in Saudi Arabia. Though evenly balanced, it was not much of a breakthrough for the American airlines, which had so far not scheduled any direct flights into the kingdom.

The real purpose of Peña's visit emerged on the final day. Peña met with King Faud for two and a half hours, and stressed once again the importance of buying planes from Boeing and McDonnell Douglas. "The meeting was productive and delightful," Peña said as he emerged from the palace, "and we will simply wait until the Kingdom makes an official decision. All I can tell you formally is that the Kingdom of Saudi Arabia will make its decision when it decides it is appropriate."

The King had been perfectly polite, but had made it clear that the $6 billion would be spent by his airline, and that he did not appreciate having its purchasing intentions announced by American senators. Faud was irritated by the intense pressure from Clinton; he still had to hear the European offer and was experienced enough to know when he had a killing hand to play. Nothing would be decided until every last concession had been wrung out of the two contenders.

If Faud was irritated, the Airbus staffers in Toulouse were smoldering with rage. Jean Pierson wrote to Sir Leon Brittan, Trade Commissioner for the European Union, complaining about the pressure the U.S. was putting on Saudi Arabia. The letter was not really necessary; as soon as Airbus salesmen were worried about the situation in the desert, Brussels would have been aware of their concerns, but it was a useful device to bring the EU into the game. Sir Leon's office quickly announced that it was investigating the affair and, by the following week, aviation officials from Brussels were flying to Washington to visit the U.S. Department of Transportation. Their purpose, officially, was to "obtain clarification" of Peña's role. The subtext was rather different. Behind-the-scenes arm-twisting should be a delicate transaction; throwing daylight on to the process can destabilize negotiations, an outcome which would suit the Europeans perfectly.

Peña, meanwhile, had been taken aback by the counter-measures Airbus deployed. At a news conference at the end of his tour of the Gulf, he said the Airbus allegations of high-pressure sales tactics left him bewildered and confused. "I frankly do not understand the allegations," he blustered. "I have not read them specifically. But I have observed with some interest the tremendous involvement of European leaders, which are far in excess, by significant numbers, of my lonely presence in the Middle East."

If Peña was charging the Europeans with hypocrisy, the accusation was accurate. It was also ineffective. European officials and industrialists are hard to embarrass, and charges of organized hypocrisy create no blushes; if anything, they are mildly flattered. Only a week after EU officials had flown to Washington to complain about U.S. pressure, François Mitterrand had flown into Saudi Arabia for his own meeting with King Faud. Of all the Airbus salesmen, Mitterrand was the most experienced and certainly the most cunning. The French President was an old hand at making airplane pitches, and was believed to know quite well the details of the models, their respective prices, their optional extras and so on. His patter was well-honed: a mixture of technological pride and political parleying — basic skills to a French politician.

Mitterrand met King Faud in Riyadh on October 14, and they were joined by the Aviation Minister Prince Sultan. Mitterrand had some strong cards to play. This was the first summit between the two leaders since the Gulf War, and the French President reminded Faud of the role French troops had played in liberating Kuwait. But Mitterrand was there to tempt as well as to remind, talking to the King about two of his favorite subjects: the defence of his realm and the promotion of the Palestinian cause. As well as the Saudia order, the two talked about equipping the Saudi Navy with a new range of French-made missiles, and Mitterrand briefed Faud on EU plans to help the Palestinians establish self-rule in the Israeli-occupied West Bank and Gaza Strip. The French President knew what he was doing in raising the Palestinian issue; America has a longstanding and close relationship with Israel, and Clinton was unlikely to offer help for the Palestinians in exchange for the purchase of a few Boeing jets. Mitterrand had no such constraints, and he pushed the issue for all it was worth.

Mitterrand slipped out of Riyadh quietly; there were no press conferences and no public pronouncements that the Europeans had won the game. Behind the scenes, however, it was known that he had done his job, and the order, which had seemed won for the Americans, was now up for grabs again. Faud, having listened attentively to Mitterrand, was to be subjected to a cluster of European statesmen crowding the tarmac at Riyadh airport. On November 2, Klaus Kinkel, the German Vice-Chancellor and Foreign Affairs Minister, flew in for a rare meeting with King Faud. He made a long pitch for Saudia to buy Airbus planes, and he too talked about the plight of the Palestinians, an issue which suddenly had high priority among European ministers. He briefed the King on European Union plans, rapidly taking shape, for political and economic help for the Palestinians. He also offered to mediate an easing of tension between Saudi Arabia and Iran, and promised that the Iranians would get no help from Germany in completing two nuclear reactors they were building. But it was planes, not regional Arab rivalries, that were uppermost in his mind: "We very much want them to buy Airbus," he told journalists as he left.

Only a week later the French were back. This time it was the French Industry Minister, Gerard Longuet, who found time to stop off on his way to an air show in the United Arab Emirates. After meeting with Saudi ministers, he announced that he was hopeful of securing for Europe at least a slice of the order; he also revealed that Chancellor Helmut Kohl of Germany and Prime Minister Major of Britain had been in touch with King Faud to add their own thoughts on the airline's fleet requirements. Longuet was followed by a man with whom Faud might have had something in common: a hereditary royal. On a tour of the Gulf, Prince Charles dropped in for a chat with the King. "We European partners are working together," said Longuet. "The latest effort is Prince Charles. He is on our side."

Back in Washington, the Clinton team working with Boeing and McDonnell Douglas were starting to sweat. Mitterrand's involvement they had expected and Kohl was always likely to intervene, but Prince Charles was a surprise. Clinton had publicly proclaimed the order won for the Americans; to lose it now would not be just the loss of $6 billion in exports; it would be a significant loss of political face.

Sensing the possibility of an embarrassing political reversal, Clinton decided on a lower personal profile, but stepped up the pressure by his cabinet. Early in January, Ron Brown, Commerce Secretary, joined the troop descending on the Gulf; he too made a pitch for the order. Hard on his heels, the German Economics Minister flew in, clutching a set of sales brochures. Then, on January 9, the French Prime Minister, Edouard Balladur, made a surprise visit to the desert, accompanied by the Defence Minister, François Leotard, and the Foreign Affairs Minister, Alain Juppé. This was a top-level delegation, and an indication of how hard Airbus was pushing to secure the order. After meeting with King Faud, Balladur came away with arms deals worth about $2 billion, but on the aircraft order there was silence. As he left Saudi Arabia all Balladur said was that he was hopeful.

In the background, the Americans had come up with a counter to the Palestinian card: Bosnia. The Saudis see themselves as defenders of the Muslim faith, and the suffering of the Bosnian Muslims in the civil war had attracted worldwide attention. Clinton advocated a firm Western policy to stop the war in Bosnia; the European Union had wrung its hands and done very little. In the Middle East, it seemed that the Europeans were doing nothing for the Muslims because of their religion; had they been Christians, the argument went, Britain, France and Germany would have intervened long since. Amid mounting Middle East hostility to the European position the Americans saw a chance to clinch the Saudia order.

Airbus saw its chances sliding away. Late in February, Jurgen Schrempp, chairman of DASA, the Mercedes-Benz subsidiary which is the German partner in the Airbus consortium, wrote to Helmut Kohl asking for more help in securing the order. "Only your personal intervention could bring at least a partial change [in their plans]," he wrote, warning that 1300 jobs at the company would have to go if the order were lost. In addition, Airbus officials knew that Boeing and McDonnell Douglas salesmen had been invited to Saudia Arabia on March 20, to begin discussing which of the company's models would be included in the order.

Kohl stayed in Germany, but Balladur made a last effort to swing the order to Airbus, arriving in Saudi Arabia on March 9. At a meeting with

Crown Prince Abdullah, the French premier was given a taste of Saudi anger over events in Bosnia. Abdullah told Balladur that the Europeans would not have a slice of the order so long as they refused to take military action against the Bosnian Serbs. "Europe's behavior is shameful," the Prince declared. Balladur was not able to give any assurances about intervention, and on the way back to Paris he told his aides that the meeting had gone badly. It had been a last throw of the dice; the order was lost.

By the end of March, Boeing and McDonnell Douglas knew that the order was theirs for the taking; for Boeing it was a victory in its bitter campaign against Airbus, for McDonnell Douglas it was a lifeline. Both knew they had the White House to thank for organizing the victory. And having won the order, Clinton was insistent that everyone knew of the role his administration had played. Vice President Al Gore was dispatched to make sure the two airframe manufacturers knew where the credit should go, and the order was announced from the White House, rather than in Seattle or Long Beach, California. "We have finally broken out of the shackles that have caused several decades' debate about the role of government," said Ron Brown at the signing ceremony. "Our international competitors figured out that role a long time ago, and that's why they are doing much better than they should be doing in international competition." Clinton, quick to claim personal credit, described the order as "a gold medal victory for American businesses and workers," which was some way from the truth. It was a victory for American power and influence; American soldiers, rather than workers, could claim the credit. This was confirmed by the Saudis. "It is your destiny to be the only superpower in the world," said Prince Bandar bin Sultan, a nephew of King Faud, and his ambassador in Washington at the signing ceremony, "You are truly the only game in town."

In Europe there was bitterness over the way the battle had gone. "When does an airline say which manufacturers it is buying from before it has even chosen the aircraft it wants?" said Jean Pierson afterwards. "It is extraordinary." It had indeed been a bizarre and unlikely saga, involving many of the world's most powerful men in an effort to sell thirty airplanes to a tiny state. But it was also an indication of the importance politicians place on the aerospace industry, and of the extent to which it symbolizes the economic struggle between the two continents.

It was also a symbol of the historical antagonisms between the two sides. Over the past forty years the European and American industries have been involved in an escalating commercial race for global dominance; a race in which the Americans have most often held the lead, but where the Europeans have made significant gains in the last few laps. If this was a game, it was a grudge match There was a history to the battle over the Saudia order which made its outcome intensely personal for both sides.

1

THE TRAGEDY OF
AN ENTERPRISE

The British Overseas Airways Corporation Comet jetliner soared off the runway at Rome airport at precisely 10:30 a.m. local time on January 10, 1954. For the twenty-nine passengers and six crew on board the sleek, modern plane, this was the last leg of a long and exhausting trip. The plane and its passengers had started their journey in Singapore; they had touched down at Bangkok, Rangoon, Karachi, Bahrain and Beirut. Now, taking off from Rome, they were within a couple of hours' flying time of Britain and home.

It looked set to be an easy flight. Only two years in service, and less than a decade since the first military jets had flown, the De Havilland Comet was one of the technological wonders of an age reared on science fiction stories and easily impressed by feats of futuristic gadgetry. Slicing through the air at over five hundred miles an hour, its passengers barely disturbed by vibration, it seemed to be a machine that could make travel between continents comfortable and fast; faster anyway than the bumpy propeller-driven planes which had taken over a week to traverse Asia and Europe, and its speed was as lightning compared with the cruise ships which had ferried an earlier generation to and from the Far East.

The plane was not quite full; its maximum capacity was thirty-six, but a one-way ticket from Singapore to London cost around £200, an expensive luxury for the time. The twenty-nine passengers were mostly English: colonial officials and commercial executives. There was also Chester Wilmot, a well-known war correspondent, who had joined the plane in Rangoon; ten were English children on their way home to boarding school after visiting their parents in the East. There were also two Americans, three from Bahrain, and a Syrian. Another American, Victor Pahlen, a film producer, had cancelled his ticket from Rome after hearing that the plane had been delayed in Beirut.

Hitting cruising altitude, Captain Gibson turned the plane slightly westwards, pointing it in the direction of Elba on a direct course for London. Gibson, at thirty-one, was an experienced pilot, and this was no more than a milk run; he had flown more than 1000 hours with the RAF, collecting a Distinguished Flying Cross along the way, and had chalked up more than 4000 hours of commercial flying with BOAC.

At 10:50, in accordance with standard flight procedure, Gibson radioed back to home a regular report of course and position. The plane was above the town of Orbetello, he told ground control, and he was heading out over the Ligurian Sea. There was nothing to report. Those were the last words anyone heard from him.

Thirty thousand feet below, in the waters between the islands of Monte Cristo and Elba, Giovanni di Marco, a local fisherman, was spinning out his nets. A rough wind was cutting up the waves, and the cold January weather made it an uncomfortable day to be on the water. He heard a low rumbling roar from somewhere above the clouds. Jet engines were an unfamiliar noise then, and disturbing enough to make an Italian fisherman look up from his net, his eyes straining into the sky.

The first those aboard knew of impending disaster was a shudder, a wrenching of the metal rippling through the plane. The cabin began to buckle and rip, and air rushed out of its body. Then it burst, exploding like a balloon, fragmenting into shards, thousands upon thousands of ripped steel strands tumbling to the ground.

Di Marco was the only person to hear it. He could see nothing, but the sky echoed with the sound of explosions, three in all, cracking through the clouds one after the other. He scanned the sky, but could still see nothing. There was silence. The explosions came and went, replaced by the sound of the waves lapping against his boat. Then, several miles away, he saw a flash of silver descending through the clouds. Smoke, black and thick, was trailing behind it. Within seconds it had hit the sea, sending up a great wall of water and foam.

The fisherman reeled in his nets and steered his boat towards the site of the crash. It took half an hour to get there, and by the time he arrived the wall had subsided and the foam had vanished. The waters were still, though the wind whipped cruelly across his small boat. But the scene before him was crueller: debris was everywhere, and so were bodies, floating bloody and lifeless in the sea. "We began to pick them up," recalled di Marco. "What else could we do?"

He fished some of the bodies from the sea, searching for survivors. But it was hopeless. Nobody could have survived the explosion and the fall. The fisherman rescued some of the floating dead, using his nets to draw them in, along with a mailbag, some coats, a handbag and two lifejackets, and sailed back to Elba. The alarm was raised. That night Italian warships, their searchlights beaming out on the rough seas, looked for more bodies. No survivors were expected.

In the town of Porto Azzurro, a small fishing village on Elba about ten miles from where the plane had crashed, the bodies were taken ashore: seven men, five women and three children were reclaimed from the sea that night. They were laid out on planks, and the local priest administered benediction. They were then taken to the local cemetery chapel, transformed into a makeshift mortuary. Candles were lit, and local children laid flowers.

Their mourning was a natural and spontaneous reaction to a disaster within a few miles of their homes. But, alongside the bodies in the cemetery chapel, there were other losses to tally, and other casualties to grieve. On that fateful morning 30,000 feet above the Ligurian Sea more than the hull of an aircraft had been broken. As the wreckage of the Comet crashed to the ground so did the ambitions of an industry which, until that moment, had seemed ready to challenge the world.

The Comet was a pivotal aircraft in the story of the twentieth-century aerospace industry; the plane upon which everything hinged. It flew on the cusp of two historical eras. Behind it, vaporized in its jetstream, was an era of pioneers: men who worked out how to build flying machines from pictures in magazines, who experimented with their machines, who broke rules and boundaries, and who, in the space of a few short decades, turned contraptions of wire and paper into machines capable of redrawing the ancient geography of seaways and continents. Ahead of it lay the era of giant, monolithic corporations, twinned and bedded with the apparatus of the state, driving the wheels of commerce but also the wheels of conflict; an era of geo-industrial politics.

Between them the Comet had its nose in one era, its tail in another. Its story, and that of the man who built it, is rich with resonance: a story which captures the erratic progress of European capitalism in the first half of the twentieth century and, through its feuds and jealousies, hopes and failures, set the pattern for everything that was to come afterwards.

Its story begins in Crux Easton, a village in Hampshire, in the summer of 1910, when, late one evening, Geoffrey De Havilland wheeled a plane out of his workshop and set it along the strip of cut grass that formed a makeshift runway. De Havilland had never flown before — he had tried once, but the plane crashed and broke up without rising even a few inches from the ground. Nor, apart from one brief glimpse, had he witnessed any flights: he had seen an airman try for a £10,000 prize offered by the *Daily Mail* for the first flight from London to Manchester. His knowledge of aeronautics was restricted to pictures of the Wright Brothers' machines that filled the pages of popular magazines.

His ignorance was perhaps a blessing. The machine he wheeled out was not a contraption to inspire confidence. To the modern eye it looks like a three-wheeled bicycle, with two canvas wings precariously strapped to the crossbar, and an engine and propeller stuck on the back. De Havilland sat himself in the makeshift seat, trying out a few practice runs. He taxied across the field, testing the rudders of the plane's wings. As he rode, he felt a lightness caused by the air rushing beneath the wing, lifting it. Eventually he pulled up next to his colleague, Frank Hearle. This time, De Havilland suggested, Frank should lie down on the grass beside the plane to see if he could discern daylight between the wheels and the ground. Frank lay down. De Havilland turned the plane and taxied up a slight slope from the workshop to the back of the field. Turning the machine again, he opened the throttle, and brought it down the hill, accelerating towards the thirty miles an hour that was its maximum speed. Holding firmly to the rudder, he passed his prostrate partner, unaware whether he had flown or not. He brought the plane to a halt and switched off the ignition. Frank was waving his arms. "You were several inches off the ground for about twenty yards," he reported.

Those few inches marked the debut of Geoffrey (later Sir Geoffrey) De Havilland's flying career. They also marked the beginning of the European aerospace industry, insofar as any modern Airbus aircraft can trace a direct lineage back to that three-wheeled flying tricycle. Between then and now, naturally, there are many twists and turns. Even before De Havilland flew, his story had taken a few curves. The aerospace industry, after all, though it grew into one of competing monoliths, drawn eventually towards monopoly, was the creation of cranks and dreamers.

The first flight of a heavier-than-air machine had been made by Wilbur and Orville Wright at Kitty Hawk, North Carolina, on December 17, 1903. Wilbur had flown the machine across the sand dunes for 120 feet, and brought it safely down to land. The story of the Wright Brothers is too well known to need replaying here, except for the observation that Wilbur and Orville never made any money worth talking about from their invention. As well as discovering the principles of heavier-than-air flight, the brothers found that the aerospace business is a tough way to make a living. It was not that they were uninterested in the wages of their ingenuity; they fought long and bitter patent battles through the U.S. courts to collect royalties from their many imitators, but were ultimately unsuccessful. Wilbur died in 1912, and in 1915 Orville sold The Wright Company, the most famous name in aviation, for a little over $1 million in cash to a group of Wall Street investors led by the mining tycoon, William Boyce Thompson. Thompson renamed the company Wright-Martin, and, during a feeding frenzy among investors hungry to cash in on First World War rearmament, floated the business amid angry allegations of price rigging and insider trading. For this illustrious invention to wind up the tool of a group of market manipulators was an ignominious end, but a useful early lesson that aeronautical pioneering is not always rewarded with commercial success.

The world the Wright Brothers had spawned was one of eager entrepreneurship. Few doubted that flying machines would be a profitable business. Men had dreamed about flying for so long, the demand for the machines would surely be limitless. Creating an aerospace business was an irresistible, though often insurmountable, challenge to entrepreneurs around the world.

De Havilland was only one of the young men whose imaginations were caught by the new science, but he was to be one of the more successful. He was born on July 27, 1882, in High Wycombe, the second son of an eccentric parson. His father, Charles De Havilland, was Oxford educated, and whiled away his life gardening and working on a great book to change the course of history; upon his death, it was found to consist of nothing more than a few notes and several pages about geographical mistakes in the Bible. However, the family had talent to offset eccentricity in its gene pool; as well as his son, whose career we will follow, Charles De Havilland was uncle to Joan Fontaine and Olivia De Havilland, both able film actresses.

There was little money in the large family of three sons and two daughters. What little there was came from Geoffrey's maternal grandfather, Jason Saunders. If Geoffrey inherited his romantic ambition from the De Havillands, what business sense and diligence he possessed came from his mother's side. Jason Saunders was typical of the socially mobile Victorian businessman. He came from a poor farming family in Oxfordshire but built up a successful transport, warehousing and removal business, and became Liberal Mayor of Oxford. It was he who financed his grandson's early ambitions.

Throughout his boyhood, Geoffrey De Havilland was fascinated by mechanical objects, and despite the assumption that he would follow his father into the church, he went to an engineering school at Crystal Palace in London. After a three-year course he joined Williams and Robinson in Rugby in 1903, a firm with a virtual world monopoly in making steam engines for generating electricity. There he did some work on early petrol engines, considered novel at the time, which led to a job at the Wolseley Tool and Motor-Car Company in Birmingham (a firm which still exists, though it is now a major distributor of plumbing equipment). The company was then run by Herbert Austin, who left later to found the Austin Car Company, which ended up as a subsidiary of British Aerospace, as did De Havilland. Geoffrey lasted there for about a year, before chucking it in, and returning to live with his parents, temporarily unemployed.

It was about this time that his interest in planes was sparked by news reports of the Wright Brothers' visit to France in 1908. He became determined to build his own flying machine, and called on his grandfather to see if he would provide a loan. Jason Saunders talked to him about the potential in building buses — he was aware of the Morris company setting up in Oxford — but was soon attracted by his grandson's talk of planes.

By the end of the meeting, he told Geoffrey he had planned to leave him £1000 in his will, but if he preferred to have the money now, he was welcome to it — so long as he understood there would be no more. Armed with the money from his grandfather, Geoffrey rented a flat in Kensington, and hired an acquaintance, Frank Hearle, to help him. His sister Ione kept house for them, and later married Hearle.

Creating a basic airplane was a haphazard but not particularly expensive business. De Havilland designed an engine, and had it built for £220; the tools for the airframe cost another £20, and the rest was made up of canvas and wood, plus a small amount of steel for the undercarriage. The most arduous task was stitching the canvas for the wings, a task delegated to a former governess of his sisters, Louie Thomas, who also made the tea in the workshop. To keep her on board an enterprise which she regarded as on the lunatic side of eccentricity, De Havilland married her while the first plane was being built.

By December 1909 the first plane was ready, but on its test run collapsed into pieces. Undeterred, the two men began building a second, stronger plane, completed by the summer of 1910. This time it flew, for those twenty yards. Once De Havilland had more confidence — he was, after all, teaching himself to fly as well as testing his contraption — the machine proved airworthy; it climbed to a hundred feet or so, and soon he was taking his wife and eight-week-old son for spins.

The machine worked, but Jason Saunders's money was just about exhausted, and there was no prospect of selling the plane — nobody was interested. An acquaintance put him in touch with the superintendent at Farnborough, an establishment set up by the British government for aeronautical research. The superintendent's name was Mervyn O'Gorman, and though he warned De Havilland that his political masters were unimpressed by airplanes, having decided that airships were the future, he offered £400 for the machine. He also offered De Havilland and Hearle jobs at Farnborough to supervise further development.

De Havilland leapt at the offer. Thus, early on, two of the key characteristics of the European aerospace industry were implanted: government support and notable financial losses. The plane had, after all, cost £1000 to construct, and recouped only £400.

Farnborough's main research work in those days concentrated on airships and man-carrying kites, technology the British government (with the scientific ineptitude for which it is justly notorious) had identified as particularly important. Airplanes were strictly in the third division; a year before De Havilland joined there had been a decision to abandon all work on planes, though that was soon reversed.

De Havilland stayed there until January 1914, when he joined George Thomas, the son of the owner of the *Daily Graphic*, as chief designer at his small company, Airco. On the outbreak of the First World War, as a member of the reserves, he was called up, and initially posted to Montrose in Scotland, from where he and a sergeant, with two planes, were charged with defending Scotland from sea invasion. In time the pointlessness of this posting became clear even to the War Office, and he returned to Airco to design warplanes. The German Fokkers were considered formidable machines, and the British had little to counter them. De Havilland designed the DH4; though known among military pilots as the flying coffin, it became the mainstay of the Allies' air force, and by 1917 300 a month were being manufactured. The circumstances of war had created his first successful product.

The First World War turned the airplane into an industrial product. Until then it had been little more than a hobby. The new machines were weapons of war less than a decade from their invention. The first recorded bombing raid was in the spring of 1913, during the Mexican revolutionary war, when a twenty-seven-year-old French mercenary, Didier Masson, was hired by the constitutionalist forces to bomb the ships of their federal opponents. With eight bombs strapped to his lightweight plane, he sprayed ships anchored offshore; all the bombs missed their targets, but terror sent the sailors diving overboard, disrupting if not disabling the ships. Its military possibilities were not lost on others. As the western front became bogged down in trench warfare, the potential of the airplane to create damage behind enemy lines was apparent even to the lacklustre generals of that war. The Germans seized on the new technology, and Manfred von Richthofen, better known as the Red Baron, was the first popular hero of aerial combat.

For the pioneers of the industry, war was a godsend. For the first time they had other people's money and resources to play with, and the chance of substantial production; by the end of the war the Holt Thomas factory manufacturing the DH4 covered several acres and employed thousands of workers. It also created the first wealth that any of the pioneers had enjoyed. De Havilland had a royalty agreement with Holt Thomas, which the build-up in military production turned into a very lucrative contract. Soon after war began, and the first orders for the DH4 were placed by the War Office, he received a royalty cheque for £1500, and the cheques kept coming. He bought a big house in Edgware, a suburb of London, and a couple of fancy new cars. The strain, however, took a toll on his health. Shortly before the end of the war, he suffered a nervous breakdown and moved to the country.

Nothing that happened later made his life any more peaceful: the end of the war was a testing time for all the early manufacturers. By 1919, a year after the peace, the people at Airco, blessed with a handsome balance sheet and extensive plant and machinery, had dreamt up plans for a civil aerospace company to match the grandeur of the military enterprise: plans for passenger planes that would ferry travellers between a network of European cities. But without military orders to support them, the dream quickly crumbled. Civil airlines who might order their planes did not exist, and no one was in any hurry to organize them. Very soon the company was in dire financial trouble, and by the end of 1919 Airco was taken over by the Birmingham Small Arms Company, which made it clear that planes were not among its plans. The takeover was a cheap purchase of plant and machinery.

This shake-out was repeated throughout the industry. The men who had built the military companies, however, were dreamers, not businessmen. Their factories could be converted to other products and different lines, but their hearts could not be turned from building airplanes. De Havilland was no exception, and together with four other senior figures at Airco, he resolved to start a new company.

Holt Thomas, personally devastated by Airco's failure to survive the peace, put forward £10,000 towards the new business; De Havilland put up £3000, and the others found or borrowed £7000, a total of £20,000 for the new venture. Work was meager, but the company took with it from Airco an order for two DH18s, a new passenger plane with room for eight people which had been designed at the old company. The planes were purchased by Holt Thomas, who had started Air Transport and Travel, the first civil airline in Britain, flying between London and the Continent. In its early days the new company was constantly courted by disaster; orders for civil airliners were sporadic, and the government had little interest in buying new planes for the air force. At one stage it was kept alive only by an investment of £10,000 by Alan Butler, a wealthy aviation enthusiast who later became its chairman.

Its salvation lay not with passenger or military planes but with machines for fellow enthusiasts. After the war, aerospace returned to the realm of hobbyists. In 1923 the company created the Cirrus Moth, a light airplane built for instructors and weekend amateur flyers, selling at £650 and able to carry two people plus some luggage at a cruising speed of 70 m.p.h. It was the first of a long series of Moths, including the Gipsy Moth and of course the Tiger Moth, which for many years was the standard military training plane. "With the Moth, in all its guises and derivatives, we had not only started a new era of cheap and convenient flying; we had built ourselves security and the foundations on which the large De Havilland enterprise of today was erected," De Havilland wrote many years later.

He was only one of the early aviation enthusiasts who created the European aerospace industry. There were others in Britain, and there were others across Europe. Perhaps the most illustrious, one who contributed to the shaping of the modern industry, was Willi Messerschmitt, whose name became synonymous with the Luftwaffe fighter planes of the Second World War. His story reflects the roots of the European industry and is worth a detour.

Messerschmitt was born in Frankfurt on June 26, 1898, a near contemporary of De Havilland, whose life and work he was in many ways to emulate. His father was a wine merchant, and in 1910 the family moved to Bamberg, where he befriended Friedrich Hart, a young man who had made a local reputation as a pilot of gliders. By the age of fourteen Willi had made his first flight in a glider, and the romance of aviation had captivated him. He was at work on building his own glider.

Messerschmitt was too young to see much of the war, being drafted into the flying corps only at the beginning of 1918. When peace came, he attended the Munich Technical School to study engineering, and after graduation, with the help of his family, set up his own aircraft company, Flugzeugbau Messerschmitt, in 1924. He started by building gliders and sailplanes, but by 1925 had designed his first proper aircraft: a three-passenger monoplane, one of the first made entirely from metal instead of the lighter but flimsier wood and canvas still prevalent in the mid-1920s. An order for twelve planes was placed by Theo Croneiss — later a senior SS officer — who was then forming a regional German airline.

On the back of that success, the Bavarian state government took the first step in what was to be a long history of promoting the aerospace industry. Messerschmitt, a dark and uncommunicative man, had few friends among the industrial establishment; indeed, Erhard Milch, managing director of the state airline Lufthansa, had told him that he was of no value to the German aircraft industry and advised him to go and work abroad. The Bavarian government saw things differently. They offered Messerschmitt a subsidy to build the planes for the Croneiss order on condition that he merge with another local manufacturer, Bayerische Flugzeugwerke (known as BFW). Among the founders of that company was Ernest Udet, a First World War flying hero second only to the Red Baron, who rose to high rank in the Luftwaffe before shooting himself.

BFW had already received generous subsidies from the Bavarian government, but lacked a talented designer. With Messerschmitt in charge — under an arrangement whereby his company kept design rights and patents while BFW built the planes — the company produced the M20, a ten-seat passenger plane. Despite Milch's opposition, an order was placed by Lufthansa for ten of the new aircraft. Little went smoothly for the company, however; the first prototype crashed, and Lufthansa cancelled the order. The second worked well and the order was restored, but the losses caused by the accident forced the company into bankruptcy.

By 1933 Messerschmitt was back on his feet with his own company, but with Milch now Minister of Aviation in Hitler's government, the way forward was not promising. No contracts were awarded for his own designs but the company was allowed to manufacture other designs under contract, which was at least profitable, and some orders for his own planes were won outside Germany. A government contract to design a competition plane gave Messerschmitt the chance to prove his worth, and he came up with one of the most advanced planes of its day, featuring a flush-riveted skin, a retractable undercarriage, an enclosed cabin, and wings with movable slots and flaps. Soon afterwards, he designed the Bf109, the Luftwaffe's main fighter right through the Second World War. Fleets of the planes provided the spearhead for the Nazi advance through Europe and Russia.

Messerschmitt was responsible for creating much of the technical expertise of the German aircraft industry, an expertise that lay dormant, to emerge several decades later. He departed for Franco's Spain after the war, where he worked at a Spanish aircraft company. He eventually returned to Germany, and became honorary chairman of the re-formed company which still bore his name; this eventually became part of Messerschmitt-BolkowBlohm, later taken over by Daimler-Benz, one of the partners in the Airbus consortium.

That De Havilland and Messerschmitt should wind up as subcontractors and partners on the same aircraft would have struck both men as bitter irony. War was the savior, and ultimately the destroyer, of Messerschmitt; it did the same to De Havilland. Just as the First World War transformed the pursuit of flight from an eccentric hobby into an industry, so the Second World War transformed it again: this time from a fringe industry into a massive industry, entwined forever with politics, with the military and with war.

During the 1920s and 1930s, the beginnings of a global airline industry emerged. Indeed, most of the modern airlines trace their origins to those two decades: Imperial Airways in Britain, KLM in Holland, Lufthansa in Germany, Air France in France. Across the Atlantic, Pan Am and TWA were all up and running by that time. By the mid-1930s, air travel was common enough for the first monthly air travel guide to be published in London, listing such possibilities as Berlin to Buenos Aires via West Africa and Brazil, or London to Cape Town. But flights were more expensive than the equivalent boat trip, and, despite the efforts of airlines already competing with comfortable seats and fine foods, flying was more hazardous than taking a ship. Air travel was a market restricted to the rich and adventurous.

The existence of a civil airline industry provided the beginnings of a civil market for the products of the airframe manufacturers, but it was a small and dangerous market in which to operate. Only with the looming threat of war, and consequent rearmament, could the manufacturers hope to win the kind of bulk orders they needed to make their work profitable. "Every new means of transport since the industrial revolution has had its romantic period, this usually occurring between the first experimental day and the time when it becomes accepted by the masses and develops into big business," Geoffrey De Havilland wrote many years later.[1]

For him, that transition came in the 1930s, and it was a period he was never entirely comfortable with. Though he adapted to the demands of big business, a part of him always craved the excitement of testing a hand-built plane on a remote field. The Moth series was De Havilland's mainstay, but the company also developed through the decade into the emerging market for passenger planes. Its most successful model was the Dragon and Dragon Rapide, an eight-seater plane which sold for about £4000. At the same time the company moved its plant to Hatfield, outside London, on a site where British Aerospace still has a major factory.

Then in 1937, discussions began with the government about a new generation of warplanes. De Havilland's contribution was to be the Mosquito, small, versatile and all-purpose, which could adapt to the roles of bomber, fighter and reconnaissance plane. Light and agile, its main task during the war was to sneak at high speed through the fighters and flak to hit targets with deadly precision, and it found a place among the legendary British warplanes, alongside the Spitfire, the Hurricane and the Lancaster. Throughout the war Mosquitoes were manufactured in Britain, Australia and Canada. A total of 7781 had been made by war's end, bringing in a solid flow of money which made De Havilland a rich man.

The Second World War, in which aerial power would be dominant, was a tremendous boost to the British aircraft industry, as it was to those of all the nations involved in the conflict. Growth was explosive: in 1935, the aircraft industry employed 35,000 people, and had an annual output worth £14 million. By 1943, with the Battle of Britain won, it was the country's largest industrial sector: 1,750,000 people worked in it; expenditure, all of it by the government, totalled £800 million in 1943 alone, and 26,461 planes were manufactured.[2] The industry was never particularly efficient or productive. It matched the German and American industries in nothing but ingenuity, and that only by a whisker. But it was large.

Large, but chaotic; chaos which could be tolerated in the muddle of war, but which was to lead to an almighty struggle once peace descended. At the end of the war there were twenty-seven different aircraft manufacturers in Britain, and eight aero-engine manufacturers. As well as De Havilland, the manufacturers included Armstrong Whitworth, Avro, English Electric and Handley Page, as well as obscure, little-remembered players such as Percival Aircraft and Portsmouth Aviation. Peacetime could not support such an industry, and the massive debts coupled with the huge expenditures of the post-war Labour government meant there was no prospect of the aerospace industry maintaining wartime levels of demand.

Just as it had after the First World War, but this time on a far harsher scale, the industry faced rapid contraction. Despite the Cold War and the war in Korea, military orders were still few and far between. As before, manufacturers would have to turn to the civil market and see if they could make a living from planes for commercial transport. This proved no easier than it had been three decades earlier. Even in 1946, air travel was only for the rich few. And its internationalization meant that British manufacturers would have to compete with their American rivals for orders. According to a division of responsibility agreed between the powers, the Americans had specialized in big bombers and troop carriers while the British concentrated on nimble fighters; building bombers had taught the American companies much more about the construction of large passenger planes. The only consolation for the British industry was that their German and French counterparts had been destroyed and, for the time being at least, were out of the running.

"We first gave consideration to the Comet project in the closing stages of the War," De Havilland wrote.[3] "It was clear that, by reason of her concentration on transport and bombing aircraft during the war, America would have a big lead when the inevitable competition for long-distance airliners began in peacetime. It was no use following what they were doing and making something slightly better; our only chance, in contradiction to our old step-by- step policy, was to make one great leap and by this gain a lead which would take years to whittle down. The answer seemed to lie in the jet engine, in which we knew we had a big lead over America." So began the British aerospace industry's greatest and grandest adventure: the world's first passenger jet. It was the first deadly strike in the competition between the American and European aircraft industries, a contest which would continue to the present day without resolution.

The story of the Comet begins with Frank Whittle. Whittle is one of the men the English have come to eulogize in their long century of national decline, a heroic figure with fabulous ideas, who winds up bitterly disappointed; one who symbolizes, in some way, how the country feels about itself. Whittle was the inventor of the jet engine (a matter of some dispute, in truth, since it appears to have been invented simultaneously in Germany; the precise moment of origin has been lost among squabbling engineers). His engine was developed during the war, and fitted to a Gloucester warplane for testing. By chance, De Havilland and some of his colleagues witnessed one of its first flights. The company's chief engine designer, Frank Halford, was an enthusiast for jets, and was asked to design a production jet engine, while Ronald Bishop, the chief designer, was to provide plans for a single-seat jet fighter. The result of those early designs was the Vampire, a jet fighter powered by the Goblin engine, which went into large-scale production for both the RAF and overseas air forces, providing the company with some badly needed revenue in the years immediately after the war. It was a successful plane, taking De Havilland to the forefront of the new technology. In 1947, for example, the Vampire took the speed record of 496 m.p.h., and the height record of 59,446 feet. For one relatively small player in the fragmented world industry to have captured both these records was a distinguished performance.

In putting together a military plane, the designers noticed two interesting features. Apart from being far faster, the new jets were quieter and suffered from much less vibration than propeller-driven aircraft. Whether planes would become significantly more attractive to passengers as a result of being faster was a debatable point in the 1940s — most people still travelled by trains or ships — but the jet held the promise of being more comfortable to fly in, a factor which might tempt more passengers away from rail and sea and into the air.

Although development of the jet was a return for De Havilland to the early romance which had drawn him to aviation, it was to be a machine of tragedy. In 1946 his son Geoffrey was killed while testing one of the company's jet fighters (another son John had been killed in a Mosquito during the war). A few weeks later his wife Louie also died, from cancer according to the medical report, although De Havilland attributed her death as much to grief over her sons as to the disease. Yet he persisted with the jet; he was a practical man, and accidents were part of the price of aeronautical progress.

As well as making airframes, De Havilland manufactured airplane engines, a rarity among the manufacturers. It therefore had in-house the technical skills and expertise. To the engineers the solution seemed obvious: build a conventional passenger airframe and fit it with four jet engines. During the design stage a plan for a plane with three engines at the tail was drawn up, but was soon abandoned for a more conventional design with four engines fitted into the wings.

The plane was not feasible without government assistance. For the Comet, as the new plane was named, it came in the form of an initial order for eight planes from the British Overseas Airways Corporation, the long-distance British airline (later merged with its short-haul cousin British European Airways to form British Airways), a deal agreed between the company, BOAC and the Air Ministry. An order for another six came from British South American Airways (which soon merged with BOAC) and two were bought by the Ministry of Supply. All these orders were either organized or financed directly by the British government, which also chipped in with a grant of £2.5 million, paid for out of the defense budget, for the development of the Ghost engine that would power the new plane.[4] Since there were no other orders at the time the project was launched, the plane was effectively paid for by the government.

The Comet was designed in close cooperation with BOAC. Indeed, it was on September 27, 1946, after calling the airline to agree to a major design point, that De Havilland gave the final go-ahead to build. The plane was designed by Ronald Bishop, a largely self-educated engineer, who had joined the company in 1921 as an apprentice. That Bishop should have been self-educated is in keeping with the British tradition, where pioneers tend to teach themselves, a system which is woefully haphazard, but which, through its lack of formality, seems to supply a certain inventiveness.

Certainly, its design showed all the British skill for making things up as you go along. Like the Mosquito and many other De Havilland planes, it was built "off the drawing board," meaning that the engineers designed and put it into production without first testing a prototype to see if it worked before reaching a final production version. The reasoning for this risky approach was that it saved both time and money, commodities in short supply within the company. A gloss was put on the decision by arguing that the approach minimized the chances of the design team throwing in too many new ideas, since there would be little chance to cover up flaws later on. But, in reality, they were improvising wildly, which is what the British like to do best.

Bishop had a group of four designers around him, with De Havilland, an inveterate dabbler in aircraft design, dropping by to add his penny-worth. There were few formal meetings. The designers discussed their ideas over lunch or tea breaks, which were taken religiously every after-noon in British offices in those days. Outsiders were never present; the

Comet was designed and built in great secrecy lest too much of its lead in the marketplace be leaked to rival manufacturers. Whatever its drawbacks, the approach was certainly quick: the basic layout was ready by 1947, and the first plane two years later.

The first test flight was slated for July 27, which happened to be both De Havilland's birthday as well as that of his chief test pilot, John Cunningham. At Hatfield, factory staff and a few onlookers watched in amazement as the first jetliner taxied off the small runway into the air, taking a few quick turns around the Hertfordshire countryside before landing safely a few minutes later. Inauspiciously, and with little fuss, the era of modern jet travel had begun.

A test flight is only the beginning for a new plane. For the Comet there were still three more years of extensive modifications, testing, and checking for its Certificate of Airworthiness before it could be handed over to its first customer. It first flew commercially on 2 May 1952. Though the first test flight had been a quiet, almost private affair, this debut was a grand public occasion. A large crowd gathered at London Airport, the old aerodrome in the suburb of Croydon which served the capital before Heathrow. Its maiden flight was to be a BOAC route from London to Johannesburg, via Rome, Beirut, Khartoum, Entebbe and Livingstone, the total journey lasting 23 hours and 40 minutes.

Newsreels and cameras recorded the moment as the thirty-six passengers (paying £175 one-way or £315 return) climbed into the steel frame. De Havilland and his team watched as the engine purred into life and at 3:12 that afternoon the plane slipped quietly through the clouds on its maiden voyage. The jet age had begun for real, and in Britain the country's technical prowess was taken as a great national achievement — a reflection of a brave new Britain entering the second Elizabethan age, an age to be marked, many hoped, by renewed technological and commercial vigor. "This distinction shared by a British operator and a British product set the seal on this country's lead in applying the gas turbine to civil aviation," *The Times* declared the following morning, allowing a hint of patriotism to creep into its reporting of the event.

Even before that first flight — a huge public event not just in Britain but around the world — the Comet had all the makings of a great commercial success. BOAC revelled in being the first airline with the new machine, claiming in its publicity material that it "had fathered the jet age," and promising to deploy the jet along "all the main arteries of the Commonwealth." Other airlines eyed its lead jealously. After the initial round of British orders which had enabled the plane to be built, the Comet began attracting overseas orders. The first purchaser was Canadian Pacific Air, which bought two in 1949 for a planned Vancouver, Hong Kong, Tokyo route (which never actually materialized); others came from the Royal Canadian Air Force, Air France and Union Aeromaritime de Transport, another French airline. Modest orders, but by the standards of British civil aerospace exports of the time it was impressive.

The Comet 2, an upgraded successor, went into design soon after the first plane was finished. By the time work on that was completed, there were forty-seven orders for the Comet — nineteen for Comet 1, and twenty-eight for Comet 2 (including Japan Airlines). More significantly, in October 1952, De Havilland made its first breakthrough into the American marke, when Pan Am, the most expansionist and adventurous of the U.S. airlines, placed an order for three Comet 3s, another upgrade then in the design stage. In the transatlantic race to dominate the industry, the Europeans had landed their first blow in the home territory of their rivals.

To De Havilland it must have seemed that his great gamble was paying off. The Comet had been the first jet in service, and by 1954, although there was much discussion among its rivals about building a competitor, none had gone any further than doodlings on the drawing board. De Havillands and the British had an important new global market to themselves, and looked set to achieve a global dominance which would be very hard for any competitor to undermine.

And then it crashed. Not once, but three times. The first crash, off the Italian coast, was one thing. Planes crash. They always had, ever since flying began. It was a shock, but it was accepted as inevitable. After that crash, the Comets were temporarily withdrawn from service and taken in for inspection. Endless theories were put forward for the disaster: a collision with another aircraft, a blackout by the pilot, engine failure. But neither inspection of the other planes nor examination of the wreckage established a definitive cause.

On March 23, 1954, two months after the crash, the Comet was pronounced airworthy again, and the planes resumed service. Its rehabilitation was to last only a few weeks; on May 2, a BOAC Comet taking off from Dum Dum Airport in Calcutta on the Singapore-to-London route crashed, killing its thirty-six passengers and crew of six. This time the inquiry concluded that the disaster was the result of the plane's running into an unexpected thunderstorm. Then on May 8, the Mediterranean, by a sinister coincidence, claimed another Comet; G-ALYY took off from Rome airport at 6:25 p.m., heading for Cairo on the second leg of the London-Johannesburg route. It had been delayed at Rome for twenty-four hours while minor repairs were made to a fuel gauge. The last heard of it was a routine message radioed back to Rome at 6:57 p.m., reporting its position over the sea off Naples. It was due to land at Cairo at 9:20 p.m. and when it did not arrive was reported overdue. Later that night a BEA plane spotted an oil slick over the sea, creating suspicion of a crash. This was confirmed when the crew of the British aircraft carrier *Eagle,* part of the Mediterranean fleet, spotted six bodies and the wreckage of a plane floating in the waters off the southern Italian coast. Inexplicably, the Comet had crashed again, killing fourteen passengers and seven crew members.

The excuses were starting to look threadbare. This was the third Comet crash in quick succession, and although the Calcutta disaster appeared to have a rational explanation, both the Italian crashes defied everything then known about aeronautical science. Nobody knew why they had crashed or whether they would crash again.

Immediately after the third disaster, BOAC withdrew all the Comets in service, and other airlines grounded their planes. "BOAC have given the Comet all the support, encouragement and promotion that any operator can expect to give a new aircraft," said Sir Miles Thomas, chairman of BOAC, in a statement. "We have had three inexplicable tragedies. They all follow a certain pattern on reaching or approaching maximum altitude at full power, and until the manufacturers can tell us that they have discovered and rectified the cause of these tragedies, we certainly cannot carry passengers in Comets."

The trouble was that De Havillands had absolutely no idea what had happened. Because both the planes that crashed in the Mediterranean had come down after taking off from Rome airport, sabotage was immediately suspected, both by the company and by the British government. MI5 carried out an investigation and, although security at Rome airport was notoriously lax, it could find no evidence of a bomb on the plane or come up with any idea why anyone should want to bring down the planes. It appeared that mechanical failure was the cause, although of what kind no one knew. That was to be discovered later; for the moment all that was certain was that the Comet was not safe. Its Certificate of Airworthiness was withdrawn and the bright hopes of De Havilland's dominating the new world industry sank as deep as the twisted remains of its planes. In an editorial the week of the second crash, *The Times* considered its prospects: "Every air disaster leaves in its train personal tragedy, but yesterday's disaster off Naples adds further to what must now be thought of as the tragedy of an enterprise."

As the events of the next few years proved, those words were prescient. The months after the second crash were consumed by trying to figure out what had gone wrong. The Royal Navy salvaged as much wreckage as possible; it was then sent to Farnborough for government scientists and engineers to work on. The answer, coincidentally, arrived on a day when De Havilland happened to be visiting the research establishment. Summoned to a pressure chamber where the structure of the plane was being tested, he was shown how a tear had developed in the side of the cabin. Exhaustive testing had revealed that after a year or so of flying metal fatigue was causing the fibric of the plane literally to come apart in the air. The reason for the crashed Comets was at last clear.

Metal fatigue was a little-known subject at the time; the Comet flew faster and at greater pressures than had any machine at that time; military fighters went as fast, but were never in the air for anything like the same time as a commercial jet. Indeed, a Court of Inquiry into the Comet disasters absolved the company of any blame for the crashes, concluding that the design team had used methods and technologies standard in the aerospace industry. Those techniques, however, were not advanced enough to build a passenger jet, and De Havilland had learned the hard way how risky it can be to pioneer a new technology. It could have happened to any company that risked pioneering passenger jets, but it happened to De Havillands, and its consequences were to haunt the company for years to come. The crashes were primarily a technical and publicity disaster, but they were also a financial calamity. In their aftermath, the company came close to bankruptcy. Orders for Comet 2s and Comet 3s had to be put on hold while the cause of the crashes was investigated. That hit the company's cashflow immediately. More seriously, the company and the plane were now tainted; few airlines would try to entice their passengers aboard a Comet. De Havilland considered changing the names of the revised, upgraded versions — with structures reinforced to overcome the problem of metal fatigue — but decided against it. That, he felt, would smack of defeatism, and would not disguise which plane it was.

Money became tighter and tighter, so tight that in 1955 the British government stepped in to bail out De Havillands. It placed an order for eighteen Comet 2s for the Royal Air Force, and advanced the company money for further development of the plane. When those funds ran out, it stepped in again, this time with a direct grant of £6.5 million to keep the company alive. The injection worked for a time, but De Havillands was a desperately weakened company. It modified the existing Comets to make them stronger, but the completely revised Comet 4 took many years to complete and was not ready until 1958. BOAC ordered twenty of the new planes, but other orders were hard to come by. The aircraft was finally launched on September 30, 1958, but even though it was still the only passenger jet in the world, the celebrations were much more muted than for the Comet 1. The Prime Minister of the day, Harold Macmillan, sent a telegram to De Havilland to mark the occasion: "The resurgence of the Comet airliner is a fitting reward for the faith in the future of this fine product and the whole nation takes pride in the fact that a British aircraft has led the world into the new turbojet age," he wrote. Fine and encouraging words. He did not show up in person.

Praise was forthcoming elsewhere. In America, the company was presented with an award by the rest of the aerospace industry "for the vision, courage, and skills displayed in conceiving, developing and producing the world's first jet-powered passenger transport aircraft." Fine words again, but words are poor currency; everyone knew that the dream was shattered. By the time Comet 4 was ready, other manufacturers had their own jets close to launch, and the Comet would now be one in a field of many. A permanent British lead in the industry had been destroyed, and would never come again. The balance sheet of the company was in tatters, and much of its spirit broken.

By the close of the decade, punch-drunk and battered beyond repair, it was ready to throw in the towel. On December 17 1959, De Havillands and Hawker Siddeley agreed to a merger. The company which De Havilland surrendered had net assets of £87 million, and 80,000 employees. As a return on the £1000 gifted to him by his grandfather all those decades ago, it was an impressive achievement and one that would have made proud the Victorian merchant who bankrolled the adventure. But it was also a bitter defeat; its independence had been surrendered — no plane would ever carry the De Havilland name again.

The Comet limped on in production for a few more years, but never recaptured its original magic, and the production lines shut down in 1962. Geoffrey De Havilland stayed on for a few years as president of the merged company, largely an honorary position. He lived near the Hatfield plant, and the company provided a small house close to the airstrip where he and other retired directors could meet and pass the time of day while keeping an eye on their progeny. But he was an old man by now, and the developments in aeronautical science had passed him by: Sir Geoffrey, as he now was, could contribute only memories.

When he was composing his autobiography some years before his death, the loss of his two sons struck him as his greatest tragedy, but the death of the Comet consumed him with almost as much sadness and regret; it, too, had been a child to him. "The material loss to BOAC and to ourselves amounted to many millions. But to many of us it was the shattering blow of sudden and complete failure following on notable achievement that was hardest to bear. The whole nation had formed an affectionate regard for the Comet, and we had failed."[5]

2

AN EMPIRE
IN THE SKY

Bill Allen, chairman of the board of the Boeing Company of Seattle, Washington, stayed at the Connaught Hotel on his visit to London in the autumn of 1952. He had come to visit the airshow at Farnborough, even then a vital jamboree for senior aerospace executives from around the world. He was there, as he was at all the major airshows, to keep tabs on the opposition, to gossip with the movers and shakers of the industry, perhaps even to hustle a few airplane orders; though hustling was not part of Allen's patrician manner. This year, however, even by Farnborough standards, was to be special. Among the new planes to be unveiled was the De Havilland Comet. Allen, who knew exactly what De Havillands was building, and why, would not have missed this. He believed that passenger jets would be the transport of the future, and he wanted to see how big a lead the British had.

He was escorted to the airshow by the managing director of one of his rivals, the Bristol Airplane Company. The fields next to the exhibition runway were packed with spectators, anxious to see the new plane, which had whipped up a mixture of curiosity and the nation's hopes for a prosperous future. They waited in near silence. The Comet, its sleek wings swept back, taxied quietly along the tarmac to an appreciative murmur. Allen watched intently as the four Ghost engines purred softly. Over the crackly loudspeakers, a voice introduced the plane: "This aircraft has an unrivalled cruising speed of 490 miles per hour at 35,000 to 42,000 feet," it intoned. "An aircraft with extraordinary commercial capabilities."

The demonstration Comet was painted with a silver underside, white top and a blue streak running along its side: an illustrative touch which car manufacturers call "go-faster stripes," put there to emphasize the speed and power of the machine. It gathered pace and pulled gracefully into the sky. "A magnificent combination of speed and beauty," the announcer continued. And as the plane disappeared there was a ripple of applause from the crowd.

Allen was impressed. Like the other aerospace executives there, he knew he had seen a plane which marked a clear dividing line in their industry, a clean break between the past and the future. He sensed, too, that a transatlantic battle for control of the aerospace industry had begun; improbably, he looked like being on the losing side. Back in London, Allen spent the evening dining with his wife and some of his Boeing colleagues — Maynard Pennell, head of preliminary design, and Ken Luplow, his chief sales engineer. Pennell was an enthusiast for passenger jets and had already begun lobbying for Boeing to follow the De Havilland lead. Luplow had been talking to the airlines, picking up the feel of what planes they wanted to buy in the future. He was acutely aware of the stir created among them by the Comet, and how close De Havillands was to major international success. The Comet seemed to be a plane that would sweep Europe and might even make substantial inroads into the American market.

"Do you think we could build one as good?" asked Allen.

"Oh, better, much better," replied Pennell,[1] going on to describe the design improvements he would make in engine positioning and wing sweep. Luplow chipped in with information from the marketplace. Airlines, he said, were already wondering what they should do about the arrival of the jet; how soon they should introduce it to their schedules, and whether they should buy the Comet now or wait for later models from its rivals. They would wait for a while before making any decisions, but not for long. They were asking if Boeing planned to introduce a jet of its own; if he could say they were, the airlines might hold off ordering the Comet, at least until they saw what Boeing came up with. He needed an answer from Allen; he could not go around promising a jet the company might not build. Right now, Allen couldn't say — he was not sure. And for the rest of that year, when the question was put to him by staffers or airlines, he kept to a simple formula: We are reviewing the situation.

For Allen, for Boeing, and for the American aircraft industry, this was a crucial time. A decision to proceed would be a costly and risky enterprise. De Havillands had little to lose; for it, as for the fragmented European industry, it was all or nothing, and you might as well have a go. For Boeing the situation was different: it had a secure if far from dominant place in the American industry, the world leader in size and strength. It had a world to lose. This decision was to be the most significant Allen had taken since he had inherited stewardship of the company from its founder, Bill Boeing. It would be a tremendous gamble, which would put in jeopardy everything the organization had built in its thirty years on the distant northwestern shores of the United States.

Boeing then, as it is now, was something of an exception in the aerospace industry; a company driven as much by the desire to make steady profits as to build planes. That wish, to bring commercial order to a wild and uncivilized industry, had been the core around which it was founded, and its roots and origins are worth tracing. Boeing's arrival at the edge of the jet age had also been a wild and turbulent trip, but it had been guided by a single principle — dominance of a global industry.

Like Geoffrey De Havilland, William E. Boeing's fascination with flying can be traced to the early origins of aviation. It begins at Dominguez Ranch, a dusty outpost a few miles south of Los Angeles, in January 1910. The event was a flying show — a public spectacle, amusing the crowd with the newly invented flying machines; balloons and airships were on display, together with some of the early planes. Boeing, a businessman from Seattle, several hundred miles to the north, was filling in a day when there wasn't much else to do. Tall, slim, with a dark moustache and rimmed glasses, he was a studious and serious figure among the crowds of tourists. But something about the new flying machines appealed to a vein of romance in him. He watched all day, witnessing the stunts and marvelling at the agility of the planes. Finally he approached one of the aviators, a Frenchman named Paulham, to ask if he might take a ride in a plane. The pilot told him to come back the next day; Boeing did, but Paulham was busy. And the next day as well. Boeing didn't get a ride in the plane, but, by the time he returned to Seattle, a fascination with flying had developed — and so had the germ of an idea.

Boeing is a German name, and Bill's father had emigrated to America in the nineteenth century. Boeing senior died when Bill was only eight, but he had done well in the years since he arrived; he left his son and his Viennese wife substantial holdings of timber and iron ore in Minnesota's Mesabi Range. Bill was sent to boarding schools both in the U.S. and Switzerland before going to Yale, where he studied engineering. But he was an adventurous spirit, and the academic establishment atmosphere of Yale was not to his taste. A year before graduation he quit school, at the age of twenty-two, and heeding the siren call to "go west," departed to set up a timber business in the vast forests of the Pacific Northwest.

Seattle then was a small, rough frontier town, developing fast because of the timber trade, a fine natural harbor and plentiful supplies of local coal to fuel the steamships that arrived to collect the wood. Here, in the little timber town, Bill Boeing settled. At Seattle's University Club, Boeing made the acquaintance of Conrad Westervelt, a fellow Yale alumnus, who was working as a naval constructor at the shipyards. The two young men became firm friends, and together developed their fascination with flight. In 1914, a freewheeling travelling aviator named Terah Maroney brought his plane to Seattle, and Boeing and Westervelt leapt at the chance to book a flight. They took turns going up in the flimsy two-seater biplane, marvelling as the machine circled the sky around the bay. After several flights, however, Boeing tired of being a passenger in someone else's machine. And Maroney would soon be gone, taking his plane with him. With little thought for the technical difficulties, Boeing and Westervelt decided to build their own plane. It struck them as not a very difficult project, and one that would be great fun.

Neither knew anything about building a plane; neither knew how to fly. Unlike other pioneer manufacturers, Boeing's enthusiasm was for organising the production of planes; designing, building and flying them he left to others. Herb Munter was an aviator who lived in Seattle and had his own hand-built plane which he flew for exhibition money around the northwest. Boeing and Westervelt hired him for their new company, provisionally called B&W. Then Boeing headed for Los Angeles again, buying a seaplane from a pioneer American aviator named Glen Martin, who had appeared in some films, acquired a measure of celebrity, and formed his own airplane manufacturing company (which is now part of the defense contractor Martin Marinetta). The plane cost Boeing $10,000; flying lessons were extra.

With the outbreak of war, Westervelt was transferred to active duty by the Navy. Boeing persevered on his own, hiring a young Chinese engineer, T. Wong, a recent graduate of the Massachusetts Institute of Technology, who was recommended by Jerome Hunsaker, the leading authority on aviation at the college. By June 1916 the first B&W machine, a wooden biplane, was complete. It was tested, and it flew. Boeing, who already had twenty-one men working on his infant project, decided it was time to incorporate. The company made its debut on July 14, 1916, as the Pacific Aero Products Company, with himself as president.

The name did not last long. By 1917, Wong, who was an engineer of rare genius, had designed a new plane. Wong utilized wind studies to make it more stable in flight, and the plane appeared to be technically the equal of anything available in the U.S. — possibly even ahead of anything else. The company changed its name changed to the Boeing Airplane Company, and Boeing headed for Washington to see if he could convince the U.S. government to place an order. After rigorous testing, the Navy pronounced it a success, and decided to buy fifty. Its first order secured — a large one at that — the Boeing Airplane Company was in business.

A factory was built to produce the planes, as was a wind tunnel at the University of Washington to give the company access to the latest aeronautical research. Boeing sensed from the beginning that making planes was a task for large companies, and he was keen to establish the infrastructure of a major business as quickly as possible. The development of the company did not run smoothly, however; after the initial fifty planes were built, the Navy decided no more were needed. Boeing was offered work as a subcontractor, producing planes to another company's design. Although the work was accepted — it was badly needed, since the factory had nothing else to do — this was not what Boeing wanted. If the company were to succeed in the long term, it needed its own technology and its own planes. Making other people's planes would never put Boeing at the forefront of the new industry.

As it had been in Europe, the First World War was a tremendous boost for the emerging American aircraft industry. Though the airplane had been invented in the U.S., a serious industry had been slow to emerge. For a decade after the Wright Brothers' first flight, there was little real investment in the new machines. In 1907, largely because of President Theodore Roosevelt's personal interest in flying, the U.S. Army established an aeronautical division. It was staffed by only three officers and ten men, and had one Wright plane and some balloons to play with. Although The Wright Company was capitalized at $1 million in 1909, that was largely the result of speculation and stock ramping by Wall Street financiers such as Cornelius Vanderbilt.

Despite the Wright Brothers' invention, the technical lead was quickly surrendered to the Europeans. By 1912, for example, the French company Deperdussin had built a 100 m.p.h. plane, the technological achievements of which were far in advance of anything in the United States. European governments were starting to spend significant money on military aviation, beginning the cycle of subsidy for research and development that was to become a permanent feature of the industry; the French spent the most, followed by the Germans and the Russians, with the British and the Italians in the rear, a pattern of subsidy which suggests ambitions in aerospace have deep nationalistic roots.[2]

The war changed the American attitude. In August 1916, Congress agreed to spend more than $13 million on planes for the Army, and another $3.5 million on seaplanes. Their decision had been influenced by the Battle of the Somme, which began in July 1916, when the British first sent aircraft across the battle lines to attack enemy trenches (hence, incidentally, the term "strafe" from the German word for to punish). The American industry looked as though it had a serious purpose at last, and some serious government money to play with.

Boeing was by no means the only young entrepreneur to cash in on the war boom. Around the U.S., dozens of small airplane companies had been established or were quickly set up to take a slice of the government dollars. The most significant in the long run was the man who was to become Boeing's most serious American competitor, Donald Willis Douglas. Douglas was descended from Scots. Like Boeing's father, Douglas's father had emigrated to the U.S. in the nineteenth century and prospered. He was not rich but, by the time Donald was born in 1892, he was working as a bank cashier on Wall Street, and the family was solidly middle class. Donald, like Bill, was bright, but had trouble settling down. He joined the Navy but left after a couple of years, and enrolled at MIT to study engineering. Though he studied mechanical engineering because there was as yet no course in aeronautics, he fell under the influence of Hunsaker, who had recommended Wong to Boeing. Douglas graduated in 1914, but stayed on as research assistant to Hunsaker, who had tried, unsuccessfully, to dissuade him from a career in aviation, which he believed had bleak prospects. A year later, on Hunsaker's recommendation, Douglas was hired by Glen Martin, who had sold Boeing his first plane.

Martin's company concentrated on military aircraft. Douglas's first design was sold to the U.S. Army; his second to the Dutch government, for use against guerrillas in Java. As one of the most respectable of the aerospace companies, Martin was to be a prime beneficiary of the war spending. On the back of the jump in the U.S. budget for warplanes, Martin merged his company with Wright, to form the Wright-Martin Aircraft Corporation, with a capitalization of $5 million. Orville Wright remained on the payroll at a salary of $25,000 a year, but was primarily a figurehead to give the company stockmarket glamor.

The new company had no room for Douglas, who was replaced as chief engineer and went to work in Washington as head of the Army Signal Corps's in-house engineering department, where he was involved in the build-up of aircraft production. This build-up degenerated into a costly fiasco amid allegations that money was being squandered, that the British and the French, upon whom the Americans now relied for technology, were more interested in squeezing royalties from the U.S. than in getting planes delivered to the front, and that the Europeans were holding back from their allies crucial technical advances to maintain the competitive position of their own aircraft industries. Had Douglas been listening, there were intimations here of future trade battles in which his company would be embroiled.

In 1917, Douglas returned to Wright-Martin as chief engineer, remaining there for another three years. But the disorganization convinced him that he would have as much chance on his own as with the chaos of the hucksters and dreamers who controlled the company. In 1920, with a wife and two young children to support, he quit his $10,000 a year job to set up his own company, a decision which struck his colleagues as willfull and peculiarly crazy.

His move was poorly timed. As in Europe, the immediate postwar years meant a vicious slump in the aircraft industry. The federal government was determined never to be so badly caught out in aircraft manufacturing capacity again; it was to be an article of policy that America needed a strong commercial aerospace industry which could be turned over to war production if the need arose. The U.S. did not want to depend on European technology. Money would be made available to make sure of this, but not unlimited money, and nothing like that spent during the war; funds and orders for military aircraft, still the only realistic market, were heavily cut after the peace.

Douglas had few resources to start his company: $1000 he had saved and $2000 his wife had inherited. Raising money from bankers was unsuccessful, and Douglas was so worried about going broke that he planted potatoes in his garden — which rotted. He was rescued by a wealthy sportsman and aviation enthusiast, David Davis, who put up $40,000 for a plane that would fly across the American continent, and took a quarter share in the company. Then in 1921 Douglas won — from Hunsaker, his old tutor — a $120,000 contract to build an experimental torpedo plane for the Navy. Davis pulled out of the company, leaving Douglas strapped for cash once more; he had the order but no way to finance it. Eventually he was rescued by Harry Chandler, publisher of the Los Angeles *Times,* who persuaded a group of financiers to guarantee a bank loan. The prototype was successful, and Douglas's company was in business. Of the two great conglomerates that were to dominate the American aerospace industry in the latter half of the twentieth century, one at least now had the private financing and the government orders as the base for a solid enterprise.

A few hundred miles north, in Seattle, Bill Boeing was having a tougher time with his new company. As the war machine wound down, Boeing had told his colleagues that he foresaw a splendid future for the business, but it would be hard going for the first couple of years. It was harder going than he or anyone else imagined.

To keep the plant ticking over, Boeing suggested the company look for some other line of work; interior woodwork was one idea that sprang to mind, a plane factory in those days being easily adaptable for any form of carpentry. In the meantime, like everyone else in the industry, Boeing's mind was fixated on finding a commercial market for his plane. Again, as for everyone else, no commercial market existed; there were few if any passenger services. But Boeing found a way out of this conundrum; his company would make flying boats.

Less than a couple of hundred miles north, across the Canadian border in Vancouver, a local businessman named Knowlton had hit on the idea of starting an airmail service, ferrying the post over the border by plane. He asked Boeing if could provide a plane, a request Boeing was only too eager to meet. The first airmail service anywhere completed its first trip on March 3, 1919 — a Boeing seaplane which took off from Lake Washington in Seattle, and landed at the Royal Vancouver Yacht Club, 125 miles away. One of the first useful and peaceful applications of flight had been discovered, and Boeing had learned a crucial commercial lesson: sometimes you must create a market to justify a product.

That achievement aside, 1919 was a dismal year. By the winter, with no sign of other work coming in and the calculation that the firm would show a loss for the year of $90,000, Boeing seriously contemplated closing down. Only a certain Germanic determination prevented him from taking that step; he did not like to start something and leave it in mid-air. Another year dragged on with nothing more than scraps of airplane work, and even the furniture business was losing money. By December 1920 the company was recording a loss of $300,000, a tremendous sum for the times.

Salvation arrived with a government order for 200 pursuit planes, which were to establish Boeing as a serious player in the airplane business. He had bid low for the contract, knowing that every other manufacturer would be pitching for the business, and won it at a price which still permitted a small profit. By December 1922 the balance sheet was in better shape, and the three hundred company employees were paid a Christmas bonus for the first time since the war.

By the middle of the 1920s, a decade of great commercial optimism, the aerospace industry in the US. began its transformation from a ramshackle collection of eccentrics supplying the generals with war machines into a modern industry, serving civil as well as military markets. It began with the realization that the plane was a permanent feature of modern warfare; a separate Air Corps was created, and a five-year procurement plan put in place. At the same time, in 1926, the Air Commerce Act was passed, establishing federal rather than state regulation of the small commercial air services springing up, and, more importantly, providing federal funds for beacon lights to guide the network of airmail services being established. Through government intervention, a civilian market was at last in prospect.

With the ruthless efficiency and market opportunism that would always characterize the company, Boeing was among the first manufacturers to understand the possibilities. In contrast to other entrepreneurs of the air, Boeing modified his involvement in the business. In 1926 he made himself chairman of the board, appointing Phil Johnson president of the company. Johnson had joined the company during the war after graduating in engineering, and had stayed with it ever since. By putting him in charge, Boeing was planning early the structure of a major corporation, even though the size of the company hardly justified it.

Boeing and Johnson realized that development of the civilian market was crucial to the development of the company. But to sit back and wait for it would be disastrous; the market could take years to establish and their company would be scrabbling for orders with all the others. They decided to act.

With the U.S. Post Office tendering airmail contracts to private companies, Boeing put in a bid to carry the mail across the western half of the country. The bid they put in was far below any of their competitors, and although the Post Office officials doubted Boeing could make money on the deal, it was accepted. The Boeing Air Transport company was formed to carry both mail and passengers from Chicago to San Francisco, a twenty-three-hour journey at the time. To service the line, a fleet of twenty-five planes was built. Boeing had its contract, minimally profitable in itself, and it had awarded itself its first significant order for civil airplanes.

The move into air transport was an inspired breakthrough. With the introduction of the five-cent airmail stamp, and the growing reliability of the planes carrying the mail, the demand for postal and passenger services was rising rapidly. The plane was becoming a serious competitor to the train. In 1928, Boeing took advantage of the upswing in the company's fortunes, coupled with a booming economy and stockmarket, to float the company: the business was listed as the Boeing Airplane & Transport Company. Soon afterwards, in a bold series of mergers, the United Aircraft & Transportation Corporation was formed — a new aeronautical giant which took in the Boeing Airplane Company, Boeing Transport, the engine maker Pratt & Whitney, as well as a propeller manufacturer and several young regional airlines. From the moment of its formation, United was the largest aerospace conglomerate in the world, and the only one whose universe included every aspect of the business, from building the airframe and the engines to operating the planes for passengers and mail. Bill Boeing was its president.

The internal logic of the conglomerate was expansion and market domination. The airline would boost demand for the planes; the plane division would plough profits back into production of bigger and better machines; the better planes would tempt more passengers into the air, which would generate more cash for production, and so on. A virtuous financial circle would have been established. For a time it seemed to work as well in practice as in theory. Boeing's early mail and passenger services had used a four- seater plane. In 1928 they were replaced with the Model 80, a twelve-seater, which, with good reason, became known as the "Pullman of the Air." Before many of his competitors, Boeing realized that flying had to reach beyond the enthusiasts to people looking for speed and comfort. The Model 80 pioneered many of the features now familiar to passengers on any modern jet: reclining seats adjustable to four positions; ventilation and heating; a soundproofed cabin; a lavatory with hot and cold running water; large and shatterproof windows for admiring the views, dome and wall lights, and facilities for meals. Stewardesses were introduced for the first time, and they were, inevitably, young and pretty.

The great stockmarket crash of 1929 was not a tremendous setback for the booming airplane business. Though prices fell — the combined value of quoted air companies was more than $1 billion before the crash, even though their combined profits were only $19 million — the underlying business was still growing strongly. The airlines operating under the United banner had grown by the new decade to a fleet of 120 planes flying 32,000 miles a day. With the outlook set fair, the board of United agreed to spend $3 million on replacing the fleet with the most modern plane that could then be built.

The Boeing 247, completed in February 1933, brought about another revolution in standards of comfort and speed. Flying at 11,500 feet, and with a top speed of 200 m.p.h., it allowed the company to advertize average speeds of three miles a minute. It meant United could introduce a coast-to-coast service spanning the continent in twenty hours with seven stops along the way, far faster than the transcontinental railways. And for the Boeing division of the conglomerate, the seventy-five orders for the plane — including two from Deutsche Lufthansa — meant that it was starting to get substantial orders from the civil market, which it now dominated.

Between 1929 and 1933, the conglomerate accounted for 48 percent of all aircraft and engine sales to the Navy, 29 percent to the Army, and a huge 48 percent of the commercial market.[3]

This was the closest Bill Boeing got to his dream of creating the unchallenged leader of the U.S. aerospace industry. He had promised himself that he would retire at fifty, and, a year adrift, he withdrew from the organization in August 1933, promoting Phil Johnson to the presidency of the United conglomerate. His life's work appeared complete.

With cruel timing, that dream was punctured. If 1933 was a high point for the company, 1934 was a dramatic low. Boeing had established its position through the classic commercial strategy of combining the different arms of an industry — production, distribution, retailing — into one unit, and used that combination to control the market. Though successful, it has never been politically popular in the U.S., where the interests of the consumer and free competition have as high a priority as the sustenance of industrial giants. The watchful guardians of anti-trust legislation, which a generation earlier had broken up the great oil and railroad empires, turned on Boeing's United monolith.

In the early thirties the tide of opinion in the U.S. was running against business, and the aerospace industry was caught up in the waves. Early in 1934 a book on the aerospace industry, *Merchants of Death,* topped the bestseller lists, and Congress began a series of investigations into the incestuous webs of alliances between the military and the manufacturers and between the manufacturers and the airlines. Allegations of profiteering and monopoly abounded, and one of many inquiries centered on the award of airmail contracts by the Post Office, which had proved so lucrative for Boeing. A Senate committee charged that many of the routes had been granted without competitive bidding; Boeing/United protested that this had happened only where there was one bidder in the frame, or where it had been asked by the Post Office to operate the route. Their pleas were of no avail. After a long examination by the Senate, Bill Boeing saw his company go down to a humiliating defeat.

In 1935 President Roosevelt ordered that the Army should take over the operation of airmail routes; a short-lived experiment. since the Army had little experience in that kind of flying, and twelve of its pilots died in the first two months. The routes went back to the airlines, but the U.S. government decreed that no executive involved in the earlier route awards could participate. For United, that created a crisis: Phil Johnson had to resign to prevent United's being barred. But the government did not leave it there; a law was passed preventing an airmail contractor from having any connection with an airframe manufacturer. For United, the law spelled the end of the conglomerate — without the mail, its routes would not be profitable; passengers alone would not sustain the service.

Bill Boeing was bitter about the defeat, and sold his remaining stock in the company. His managers dealt with the new law by breaking up the conglomerate; the airline went into United, the engine manufacturing into Pratt & Whitney, and the airframe plants returned to Boeing, its headquarters once more in Seattle. After such huge expansion, the company returned to where it started — a small and financially weak airframe manufacturer in the distant Northwest. Apart from a brief return as a consultant during the Second World War, Boeing had no further involvement in the company. Nor was his legacy anything like as powerful as he had hoped.

Boeing's first figures as an independent company again showed how great had been the damage inflicted —it recorded a loss of $225,000 on sales of a little over $1 million. The payroll dropped from over 2000 in 1933 to only 600 in 1934. More ominously, ferocious competition was looming. The United conglomerate had made Boeing the leading manufacturer, but muscle rather than skill had been the method. Independent again, its skill was to be tested and found wanting.

Since his early hustling days, Donald Douglas had prospered on the back of a steady stream of military contracts. In 1932, TWA, one of the fledgling airlines of the time, asked Douglas to build a commercial plane. The airline wanted a supplier outside the United conglomerate. Reluctantly, Douglas agreed, building the DC-1. At TWA's prompting, the plane was designed to leapfrog the competition from Boeing and establish the company in one bold step as a serious competitor in the civil market. By July 1933, the new plane was ready. Made entirely from aluminium, it seated twelve passengers and set new technological standards. By the time it was launched into service, with slight improvements, it had been rechristened the DC-2, and it carved a name as the most formidable passenger plane yet built. In 1935, it established a new transcontinental speed record, traversing the U.S. from west to east in twelve hours forty-two minutes, which made the Boeing 247 seem cumbersome.

Douglas gambled not only on a technological lead on Boeing, but a commercial lead, as he set the price of the DC-2 low enough to squeeze his competitor out of the skies. Each DC-2 cost $65,000, which, given its development costs, meant that seventy-five planes had to be sold for it to break even, a huge number by the standards of the time — and as many 247s as Boeing ever sold. With the United monopoly cracked, expanding the market by making the product more affordable seemed a good strategy. Eventually 132 DC- 2s were sold, netting a huge profit, and establishing Douglas as the leader in the market for civil transporters.

At the same time, also in California, another competitor had emerged. Lockheed, a pioneer of the early aviation business and one of the companies caught up in the stock market frenzy in the late 1920s, had gone bankrupt in 1932. It was bought from the receivers for $40,000 by an investment banker named Robert Gross, who, though he had little experience in the industry, was convinced there was an eager market for civil airplanes. Investing $120,000 in a new plane, the company created the Electra, a state-of-the-art machine for its time; it was a ten-seater, all-metal plane; it sported retractable landing gear, trailing edge flaps, and variable pitch propellers (with different blade angles for take-off and landing), all of which added to its sophistication. The makers took it aggressively into the export market, particularly in Europe — so far ignored by Boeing and Douglas — and the Electra soon established Lockheed as the third force in the American aerospace industry. Of the three, Boeing, with the 247 looking dated, had been relegated from first to third place with indecent speed.

For the rest of the 1930s, Boeing struggled to regain its place in the civil market. The decade saw the industry grow steadily, as air travel became accepted, particularly within the United States, even though it was expensive and relatively uncomfortable. It was also the decade during which the American manufacturers, backward compared with their European competitors for the first two decades of the century, came to dominate the world industry. Between 1935 and 1938, U.S. aviation exports to Europe amounted to $42 million, or 43 percent of all American exports to that continent (surprising, given that the industry accounted for only 0.6 percent of U.S. manufacturing employment); already, as it is today, aerospace was becoming the major American export industry. In Asia, demand was even greater, with $58 million of equipment being sold to the region over the same period. Exports were crucial; overseas sales accounted for one third of the industry's output, and allowed planes to be profitable which could not have survived in the domestic market alone. Global market domination was becoming the key to success; but once it was established it could not be surrendered without terrifying financial consequences.

The Americans' was not a success that passed without reaction. In the 1930s the Europeans were fretting about their relative inferiority in the worldwide aerospace industry. "The aircraft industries of Europe are now on the defensive," wrote the Swiss-based trade journal *Inter Avia* in 1934. "The struggle will not be an easy one, for if last year the American invader was yet encamped outside the gates, he now has a secure foothold within, and he shall show what he can really do."

Simmering hostility lurked between the European and American industries — a faint signal that would became overt only many years later. The American manufacturers were deaf to it, hearing only the exchange of gunfire between themselves.

With Johnson stepping aside, day-to-day control of Boeing fell to Clair Egtvedt, another of the young engineering graduates who had joined the company during World War One. Boeing was financially the weakest of the three U.S. contenders, with just over $500,000 cash in the bank, hardly enough to keep going for a year. At the first board meeting of 1934, a decision was taken to pump $275,000 into designing a four-engine plane — the B-17 — to be sold to the military as a bomber; if successful, it would be the largest and most powerful plane yet built. The Army was in the market for a new bomber, but it chose a two-engined machine from Douglas. An order for fourteen B-17s was placed as an experiment, but the plane languished on the fringes of the Army's plans for many years until resurrected during the Second World War as the Flying Fortress, when it became the workhorse of American bombing campaigns throughout that war.

Building the B-17, though commercially a flop, yielded new and valuable experience in manufacturing bigger planes. By the middle of the decade, with the lead in the civil market lost to the DC-2 and the even more successful DC-3, Boeing put that experience into expanding the size of passenger planes. In 1936 an order came through from Juan Trippe, of Pan American, the most ambitious and expansionist of the American airlines, for six giant seaplanes at $500,000 each. The Boeing 314 was 106 feet long, with a wingspan of 152 feet, and could carry 74 passengers 3500 miles without refuelling. It was the Jumbo of its day, ferrying passengers from the U.S. to Europe and the Far East. But it was not launched into commercial service until 1939, and the outbreak of war meant that it had no chance to establish itself as a major commercial product.

Still, big planes were what Boeing did best, and what the company would continue to make. Work began on the 307, a land equivalent of the 314, called the Stratocruiser. A limitation on the speed of planes then was altitude. The higher a plane goes the faster it can fly (because the air resistance is much lower), but at great heights the air pressure is too weak for passengers to breathe. The 307 became the first passenger plane to solve that problem by introducing a pressurized cabin, which meant it could climb higher and move faster than any of its predecessors. With four engines and two decks, it was the biggest and most luxurious civil transporter yet built.

But again it was not a commercial success: only ten Stratocruisers were ever built. Worse, it was soon trumped by Douglas's DC-4, a forty-two-seat plane with a pressurized cabin, which would outgun the Boeing 307 for both size and comfort. Pioneering new technologies was not enough if Boeing was constantly being trumped by its Californian rivals. By the end of the decade, Boeing was no stronger. In 1939 the ranking of the top three commercial manufacturers showed Douglas well ahead, with 183 planes flying in the U.S., followed by Boeing with 45 and Lockheed with 42.[4] The balance sheet reflected its weakness, recording a loss of $2.6 million in 1939.

The Second World War, with its insatiable demand for machinery and emphasis on bombing as a strategic weapon, was to consume planes voraciously. A few figures illustrate the tidal wave of iron and steel on which the manufacturers rode. Between 1939 and 1945, America built 304,139 planes for the military. Over that period the industry jacked up its output by 13,500 percent, measured by pounds weight of airframe (of which the Army alone bought more than a billion). Production was incessant; in the peak month of the war, March 1944, the U.S. Army received 6800 planes, and the Navy 9113. Money, naturally, flowed like water; of the $185 billion the U.S. spent on weaponry, $46 billion was spent on planes.

Boeing participated in the avalanche of money. Soon after the outbreak of the war, the Army began buying the B-17s which had been so long neglected. The Stratocruiser and 314 Clipper lines were shut down and the entire plant converted to war production. In full spate the Seattle plants were turning out over 200 B-17 bombers a month, most of them flown to England for the raids over Germany which were a key component of Allied strategy. The B-17 was followed by the B-29 (the Superfortress), in production by 1944. Almost 4000 were built during the war, mainly for the long bombing missions over the Pacific and into Japan; B-29s carried the atomic bombs to Hiroshima and Nagasaki.

The war had been a blessing for the company; from a financial weakling, its purse had been refilled with government dollars. The same was of course true for the other manufacturers; Lockheed and Douglas had also had "good wars," making millions from military contracts. But, as after the First World War, the aerospace industry was both rich and poor: rich in financial and physical resources, but poor in prospects. With victory, the industry faced another drastic round of cutbacks in orders and production.

The insatiable demands of military production — Allied commanders wrote off two hundred bombers a night in the largest raids over Germany — left little time for wondering what would become of Boeing when the war was over. And indeed, the company was ill-prepared for peace. Phil Johnson, now back at the helm, put a small team to work on post-war projects; it quickly arrived at the same conclusion as Bill Boeing after World War One: manufacture anything other than airplanes. A cheap car, and kitchen and bathroom equipment were among the projects it came up with.

In September 1944, Johnson died of a stroke. Egtvedt had the task, with the other board members, of finding a new chairman. The managers felt they wanted someone they knew and trusted, but their choice was a strange one on the surface — Bill Allen, the company lawyer. Allen came from a typical small-town background, and was a Westerner, reared in the virtues of persistence and grit. He was born in Lolo, Montana, in the Bitterfoot Mountains south of Missoula, where his father worked as a mining engineer. He had graduated from the University of Montana in 1922, and went on to Harvard, where he read law. He returned to the West, settling in Seattle in a law practice where his first major assignment was working on the Boeing account. He quickly became a close adviser both to Bill Boeing and to those who took over the running of the company, and he joined the board in 1930. Neither an engineer nor a pilot, he nonetheless had a natural feel for the aircraft business; his legal training never smothered an appetite for commercial risk, nor did it inhibit his taste for adventure.

Allen initially turned down the offer, claiming it was preposterous to make a lawyer chairman of the company, and advised his board colleagues to look a little harder. In the spring of 1945, the board offered him the post again. Allen, a widower, protested that he already spent too little time with his two young daughters, and could do without the greater responsibility: "I just don't have the qualifications for it," he told the board. The reply was that the board were at least as well able to judge as he was, and Allen conceded. A bizarre choice in many ways — even in the U.S., where lawyers dominate many walks of life — he turned out to be an inspired choice; in more than two decades at the helm Allen left an imprint on the company stronger than the founder of the business.

When the board met on September 5, 1945, Allen's election as president of the company was a mere formality. There was more pressing business to discuss that day. The government had scaled back its orders of B-29s. A secondary plant at Wichita had been closed, and Seattle plant production was to be cut from 122 to just twenty planes a month. The workforce would go from a peak of 45,000 to 15,000 in November.

No sooner had the new chairman been elected than word came through from Washington that only fifty planes would be required in September, and ten a month from the beginning of 1946. Boeing had enough planes in stock to meet this requirement and, with the payroll running a $500,000 a day, the production director suggested the plant be shut immediately; if the lines were kept running, the company would be building planes nobody wanted. It was 3:30 p.m. Allen told his executives to make the announcement before the shift ended at four o'clock. To reporters from the Seattle newspapers — covering a town where one in every six people worked in the Boeing plants — Allen said, "I haven't figured out yet whether my election caused the contract reduction or they gave me the job because they knew it was coming."

Either way, it was a bleak beginning. The next day he met with his senior executives to discuss the options. Cars and kitchen equipment were soon discounted; they'd been down that road before. Other, bigger military bombers were a possibility, but firm orders were a long way off. Commercial transports, the instant reflex of the post-war airplane manufacturer, looked the best bet. But Boeing was a weak contender: the Stratocruiser was there but, despite active negotiations with the airlines, there were no orders as yet. The new DC-6 and the Constellation from Lockheed were carving up the civil market, leaving Boeing a trailing third. Both were cheaper than the Stratocruiser, and without long production runs Boeing could not compete on price. Allen had to make his first decision as president, and, uncharacteristically for a lawyer, he chose the boldest: the path of maximum risk, maximum return. They would start building fifty Stratocruisers right away. Volume production would bring the price down to $1.25 million per plane, and the company would just have to make sure it sold them.

Initially Allen's throw of the dice appeared to have turned up a pair of sixes. In November Pan Am ordered twenty Stratocruisers; in February Swedish Airlines took four, followed by Northwest Airlines with ten, and American Overseas with eight — a total of forty-two sold by the spring. In the end, however, the plane was an also-ran in the commercial race. By 1950, when the project was wound down, only fifty-six Stratocruisers had been sold around the world, and those at a loss; the program finally nudged into a marginal profit only some ten years later on the accumulated sales of spare parts. But it had served its purpose of keeping the plants running and Boeing in the commercial game. For the first post-war decade, however, military work kept the company alive. The Cold War held the level of military spending high for what was nominally peacetime, and the Korean conflict soonafter stoked the fires higher. The emphasis put on bombing by the development of the atom bomb, and by American strategic thinking, suited Boeing perfectly. Big long-range bombers were what it knew best, and demand was good.

Making use of German military technologies confiscated by the U.S. after the war. Boeing developed the B-47, its first jet, a long-range bomber with a speed of over 600 m.p.h. This was followed by a mammoth warplane, the B-52, a bomber with intercontinental range, designed for possible delivery of nuclear bombs into the Soviet Union. The B-52 weighed in at 330,000 pounds, with a sweptback wing of 185 feet, supporting four engines on each wing. Still in regular use today (B-52s were used in bombing missions during the Gulf War), over 700 of the planes were eventually built. At the same time Boeing diversified into building missiles designed to deliver America's new atomic weapons anywhere in the world.

Experience of building two long-range bombers, paid for by the US government, took Boeing into the jet age, acquiring the skills and technology at relatively little risk or cost. But it was still a minor player in civil aerospace, and was struggling to find a foothold in the market for commercial planes.

All the manufacturers and airlines in the U.S. had watched the development of jets with ambivalent eyes. They knew that jets offered substantial advantages over propeller-driven planes: they were faster, more comfortable and often safer. And they knew that large efficient jets could be built, but remained unconvinced of the potential of the technology for passenger planes. Jets, they figured, would always be expensive, and there would be too few passengers willing to pay a premium for jet travel to make them economically viable. For now, they would watch and wait.

News leaking from England that De Havilland, supported by government money, had begun building a civil jet caused consternation and some fright among the American manufacturers. Boeing held talks with Juan Trippe at Pan Am, and with other airlines, but the $15-20 million to build a prototype plane was beyond either a manufacturer or an airline. The industry discussed its fears about the De Havilland plane swamping both the European and American markets; Trippe had also ordered three Comets, not because he thought he could make money from operating jets but because Pan Am did not want to be left out.

So fearful was the U.S. industry of the threat the Comet posed and of the Europeans capturing this new market that its posse of tame politicians put forward a draft bill in Congress to provide government funding for a civil jet, a radical step in the U.S., where government almost never subsidizes commercial projects directly. The bill was scrapped because the manufacturers could not agree among themselves how the money and the work should be split; dividing the spoils of upfront government subsidy was something they were equally unused to. But its existence was indicative of the challenge posed by the Comet, and of the simmering geo-industrial rivalries of the two continents.

By the middle of 1950, the last of the Stratocruisers had been built, and Boeing was, for the moment at least, out of the civil airplane business. In the design workshops there were preliminary designs for a jet transport. Studies of the Comet had been made, and ideas for improvements sketched out on the drawing board. But the $15 million or so needed to build a prototype was nowhere to be seen. The turning point came during Bill Allen's trip to Farnborough to witness the commercial debut of the Comet. Impressed by the achievement of De Havillands in creating a plane so far ahead of the commercial competition, Allen was now more than ever convinced that the future lay with commercial jets; airlines would buy Comets by the score, and the British would have a lead that might prove unassailable.

But discussions with the U.S. airlines still proved fruitless; none of them was prepared to order a plane that existed only on the drawing board. Reaching back into the company's heritage, Allen sensed that it would have to create the market, just as Bill Boeing had created a market with his United conglomerate. Allen ordered a detailed study of the costs and risks involved in building a civil jet transport. By April 1952, the answers came back: $13 million was now the target figure for a prototype. A board meeting was called for April 22, when the designers presented their case with flip charts and diagrams, then left. There was little discussion; Allen had squared the board in advance. By the end of the afternoon a decision to build the 707 (as the jet would be called) had been taken.

There was no percentage in delay. The Americans were already behind and the De Havilland lead could only get longer. The 707 would be a low-wing monoplane, stretching 128 feet, with swept back wings supporting four engines. It would carry 130 passengers — far more than the Comet — at a speed of 550 m.p.h., but the demonstration model would be built as a cargo plane to show to the military; the company was still hoping for military orders to dilute the risk. May 1954 was targeted for the first test flight; the new jet would have to be built in record time.

The target was met. On May 15, 1954 the prototype was ready to roll out of the factory, and great ceremony accompanied its first appearance. The workers downed tools to line the runway, and newsreel and television cameras were on the buildings to capture the moment on film. In the background a band played stirring marching music to herald a new era. At 3:53 p.m. the giant doors slid open, and the plane, painted bright yellow on top with a copper-brown hull, edged into the sunlight. It nosed towards a podium where Bertha Boeing, wife of the founder, stood ready with a bottle of champagne: "I christen thee the airplane of tomorrow, the Boeing Jet Stratoliner and Stratotanker," she said, crashing the bottle against its metal frame. Behind her, Bill Boeing, making a rare appearance, watched proudly; observers believed they detected a touch of moisture in his eyes. The plane taxied away, ready for its initial test flight the next day. The great commercial air battle between Europe and America had begun.

The contest, billed an epic market clash between the Boeing 707 and the De Havilland Comet, never became the fifteen-round clash of heavy-weights anticipated. The Comet crashes finished the British plane as a serious competitor; the early battle for control of the jet market would be fought between American manufacturers.

The 707 got off to a good start with an order from the military for its use as an airborne fuel tanker, but airline orders were still painfully slow. Then in June 1955 Boeing got wind of its first major American rival: Douglas was building his own commercial jet, a shade larger than the 707, to be called the DC-8.

Juan Trippe at Pan Am was the only airline executive in the U.S. convinced of the viability of the jet; pulling strings behind the scenes, he had brought Douglas into the race. In a style perfected during several decades at the helm of Pan Am, he started a complex game of bluff among the three major manufacturers. Trippe liked the look of Boeing's planes; the 707 would give him a fast transatlantic service, with only one refuelling stop on the westbound route, usually Shannon in Ireland. But Trippe had based his airline on a simple principle: bigger is better. To make a dramatic entry he wanted the biggest plane that could be built.

He went first to California. Donald Douglas resisted. He had just finished enlarging the DC-7 at Pan Am's request, so that it was now capable of flying the Atlantic non-stop, and he was reluctant to commit himself to another risky project. He was also worried that the heavy fuel consumption of jets would make them uneconomic. Only when he checked Pan Am's figures did he reluctantly give the go-ahead for the DC-8. Lockheed was even less keen. Despite Trippe's invitation to compete, Gross figured two players were one too many already; he had no wish to be the third.

By the spring of 1955, Douglas had finished the design of the DC-8, but Trippe was still not happy. Both planes used the largest engines then available, but Pratt & Whitney had a new engine in development, one third more powerful than anything before, which could carry a larger plane even farther. Trippe wanted that engine, but Boeing was not willing to buckle. It had spent $16 million, $3 million over budget, with no orders apart from the military; it could not afford to overhaul the design. Douglas was also reluctant. The J-75 engine was untested, and he was not prepared to risk building a plane around a paper engine. Pratt & Whitney could not even guarantee a delivery date.

Trippe cajoled the engine maker into delivery to a set specification by 1959. In return, he signed an agreement to buy $40 million in engines; he now had engines to play with, but no planes to hang them on. He went back to Boeing, saying he needed planes for the engine, and if Boeing wouldn't supply he would buy them elsewhere. Allen reckoned he was bluffing, and told him so. Trippe went back to Douglas, and pulled the same trick on him. Douglas still had only a design for the DC-8; little had been spent. With little to lose, and much to gain, he agreed to Trippe's specification, taking an order for twenty-five of the new planes, the first American commercial jets sold, and only the second jet after the Comet. Tnppe and Douglas kept this deal secret for a time: Trippe wanted to make sure he had the first U.S. jets in the sky, and would buy 707s as well. Eventually, on 13 October 1955, he announced $269 million worth of orders: $100 million for 20 707s, and $160 million for 25 DC-8s, a record civil jet order.

And the best part of it had gone to Douglas. It was a bitter blow for Boeing, which had launched the first American jet, and now appeared to have been outplayed. Not just Pan Am, but other airlines as well were playing a game of cat and mouse with Douglas and Boeing, seeing how far they could bring down the prices before placing orders. Internally, Boeing salesmen complained that they were viewed as outsiders; airline executives were not convinced that the company was a serious long-term player in civil aerospace. Douglas took the next prize also, winning an order for thirty planes from United, a critical moment for Boeing, which saw itself slipping into a poor second place. Fewer sales meant higher unit costs, which translated into a higher price and even fewer sales. Allen was desperate not to fall into that trap. The engineers proposed modifying the 707, making it larger and more powerful, in an effort to pull in more airlines, even though it meant an expensive retooling of the plant. Most significantly, it would now carry the larger engines. "It will increase our risk, but let's go ahead and do it," Allen told his colleagues. He was doubling up on a risky hand, but this was the pattern of play he had established and he was unlikely to change it now.

In effect, Allen had caved in to Trippe's demand, and that had won an increased order from Pan Am. Slowly it seemed to emerge as the right decision, even though it had been made under fierce pressure. The next major order, from American Airlines, swung towards Boeing, and orders started to come in from Europe — from Sabena in Belgium and from Air France.

The battle between the 707 and the DC-8 was to rumble on for many years. Convair entered the race briefly with its 880 model, but could make no headway against the two giants. Eventually it recorded losses on the project of $440 million, the biggest financial disaster in American corporate history at that time, and a bitter warning to any other potential competitors that the jet business was a great way to lose a fortune. Lockheed dropped out of the civil market for the time being, and never stood a chance of regaining its place when it finally produced its own jet over a decade later.

Both the DC-8 and the 707 proved tremendous hits with the passengers, fulfilling the most enthusiastic predictions of propagandists of jet transport. The first 707 was inaugurated on a Pan Am flight from New York to Brussels on October 19, 1958, and was an immediate financial success. In the first quarter of 1959, 33,400 people flew on Pan Am's jets, with an average load of over 90 percent, the sort of numbers airline executives dream about. In the five years after that first flight, overseas traffic out of the U.S. doubled. Pan Am, which had pushed further and deeper into jets than any of its rivals, quickly became the biggest international airline in the world. Trippe's boldness and skulduggery had paid rich dividends.

The financial success of the planes encouraged other airlines to sign up for the new aircraft, but the money made by the operators was never matched by the manufacturers. The cut-throat competition between Douglas and Boeing for each and every order, in which both offered near-identical planes distinguished only by price, meant that margins were screwed down to rock bottom. By the end of 1959, Boeing was recording a loss of almost $200 million on the 707 project, and it was many years before the company got its money back.

Allen's gamble on the 707 had paid off in one way: it had taken the company back into commercial planes, a market abruptly severed when the United conglomerate had been broken up. The dice were no longer loaded against Boeing, and that was an achievement. But the gains were made at a terrible cost. The company was losing money on its civil transports, which it could only subsidize by the profits still made on selling hardware to the military. In the long term that would end in bankruptcy, a fact Allen was painfully aware of. Re-establishing its dominance — as opposed to re-establishing its presence — in the civil market would take another tremendous gamble; one that would make the stakes on the 707 seem puny.

3

THE HOPE
DIAMOND

The eventual signing ceremony was a simple, downbeat affair. On November 29, 1962, the British Minister of Aviation in the ruling Conservative administration, Julian Amery, met in London with the French Ambassador, Geoffroy de Courcel. In front of them was a short document of only seven articles, but explosive in its implications for both countries and for the world aerospace industry. It marked the beginning of the most epic and misguided adventure in the industry: the creation of the Concorde, a brave but doomed attempt by the two leading European industries to take a technological leap over their American competitors.

The signing ceremony may have been accompanied by little fanfare, but it was preceded by five years of international haggling, characterized by machinations of which the plane in the turbulent two decades of its life became a symbol. And though the agreement was brief, both countries discovered to their cost that it was binding in international law — a commitment neither could walk away from.

Concorde's story is long and convoluted. It probably begins with the Comet. The failure of that plane — with its implications for the future of the European aerospace industry — created a mental universe in which men wondered about the next great stab at glory. In the immediate aftermath of its failure, the European industry was still fragmented, as it had always been; now, for the first time since the Wright Brothers flight, it seemed threatened with technological torpidity as well.

To geo-industrialists, this was a serious matter. The advent of jet travel had made it clear that the airways were becoming the sealanes of the twentieth century; the airports its docks; the planes its ocean-going craft. Control of the mechanics of world transport had been a European prerogative ever since the sixteenth century, and great wealth and empires had been founded on the mastery of shipbuilding and seacraft. But as sealanes gave place to airways, politicians and industrialists saw European mastery slipping away. It was not a sight they intended to witness with silent and careless passivity. This bleak prospect for the European aerospace industry was the deep background to the development of the Great White Elephant. More prominent were two other factors: the emerging closeness of the British and French aerospace industries and the technology of supersonic transportation.

France had a proud tradition of aerospace inventiveness: the early pioneers of man-carrying balloons had been French, and although balloons turned out to be a technological cul-de-sac, the French proved their willingness to embark on hazardous adventures. Many of the finest names among the aeronautical pioneers had also been French, but this inventiveness did not translate easily into commercial success. Though they had become a substantial part of domestic industry before the Second World War, the French aerospace companies did not compare with their British, German or American rivals.

Post-war reconstruction took it up a league. The German industry was devastated, and was not to re-emerge for several decades. In France, from almost nothing, two major companies moved quickly to the front rank. Dassault concentrated on building military planes, while in Toulouse Sud Aviation, under the leadership of Georges Hereil, became competitive in the civilian marketplace. The industry had been nationalized in 1936 by the Popular Front government, and had been consolidated into six groups organized along regional lines. Hereil had started his career as a lawyer and a specialist in bankruptcy —desirable knowledge for anyone running a French nationalized industry — and had taken command of what was then Sud-Est just after the war. In 1949, one of its rivals (Sud-Ouest) had won government funding to develop a four-engine civil jet; a plane which, had it been built, would have been a lookalike for the British Comet then being designed across the English Channel. But the French government decided this was a machine it could not afford, and Hereil stepped in with a proposal for a cheaper two-engine jet. That contract was awarded and with government funding the Caravelle was launched in 1957, rapidly establishing itself as the first serious European contender in the jet market. Hereil sold twenty Caravelles in the U.S., not a large number but a significant psychological victory over the giants of the American industry. The success of the Caravelle, which was still in commercial service in the early 1990s, enabled Hereil to absorb Sud-Ouest into an expanded Sud- Est.

The emergence of the French as significant players in civil aerospace markets changed the balance of power within Europe. Until the launch of the Caravelle, the British thought the struggle would be between them and the Americans. It now began to look like a contest between the Europeans and the Americans; and with the ill-disguised anti-Americanism of the French, it acquired a bitterness and edge which had not previously existed.

Initially, the Caravelle set the stage for continuing cooperation between the British and the French. The plane had plenty of British equipment on board; it was powered by Rolls-Royce engines; it had a Dowty undercarriage and many other British components. The French, who tend to see virtue in trade-offs, reasoned that since they had supported British industry by buying its components, the British should buy the finished plane. But no Caravelles were bought by British European Airways, even though practically every other European airline ordered them, and this struck the French as little less than treachery, and colored their already harsh views of the British as industrial partners. As in geo-politics, so in geo-industrial rivalry, the British seemed little more than lackeys of the American eagle. It now appeared that the European industry would be divided internally, weakening its challenge to American hegemony.

The French, led by the two chief designers at Sud-Est, Pierre Satre and Lucien Servanty, were examining the options for a supersonic jet transport. Supersonic flight was already well established in the military field. The American test pilot Chuck Yeager had broken through the sound barrier some years earlier. Until now speed had governed the development of new methods of transport: The fastest had always come out ahead. As early as 1958, Sir George Edwards (who was to head the British side of the Concorde project) pointed out that once two places were brought within twelve hours' journey time of each other, traffic between them went up dramatically; this had held good from the stage-coach to the jet, and it seemed reasonable to suppose that supersonic jets would be no exception. The challenge was to see who could be in the air first with supersonic machines.

That was certainly the view of the technocrats at Farnborough, and on their advice the British government set up the Supersonic Aircraft Transport Committee in November 1956, a joint study between industry and government, to inquire into the project. After three years and £700,000, it came to the conclusion that supersonic transport was both technically and economically viable, and put forward two theoretical airplanes: A medium-range craft with a speed of Mach 1.2 (1.2 times the speed of sound), and a long-range craft capable of Mach 1.8. Development costs were estimated — rather roughly — at £50-80 million for the smaller plane and £75-95 million for the larger. Both would cost about one and a half times as much to operate as comparable subsonic planes, and would sell for £3-4 million each.

The committee's report laid the theoretical groundwork for development, and built a degree of momentum. The pressure now was for the commercial opportunity to be exploited before the Americans inevitably moved in. The Ministry of Defence, which took charge of the project, moved swiftly. By September 1959, the Conservative Minister of Aviation, Duncan Sandys, had commissioned two designs. Bristol was asked to put together a proposal for a supersonic jet with a conventional cabin and a slender wing, while Hawker Siddeley was commissioned to submit a design for a more daring flying-wing design, where passenger compartments would be part of a seamless wing structure. Both delivered their designs and Bristol won favor with the government. The firm was asked for a more detailed design. Its plane — which was inherited when the company was merged into the British Aircraft Corporation in 1959 — was to be the immediate forerunner of Concorde.

So far the development of a supersonic jet had been a purely British affair, but now the wheels of geo-industrial politics began to grind. Via the Ministry of Defence, discreet conversations were held with the Americans about their plans to build a supersonic plane. The message came back that the U.S. was interested only in a plane flying at Mach 3, whereas the British team was convinced that Mach 2 was the fastest speed compatible with the existing technology (they reckoned that equipment on board would melt because of the tremendous heat — above 250 degrees centigrade — caused by travelling at three times the speed of sound). With no agreement possible on the technical issues, collaboration with the Americans was a non-starter.

Contact was now made with the French. George Edwards, chairman of BAC, met Georges Hereil and discussed cooperation on the project but little progress was made. They talked of using common parts on otherwise competing planes, but the British came away from the meetings convinced that they were technologically ahead of the French and had little to gain from collaboration. Meanwhile, the French effectively trumped the British: at the Paris Air Show in 1961, Sud Aviation put on display a model of a plane it called the Super Caravelle; a four-engined supersonic jet able to carry seventy passengers up to 2000 miles — the first public commitment to building a supersonic plane.

This dramatic French move spurred the British into exploring collaboration more seriously, and the premature announcement was a masterstroke of combative public relations. The British were seeking, belatedly, to join the European Community and, as an article of wider policy, were looking for ways to deepen Anglo-French cooperation and prove British credentials as aspirant Europeans. Whatever the doubts of the industrialists, the political imperative was clear: strike a deal with the French. The French and British ministries instructed their respective industries to come up with proposals for a joint design, no easy matter given the antagonisms between the industrialists and designers on both sides. Nor was it made easier when the Americans, who had been eyeing developments with interest, made an active attempt to intervene in the discussions.

At a late stage in the Anglo-French negotiations, Eugene Black, former chairman of the World Bank, called Julian Amery. A man of considerable influence in Washington, Black launched into a long tirade against the project. A supersonic jet, he argued, would have to be heavily subsidized, it could never be built and flown by the private sector; it was, in short, a waste of money. Soon afterwards, Amery was in the U.S. as a guest of the head of the Federal Aviation Administration, Najeeb Halaby, who was conducting his own investigation into the feasibility of supersonic civil transports. He told Amery that the President would soon appoint a high-level committee to pursue an American supersonic plane, and that the committee would be headed by Mr. Eugene Black. The British became convinced that the Americans were involved in a spoiling operation, an attempt to persuade the Europeans to back out and leave the way clear for their own manufacturers. The cabinet took the American attempt to dissuade them as proof that supersonic jets would be money-spinners and quickly committed the U.K. to the project.

American intervention had proved decisive. Both the British and the French were irrevocably committed, only the details of the collaboration had now to be arranged. The agreement was signed in November 1962 committing the two countries to develop jointly a supersonic passenger plane, sharing equally its costs and the proceeds of sales. Four companies were to be involved. Sud Aviation and BAC would build the airframe, while the engines would be built by Rolls-Royce and SNECMA of France. An integrated management committee would run the project, and a standing committee of officials from both governments would oversee the work. Because the British had greater expertise in engines, 60 percent of the engine work would be done in Britain, while 60 percent of the airframe work would be in France. Development costs were estimated at between £150 million and £170 million, a big increase on the British figures produced only three years earlier. The first prototype would be delivered in 1966, and the plane would enter commercial service in 1969.

To the people involved in the industry, a new era of cooperation and hope had opened. "The European aircraft industry felt they were in possession of a potential world-beater which was going to revolutionize all previous concepts of air travel," wrote one participant.[1] That was the theory. The practice would turn out very different.

The structure set up to make the new plane proved complex and laborious; long meetings were held with the bilingual trappings of headsets and simultaneous translation. Despite the endless man-hours spent in committees, decisions were slow to emerge, symbolized perhaps by the fact that the British persisted in calling the plane Concord, rather than Concorde, as did the French, until the plane was actually flying. (The British had originally agreed to the French spelling but huffily insisted that the "e" be dropped after de Gaulle vetoed Britain's application to join the EC.) More serious were fundamental misunderstandings about the type of plane that would eventually emerge: the French had in mind a short-haul plane that would fly overland; the British believed that the sonic boom would make it impossible to fly the plane over populated areas, and that it could therefore use only transoceanic routes.

Hostility between the British and the French crews contributed to the snail's pace of the work. On one occasion at a lunch given by Sud Aviation in Paris, Archibald Russell, the chief British designer, regaled his French colleagues with a barbed story. There was a young man in aviation, he began, who was ambitious but was making little progress. He had heard that a specialist could perform a brain transplant, and inquired about the cost. That, he was told, depended on the quality of the brain. A red brick university brain cost about £1000. An Oxbridge brain was £2000. A brain from an American technical college of the status of MIT would cost £5000, but a brain from the École Polytechnique would be at least £25,000. Why, asked the young man, did the French brain cost so much? He was told, "Well, it's quite simple. Those brains are as good as new and have never been used."[2] Sniping between the frogs and le roastbifs was to be a permanent feature of a collaboration which never achieved the internal harmony of its name.

Despite the disagreements, by the end of 1964 there was agreement on a long-range rather than a short-haul plane. The project had been launched without any customers — not surprisingly since even the manufacturers were not sure what kind of plane they were planning to build — but in June 1963, a breakthrough was made when Pan Am took out options on six planes. Selling it was not easy; Air France and BOAC were notably unenthusiastic, even though they knew they would have to buy. Nevertheless, the Anglo-French consortium predicted that it would be able to sell about 240 Concordes.

No sooner had the building plans been formalized than Concorde ran into the first of its many cancellation scares. In 1964 a Labour government was elected in Britain, and looked likely to scrap the plane. One story, taken seriously by some industrialists, was that the Americans had insisted on cancellation as the price of loans being negotiated with the hard-pressed British Treasury. It was certainly plausible, because the Americans were keen to see the plane unbuilt, and Roy Jenkins, the new Minister for Aviation, did visit Paris to discuss scrapping the plane. The French replied that a clause in the treaty forbade either side to back out unilaterally (a clause the British had insisted on because their civil servants suspected the untrustworthy French might try to pull out). The threat of legal action, which the British judged to be real, coupled with pressure from the unions, persuaded the government to continue, but it was the first of many alarms and threatened cancellations which dogged the project through its long and turbulent life.

There were other threats prompted by the mechanics of geo-industrial rivalry, but fear as much as hope drove the project remorselessly forward. As early as 1963, the British knew that they were not alone in developing a supersonic civil jet. On a government delegation visit to Moscow that year, they were shown a model of a jet the Soviet Union was working on which bore a remarkable resemblance to Concorde. The British suspected espionage, and launched an internal inquiry, but no evidence of spying was uncovered. Anyway, as the designers pointed out, once you decided to build a supersonic jet, the design — long and thin, with swept-back wings — pretty well chose itself; but in the frenzied Cold War atmosphere of the 1960s, the parallel development of Konkordski (as the Russian plane was dubbed in the West) provided a powerful spur. To back down and allow Russia to be the first in the air with a supersonic transport would be a bad loss of face for the Western powers, who prided themselves on technological and material superiority.

Competition with the Soviets may have provided political motivation for continuing with Concorde; competition with the Americans provided a commercial spur. The commercial rationale was that European industry would leapfrog its American rivals, a logic as compelling to the Americans as to the Europeans.

The Americans had lobbied to prevent the European project getting off the ground, applying pressure on the British — with whom they had a "special relationship" — rather than the French, who always viewed American intentions in the worst possible light. Even after the enterprise had begun, discreet American lobbying carried on behind the scenes, and chivvying to abandon Concorde became a feature of political contacts between the two countries. But as time wore on, the U.S. accepted that Concorde was happening, that the plane would be built. It was time to consider their response.

Talks with the Europeans in the 1950s had foundered on the technical specification of the machine. The Americans were looking at a plane flying at a minimum of Mach 3. The Europeans stuck to their view that a machine that fast was not yet possible: "There are only. . .a few minutes of world experience of level flight at Mach 3," Sir George Edwards said in 1962, "and that hardly seems a sensible basis on which to build a big airliner in which you can sell seats to Mr. Jones of Wigan."[3] But many Europeans were in awe of the capabilities of the Americans, and that awe translated into a fear that the U.S. would trump Concorde with a faster plane, making it technologically obsolete within three or four years.

For many of the players in the U.S. aerospace industry, supersonic flight was an obsession. In the late fifties, under the leadership of Ken Holtby, a group of Boeing engineers had been tucked away in a telephone building in Bellevue, a small dormitory town on the outskirts of Seattle, to design a supersonic civil transport. After two years they concluded that the cost of the plane would be well beyond the resources of any single company. But the fact that Boeing began work so early — in track with work also being done at NASA — illustrates how soon the development had become a race.

As he had been throughout the development of the U.S. aerospace industry, the chief booster and cheerleader of the new technology was Juan Trippe, of Pan Am. After President Kennedy had formed his committee to study the possibility of an American plane, some discussions were held with the Europeans. Eugene Black met with officials from BAC, who proposed that the U.S. collaborate in building Concorde, and the Europeans would later collaborate with the Americans in building a Mach 3 plane. The discussions foundered. The Americans were more interested in competition than collaboration and were unwilling to cede technical leadership to the Europeans, even for a few years.

Black's committee recommended that the U.S. go ahead with a supersonic plane, and that government funds be provided for its development; a radical step because the federal government was traditionally hostile to providing public money for private industry. Kennedy was unsure. Najeeb Halaby was instructed to inform Trippe that the President needed time and that Trippe should not commit himself to buying Concorde. Trippe, however, was not a man to take orders, even from the President. He knew Kennedy was uncertain which way to move, and he had long experience of playing politicians. When Kennedy announced that he would make a decision by the Monday following Memorial Day in 1963, Trippe saw his opening. Already being pressed by BAC and Sud

Aviation to come to a decision, he announced his order for options on six planes the day before the President was due to make his announcement.[4] He paid BAC £210,000 and Sud Aviation FF500,000 for the right to one in three of the first eighteen planes to roll off the production lines in Bristol and Toulouse.

Kennedy had effectively been bounced. Refusing to back a U.S. plane would now look as if he were surrendering the field to the Europeans, and to a man who had committed himself so publicly to maintaining the U.S. as the world's leading technological power that was unacceptable. He announced that the U.S. would build a supersonic civil transport, funded jointly by the government and by industry. For the Americans, at the start at least, this was to be a clear and open battle between the resources and ingenuity of their industry and those of the Europeans. The announcement by the Federal Aviation Administration on August 15, 1963 invited the country's aerospace companies to submit plans for a plane "superior to the European Concorde." Words were not minced; they had seen the competition and they intended to beat it.

Donald Douglas decided early that this was one game his company did not want to play, leaving the SST project (as the plane would be known) to be fought for between Boeing and Lockheed. With years of study already behind them, Boeing figured they had a good chance of coming up with a winning design. Lockheed put forward a proposal for a plane with a swept-back delta wing similar to the Concorde. Boeing, by contrast, came up with a more radical design — a variable sweep, with the wing pivoted so that the degree of sweep-back could be adjusted by the pilot during the flight.

Even at this stage development costs were heavy, and the government agreed to meet 75 percent of the bill, the 25 percent paid by the manufacturers being reimbursed if the project were cancelled. In effect, the U.S. government would bankroll the whole undertaking, as the European governments were doing. In what was now Lyndon Johnson's administration, the SST rumbled along as a controversial issue. Opponents of the plan objected to its massive cost and noise pollution; supporters argued that the U.S. was involved in a struggle with the Europeans and the Soviets which it could not afford to lose.

The Russian card — always a useful one in Washington — was played strongly by Halaby. His chief opponent was Robert McNamara, who had become Defense Secretary. To Halaby it was "a life and death struggle, so far as the commercial airframe manufacturers were concerned, with the British, French and Russians. To the winner, the guy who produces the first commercially profitable, safe, and efficient aircraft, goes a $3 billion to $4 billion market."[5] But Halaby pushed too hard, and in 1965 was replaced by Air Force General William F. McKee, who was charged with taking control of the SST project. Competition between the two rival designs had hotted up: Boeing remained relatively silent about their plans, in keeping with their staid image, but Lockheed began taking double-page ads in leading newspapers, urging the merits of its design and of the project generally. It won the argument for the SST, but not its own case; by December 1966, the Boeing design had been selected.

Money was still uncertain, and Trippe, still cheerleading from the sidelines, stepped in with some financial proposals. The airlines would contribute $1 million towards the costs of the prototype for every airplane they wanted to option, and in return would receive a $3 million discount on those they bought. The deposit would be non-refundable if the project were cancelled. Ten of the twelve leading airlines agreed to participate and strong political support was also building; sixty-three senators were in favor of an American supersonic civil jet, with only ten firmly opposed. McNamara backed down, recommending to President Johnson in April 1967 that the SST go ahead. Despite the demands on federal funds because of the escalating war in Vietnam, Johnson agreed, and requested federal funding from Congress of $198 million to develop the SST. Development contracts were placed with Boeing for the airframe, and with General Electric for the engines. Two prototypes were to be built and tested over the next four years. The estimated total cost was $1.44 billion. Boeing was jubilant: Bill Allen told the press that it would create 9000 new jobs at Boeing.

It had taken the Americans five years to decide on building a supersonic civil jet, far longer than the British and French. Yet, throughout that period, as it became clear that the Americans would travel down the same path, the Europeans became convinced that they had chosen the right road — and they had a long lead on their U.S. rivals. All they had to do was to make sure that their plane was first in the air and on sale to the airlines.

Getting Concorde airborne was no easy task, however. Despite extensive feasibility studies, there was a world of difference between a metal and a paper airplane. And antagonisms grew between the French and British teams. "Every proposal made by a Frenchman was criticized to death by the British, and every British proposal was torn to pieces by the French before some sort of compromise was reached," a senior executive wrote later.[6] Design rows were compounded by niggles over language: the French insisted on using their own. Senior managers fretted that their opposite numbers were using the project to promote their own national aerospace industry as dominant within Europe. The French were adamant that subcontracting work should go to European suppliers wherever possible — preferably to French companies; they refused to allow work to go to American companies even when components could be bought off the shelf from the U.S. and would otherwise have to be developed from scratch. On contracts awarded within Britain or France, the consortium was subject to intense lobbying by parliamentarians wanting the work for their own constituencies. Concorde had become a pork barrel, and the fight over the carcass contributed to its slow and expensive progress.

These disagreements added to the delays inevitable in such an ambitious project, and costs crept ever higher. In January 1966 an audit showed — to general dismay — that the bill had doubled since the last calculations two years earlier. The figure was now £500 million. Even in France, where the Treasury is less tight-fisted than in the U.K., this caused alarm. General Puget, who had taken over from Hereil as head of Sud Aviation, paid with his job for the cost overruns. His replacement was Maurice Papon, formerly head of the Paris police: a background which struck the British as an odd qualification for running an aerospace company, but confirmed their view that some of the overruns on the French side bordered on the criminal. The upshot was that both British and French governments began to take far more day-to-day control, scrutinizing the work at every level and exercising surveillance over all major items of expenditure. In the view of industrialists on both sides of the Channel, greater political involvement may have meant greater accountability, but it did nothing to reduce the final bill.

That said, the plane did get built, and in December 1967 the first French prototype, 001, was rolled out of the Sud Aviation plant in Toulouse, while the second, 002, appeared out of the BAC factory at Filton, near Bristol. These were no more than test aircraft for experiment before laying down the designs of the final production model. But they gave the partners something to work with and start showing to airlines.

By the late 1960s, the Americans were also selling options on their SST, even though it was still on the drawing board. A race developed between Boeing and Concorde to see who could sign up the most airline customers. Pan Am was Concorde's first notional customer; but Trippe was soon followed by Bob Six, the president of Continental Airlines, who took out an option on three aircraft, but with no firm delivery schedule. Many of the world's major airlines then fell into line: American, TWA, Eastern, United, Eraniff, and Air Canada all took out options. In the rest of the world, Middle East Airlines, Air India, Japan Airlines, Sabena and Lufthansa (as well as Air France and BOAC, who were taken for granted) all joined the queue. Seventy-four options were taken out by the airlines, each generating hard cash for the consortium (the airlines put down a deposit to be set against the final selling price, but the consortium paid no interest on the deposit). Judged on options, the Concorde looked likely to become the most successful European aircraft ever built.

But the Boeing SST did better. The American designs were scaled back from the original: the moving wing was dropped as too complicated, and the speed came down to Mach 2.7, compared with the top speed planned for production versions of Concorde of Mach 2.2. But Boeing's was a bigger plane, with better flight economics than its European rival. It was also American, which made it easier to sell in the North American market: 122 options were taken out, comfortably beating the Concorde total. It seemed this was another aeronautical battle the Americans were going to win, but the Europeans had plenty to feel satisfied about. Given that by the late 1960s U.S. manufacturers had come to control about 90 percent of the world market for civil airplanes, a 30 percent share of the supersonic market for Concorde was a dramatic improvement. And the American plane still had to get from the drawing board to the skies. Until then the Europeans would have 100 percent of the marketplace. The dream of re-establishing the European industry by leapfrogging the Americans with advanced technology looked like becoming a reality.

Deliveries were not discussed in as much detail as options. The airlines were not too interested in when their planes would be delivered. With the exception of a few enthusiasts such as Juan Trippe, most signed to protect their competitive position; if rivals were offering supersonic flights, they would have to offer them too. The expense of introducing the new planes, and the threat of obsolescence to their fleets of subsonic

planes, meant they were in no hurry to take delivery. In truth, nor were
BAC and Sud Aviation in a great hurry to start deliveries. Delays in the
testing, and the complex production system (the French measured their
parts in millimeters, the British factories made their components in inches)
had delayed the schedule for initial deliveries.

Concorde missed an historic opportunity. Had the plane been ready
by 1968 as proposed, it might have fared better in the marketplace. The
world was still marvelling at a techno-culture exemplified by moonshots
and James Bond gadgets and receptive to scientific breakthroughs. A sales
pitch of bigger, better, faster was still perfectly in tune with the times.
Airlines would have been more sympathetic to the new plane, and options
could have become firm orders. But by the end of the decade the mood
had turned, and the age of technological disillusion had begun. Concorde
was one of its first and most visible victims.

The plane was attacked by environmentalists, who complained that its
engines would contribute to the destruction of the ozone layer, which was
true, although it seemed unfair to single out Concorde from supersonic
military jets, aerosol cans and refrigerators which were also eating up the
ozone. Noise pollution was also recognized as a serious problem: the rapid
growth of airports through the 1950s and 1960s had created a civilian lobby
tired of the racket of jets. And the new supersonic civil jets were undoubtedly
noisy; even if the sonic boom were restricted to oceans or low-population
areas, the Concorde even at subsonic speeds was not a quiet plane. These
obstacles might have been overcome by a private-sector p'oject, which was
not after all breaking any laws, but it became very difficult to justify using
taxpayers' money to manufacture an extra pollutant.

The environmental lobby was vociferous in the U.S. and audible
in Britain, but it raised barely a murmur in France; there Concorde was
attacked as a capitalist endeavor, designed for the ruling class, a point
Aérospatiale neatly deflected by pointing to Konkordski. In the U.S., the
environmentalists formed a bizarre alliance with free-market right-
wingers, ideologically opposed to government funding of industrial
projects. Funding for the SST had to be reviewed each year by Congress,
and the alliance against the plane, drawing on the cost overruns and
delays on Concorde, grew in strength. In the 1970 vote, it only survived
narrowly. (In one of the more subtle ploys in the game, BAC and
Aérospatiale did everything in their limited power to keep the Boeing

project alive; they reasoned, correctly, that if the Americans failed to build their own plane, they would be hostile to the European version.) The forces ranged against SST proved too strong, however, and on March 24, 1971 Congress voted against its continued funding. At the time of its cancellation, the U.S. had spent more than $1 billion, the bill to be picked up by the Treasury, and had precious little to show for its efforts. 13,000 pieces of hardware and 2000 boxes of engineering data were among the few remnants. There was also a mock-up of the proposed plane, built by Boeing at a cost of $12 million, which was sold to a fairground promoter for $43,000. He turned it into an attraction on the road leading to Disney World — a pathetic fate for the one representation of a machine talked about five years earlier as an instrument to revolutionize world transport.

For the Concorde consortium, the American cancellation was a severe setback. Although theoretically it left them with a monopoly of the market, it posed the question of whether the market was a mirage. What if nobody wanted a supersonic plane?

For the moment the project seemed to be on track. The election of a Conservative government in 1970 had meant its finances were once again reviewed, but the new Prime Minister, Edward Heath, was a strong supporter. The bankruptcy of Rolls-Royce in 1971 threw up another scare; they were building the Olympus engines to power the plane, but that too left only a faint scar on the optimism of the Concorde team. The pre-production models were travelling the world, creating huge public interest wherever they went. Late in 1971, President Pompidou of France flew in one to the Azores to meet President Nixon; in June the following year Concorde made a 45,000-mile sales trip around the Far East and Australia to great fanfare. The Chinese signed a preliminary purchase agreement for three and Iran Air ordered two, with an option on a third. Whatever the flak — and there was plenty — Concorde appeared to be selling.

The moment of truth arrived once deliveries started falling due. In July 1972 Air France and BOAC signed firm contracts for the delivery of their first planes: four for the French airline, five for the British. One immediate consequence was that, with the planes now entering production, the clock began ticking on the option agreement with Pan Am, which provided that they would make a decision on delivery dates within six months of work starting on the British and French planes.

Early in the round of negotiations, the salesmen formed the worrying impression that Pan Am had cooled on their commitment to the plane. Trippe had now left Pan Am, and the loss of his titanic personality had sapped the boldness which once characterized the airline. Both the British and French governments became heavily involved in lobbying the Americans to stay with Concorde, but on January 31, 1973, six months to the day after the Air France and BOAC contracts had been signed, Pan Am decided not to take up its options. To try to mitigate the inevitable damage, BAC threatened to expose Pan Am's weakening financial position, and accuse them of being unable to afford their plane if the statement accompanying the release were hostile to Concorde. Nonetheless, the airline's statement made dismal reading for the Anglo-French team: "Pan Am's studies indicate the airplane will be capable of scheduled supersonic services but since it has significantly less range, less payload and higher operating costs than are provided by the current and prospective wide-bodied jets, it will require substantially higher fares than today's. Concorde does not appear to be an airliner that satisfies Pan Am's future objectives and future requirements as the company now sees them. However, Pan Am will maintain an 'open door' to the manufacturers of Concorde for any new proposal they wish to make."

The dams had burst. The kiss-off line about maintaining an "open door" had been added at BAC's insistence, but Pan Am was not proposing to buy the Concorde — now or at any time in the future. This was the worst crisis in the plane's already troubled life. In New York, London and Paris, simultaneous press conferences were called by the Concorde partners to explain their side of the story and to say that the loss of the Pan Am contract did not spell the end of Concorde's commercial future. But that was the way it was played in the papers the next day, and the way it was read in much of the industry. Ranks closed quickly in support of the project. In Britain, Michael Heseltine, Minister for Aerospace, expressed his continuing faith, as did his opposition counterpart, Tony Benn, who had been one of the great supporters all through the Labour government of the 1960s. In France, the Minister of Transport backed Concorde, and the managing director of Air France said that in the future there would be two types of airlines — "those with Concorde, and those without."

But from here on it was an uphill struggle against formidable odds. In the few months following the Pan Am decision, all options on Concorde were cancelled, with the lone exceptions of Air India, Japan Airlines and Lufthansa. In the background the economics of the plane were getting worse and worse: a report in 1972 put the cost to date at £1 billion, with a further £250 million required for completion, making the final bill about eight and a half times higher than the estimates of 1962. The price of the planes had accordingly gone up from an estimated of $11 million apiece to $25 million.

Two more blows came in quick succession. The oil-price hike of 1973 made the economics of operating Concorde even less attractive; it had never been fuel-efficient, and the cost of fuel would now be the largest component of flying costs. And an economic crisis in Britain, followed by the election of a new Labour government, put intense pressure on British funding.

Soon after coming to power in February 1974, Dennis Healey, the new Labour Chancellor, decided that axing Concorde would be one way of bringing the government's escalating deficit under control. On March 18, Tony Benn, Minister for Industry, released a statement that summarized the costs of the project so far, and gave an ominous reading of its prospects: "British Airways [as the merged BOAC and BEA were now known] estimate that the operation of Concorde could substantially worsen their financial results, possibly by many millions of pounds a year." The statement detailed the estimated selling price as now being $47.5 million per plane, which would not be enough to cover the production and selling costs, never mind the vast investment in development. Further losses, dependent on how many planes could be sold, would range between £240 million and £600 million, of which the British would have to pay half. "In view of the size of sums of public expenditure involved and the importance of the decisions that must now be made, I though it right to place all these facts before . . . the country before any decision is reached," Benn's statement concluded.

The revelation that Concorde would not and indeed could not make money had the look of a mortal wounding. "It looked like the end of the line, as the general tone of the document was so doomladen," recalled a senior BAC executive.7 British Airways twisted the knife even more cruelly. The state-owned airline outlined how in their agreement to buy five Concordes, the British government had guaranteed it would subsidise any losses from operating the aircraft. Its estimates, it said, ranged from a £6 million profit in the best-possible scenario, to a £26 million annual loss. "Unfortunately the latest estimate of the effect of operating five Concordes is, at best, towards the most adverse of that range of forecasts. Greatly increased fuel and other costs affecting all British Airways operations and uncertainties of Concorde route permits contribute to the situation."

With not even the state-owned British airline able to speak well of the plane, the outlook looked bleaker than ever. A brief respite was won when Freddie Laker, the maverick airline entrepreneur, popped up at BAC's encouragement to say he could operate Concorde profitably if the government offered him the planes on the same terms as British Airways. Despite an internal cabinet row, the government agreed to continue financing the project up to a limit of sixteen production models. But Concorde was in deep trouble.

It had to fight not only for orders but for landing rights, against vigorous opposition from environmentalists. South Africa was ruled out because then no black African country would permit it to touch down for refuelling. An Australian service was ruled out because it could not touch down in either Malaysia or Singapore, and Tokyo went because there was no new airport where it could land. For its inaugural commercial flights, the plane could only go to Bahrain, although for a brief time it could also fly on to Singapore. Entry into the U.S. was finally won, after a long and bloody set of public hearings, and the plane began flying to Washington in 1976, and New York in 1977. But that was it. In the end, it flew regularly only to New York. Apart from British Airways and Air France, no other airline ever bought the plane. The greatest and most ambitious adventure in aerospace history had ended as its most disastrous flop. In a comment of the time, Concorde was like the Hope diamond, a flawless jewel which brought bad luck to everyone connected with it.

The Hope diamond was a fitting analogy. Concorde was a technological marvel. Two decades after its introduction it is still flying safely, and has acquired a cult following on its transatlantic routes. It is still the most beautiful aircraft ever built. It was inspired in a mood of great optimism, but, like many other products of the European industry, it fundamentally missed its mark. It was a luxury product introduced into a mass market; but the people who designed and built it had not understood the economics of the airline business: pack as many as possible on to big, cheap-to-run planes.

Its failure — and such a spectacular failure — cut deep. Concorde had always been more than just a plane. The Europeans had loaded it with their hopes of fighting the technological and commercial domination of the United States. This was always clearer to the French than to the British. In continental Europe, the plane was a symbol of a longed-for industrial renaissance, a point clearly made by Henri Ziegler, president of Aérospatiale between 1969 and 1972. He believed that Concorde was a vital symbol of European freedom and independence and he drew eloquent parallels with the Greek and Roman empires: the Greeks brought progress to the ancient world but were overthrown by the Romans when they began fighting among themselves. The case was perhaps overstated, but the kernel of truth remained. "For Ziegler, Concorde is a major element in the European fight to keep its independence and freedom in the face of American or Russian dominance."[8] When it failed, not just money had been squandered. The fight too seemed to have been lost.

4

THE FINAL FLING

The *Clipper Young America,* christened by the President's wife, Pat Nixon, sat on the tarmac at Dulles Airport, Washington, on the evening of January 15, 1970, ready to inaugurate a new era in jet transport: the maiden commercial flight of the Boeing 747, the largest civil plane ever built. It was a bitingly cold winter night, and the passengers shivered as they climbed the staircase to the giant machine. When they entered, they may have marvelled, as millions have done since, that such a large beast could fly. Seated, they waited for take-off. At 7:29 p.m., the plane began to taxi along the runway, the first steps on the journey to Paris. Then, with anticipation at its height, the plane taxied back to its berth. An engine had overheated, and the maiden flight had to be aborted: a public relations disaster threatened, which, to the watching Boeing officials, seemed to symbolize the whole wretched enterprise.

The plane almost hadn't made it to the tarmac. Close to completion, the production models of the 747 had developed a series of engine problems. Annoyed by the threat of delays, Pan Am, early in December 1969, threatened to withhold half the final payments falling due on its first delivery of the new Jumbos — $4 million on each plane. Thornton Wilson, the new president of Boeing, was disturbed by the threat; Boeing desperately needed the money to plug the hole in its bank accounts. But Najeeb Halaby, who had taken over as president of Pan Am, was not in the sympathy market: "We want the progress and then the payments, not the payments and then the progress," he told Wilson.

Halaby was not really in a position to dig anyone out of a financial hole. He knew that Pan Am would report huge financial losses for that year, and was preparing 1500 "redundancies," the first layoffs at the airline in almost two decades. But Halaby dug in his heels and told Boeing that he had a case against them for lost revenues caused by late delivery of the plane. The argument bounced back and forth. Wilson said the engines and not the airframe were causing the delay; Halaby argued that the delay was ruining his competitive advantage as the first airline to have the new plane, an advantage they had paid for in hard cash. Both men pushed to the brink of scrapping the Pan Am order before realizing it would damage the reputation of both companies. Finally, on December 12, a compromise was reached. Halaby agreed to split the difference; he would pay $2 million and withhold $2 million. At 7:30 p.m., with the check issued to Boeing, the first plane was released from the plant, and a Pan Am crew flew it to Washington, ready for its debut flight.

The teething troubles on the *Young America* were exactly what Pan Am had been complaining about. Fortunately, the airline had foreseen the possibility of a technical hitch (they had plenty of reason) and had another plane standing by, loaded with champagne and strawberries, to celebrate the first flight. The passengers boarded, destination London. After six hours' delay, the *Clipper Constitution* finally took off, and just over six hours later its 324 passengers touched down in London. The age of the Jumbo Jet, the defining machine of the late twentieth century, had begun.

That its debut was late and difficult was not surprising. The Jumbo was a difficult machine: difficult to build; difficult to finance; difficult to sell; and at times even difficult to credit. Yet it can also claim to be the most successful flying machine in the world, and perhaps the most important. Certainly, within the world aerospace industry, it is now the center of gravity around which everything turns — a tribute to the adventurous recklessness of American capitalism, and in particular to two cantankerous old men, for whom the 747 was their last and finest stand: Juan Trippe and Bill Allen.

Juan Trippe's name has been a consistent skein in this story. He has made cameo appearances, pushing and cajoling the industry and taking decisions of awesome risk, but his role in the development of the Jumbo makes a full portrait essential. Trippe was born into a family which contained the mixture of convention and eccentricity that was to characterize the man. His father came from a respectable old Southern family but his mother was born out of a marriage between a barmaid and a bank robber; ancestors many business people thought contributed plenty to his character. His step-grand-father was a Cuban businessman who brought money into the family, and from whom he got the name Juan. He was embarrassed by the name, for he spoke no Spanish and had no Spanish ancestry.

After Yale, he went to work in a bank but quit after two years to form his own aviation company, Long Island Airways, which ferried rich socialites to their country retreats in surplus warplanes. He moved into carrying airmail with a small company, Colonial, backed by Yale friends such as William Rockefeller, but fell out with his partners and had to resign. He then raised money to take over a small company called Pan American, which had won the mail contract between Florida and Cuba. With his high-level contacts in Washington and an abundance of persua-siveness (he wore frayed cuffs to meetings with officials to prove he needed the money), he tied up airmail contracts throughout Latin America and the Pacific. Piece by piece he turned Pan Am into the American international airline, establishing such a close relationship with the State Department that the airline was referred to as the "chosen instrument" and often accused of running its own, independent foreign policy. (When Chiang Kai-shek wanted to pass a plan to President Truman to prevent China falling to the Communists in 1949 he used Trippe as a more influential messenger than the American ambassador.)

Trippe was a cold and ruthless businessman, who ran the airline with a cynical disregard for rivals and employees, but more than any other figure of his age he understood the role that planes would have in transforming the world's geography. He embraced the jet, and sensed that it could reduce travel to another manufactured product: standardized, mass-produced, cheap, it would make air travel a mass-market commod-ity. In the process, he turned Pan Am into the most powerful of the world's airlines. By 1965, it was making 258 flights a week across the Atlantic. He was determined to create bigger and cheaper planes, capable of carrying more people to more places than ever before. His desire for the Jumbo was part of a continuous theme that ran back to the 1920s: a quest for grandeur that overrode commercial inhibitions. For him there was no doubt. A bigger plane was a better plane, and a bigger plane as soon as possible was the best plane of all.

In Bill Allen (although they were too suspicious of each other ever to become close friends), he found a spiritual soulmate. Since introducing the 707, and surviving the cut-throat competition from Douglas, Boeing had prospered mightily. The 707 had re-established Boeing as one of the pre-eminent manufacturers of civil aircraft, and it had consolidated its position with the 727 and the 737. In May 1958, before the first 707 was delivered, work had begun on a medium-range jet, the 727, for the regional journeys which made up the bulk of the air travel market. The Trident, a three-engined jet built by the newly merged De Havilland and Hawker Siddeley, had attracted the interest of many of the airlines, and Douglas was also working on plans for a small jet. Boeing fretted about being squeezed out of the market, but their fear was groundless. In 1960, the 727 was launched with orders from United and Eastern totalling $420 million, then the largest in aviation history. In the twenty-one years of its production life (the last was delivered in 1984), 1831 Boeing 727s were sold, a record for any commercial jet, which lasted until it was overtaken by the 737 in 1990.

With the medium-range market captured by the 727, a market was developing for short-range jets, small planes to ferry passengers between relatively close cities. Boeing entered the race late. The 111 from the British Aircraft Corporation, a small twin-engined plane, captured some of the European market and, more significantly, the DC-9 from Douglas covered the bulk of the growing American market. To maintain its position, Boeing felt it had to compete in short-range jets and the final decision to proceed was made in 1965, on the back of orders from Lufthansa. Over the next two years 232 were delivered to the airlines, and the 737 is now the most commonly used plane in the world.

Across its range Boeing had built a family of jets which made it arguably the most successful aircraft manufacturer in the world by the mid-1960s. But it *was* arguable. Douglas was still a player, and so was Lockheed. Across the Atlantic, the British and the French were building Concorde, a plane still expected to revolutionize the industry as the early jets had done a decade earlier. And Boeing was in there too, competing fiercely in the upcoming battle for supersonic aircraft. It was also staking its place in the development of interplanetary travel.

From the perspective of the 1990s, the conquest of space may appear increasingly futile, a technological dead end. But in the 1960s, the outlook was very different. For a generation raised on a diet of sci-fi stories, the conquest of space seemed just another chapter in the endless story of going further, faster. There was an underlying assumption that in due course men would colonize the planets, and, indeed, it seemed obvious that ferrying people around the solar system would one day become big business. One where it was worth getting in on the ground floor. Particularly for a company in the transport business.

When President Kennedy made his speech pledging that Americans would walk on the moon before the end of the decade, the race began in earnest. America's space project was an ingenious mix of public and private enterprise. NASA, a publicly funded agency, took the lead role, and the design team was headed by Wernher von Braun, a German rocket scientist who, after working for the Nazis in the Second World War, was brought to the U.S. Although NASA masterminded the crucial design work, building the rockets was farmed out to private industry. Early in the 1960s, Boeing officials, led by Bill Allen, took the decision that rocket boosters were the part they wanted to be in; big, heavy units of engineering providing plenty of power were what they knew best, and rocket boosters seemed to be a long-term, cash-generative business beyond the immediate demands of the moonshots.

As early as 1958, Boeing opened an office in Huntsville, Alabama, the site of NASA's Marshall Space Flight Center. In 1961, it won its first contract — to build twenty-four first-stage boosters for the Saturn rocket. That was followed, in 1963, by a contract to build eight lunar orbiters (five for flights, three for testing) at a fixed price of $80 million. On the back of these pieces of work, and the company's enthusiasm for the future possibilities of space travel, Bill Allen okayed the building of a new space facility outside Seattle. Eventually the plant grew to cover 320 acres, containing enough equipment to build and test the rockets in an artificial space environment (the largest testing facility outside NASA). Boeing's space program climaxed with the landing on the moon, and fizzled out with the subsequent moonshots. Its adventures reflect the temper of the times and the technological excitement of the decade. Between supersonic travel and space exploration, the building of another subsonic civil aircraft seemed a dull and pedestrian task. The building of the Jumbo, the great transformational vehicle of the late twentieth century, created little excitement at the time.

It began, as had many previous Boeing projects, as a military plane. In the early 1960s the Pentagon began putting together plans for a rapid deployment force which could be moved anywhere in the world in a crisis. It meant transporting men and equipment far faster than the traditional ships had done. The Pentagon was looking for a plane capable of carrying a division of troops — the largest plane yet built, dwarfing even the giant B-52 bombers.

Boeing, the masters of the big plane, naturally wanted to bid. As early as 1961, as forward military strategy was just starting to take shape, the company was working on plans for a giant troop carrier. By September 1964, after four years' work and $10 million of research money, a 4000-page proposal for the plane, dubbed the C5A, was submitted to the U.S. Air Force. Boeing was not the only company lobbying to build this plane: both Lockheed and Douglas had joined the race.

Boeing's bid was judged in defense circles to have the best technical work, and the company was certainly qualified to build a major military plane. But Robert McNamara, Kennedy's Secretary of Defense, had already revolutionized military procurement, focusing on value for money and cutting back costs. He had been hired to bring into the military the same financial disciplines he had used at Ford. Boeing's proposal was good but it was not cheap: for the 115 planes the Air Force wanted, Boeing had bid $2.3 billion. Douglas offered the same fleet for $2 billion. And Lockheed wanted just $1.9 billion. Cynics within the industry believed that Lockheed had bid just low enough to win the contract, reckoning the price could always be renegotiated upwards when it was too late to switch to another company. Whether true or not (and had Boeing won it would probably have renegotiated as well), the tactics succeeded. It was later revealed that the Lockheed plane never ranked technically higher than third of the three proposals put before the Air Force, but that did not matter greatly. The company had recognized the dedication of McNamara to paring the budget as thinly as possible. And Lockheed had observed the politics of the order: though it was a California-based company, with all its plants in the west, it decided to build the C-5A in an old Second World War plant in Marietta, Georgia, the same state which, by transparent coincidence, elected the head of the Senate Armed Service Committee,

Richard Russell. Pork-barrel politics was as successful as ever, Lockheed won the C-5A contract, and Boeing was stuck with the costs of four years' laborious technical work on a giant subsonic aircraft, and no plane to build.

In the event, its defeat was probably a stroke of luck. The C-5A was one of the Pentagon's more disastrous purchases. Its costs overran by more than $1 billion, and the wings developed cracks, which had to be put right at the cost of another $2 billion, bringing the final cost of the program in at more than twice the Boeing bid. The planes were not much use — their size made them too vulnerable to small-arms fire to be used anywhere but far behind the lines, where smaller aircraft could have done the job just as effectively. But nobody knew that at the time. When the news of the Lockheed award broke on September 15, 1965, it was a shock to Boeing, which until then had basked in its reputation for military planes. The news was announced to the workforce (ironically during a strike so that relatively few heard) by Thornton Wilson, an executive vice-president at the time: "I regret to report that Boeing has lost the C-5A contract to Lockheed," he said over the public address system in the Seattle headquarters. "It is an understatement to say we are disappointed; however, we are not disappointed in our people. What we learned will be applied to our other business efforts." [1]

There was truth in the last sentence of Wilson's statement. Though the Pentagon's decision had come as a bitter defeat, two consolations were available to soften its impact. One was the SST, the great hope for the future, which Boeing was already working on with ample government money. The other was the proposal in the industry for a giant subsonic aircraft.

The idea was mooted primarily by Juan Trippe. In the summer of 1965, shortly before the C-5A decision was announced, Trippe and Bill Allen had gone fishing together in the frozen seas of Alaska. They hired a classic old yacht, *Wild Goose,* owned by John Wayne and rented out to rich tycoons, who hoped perhaps that some of the old movie cowboy's stage grit would rub off on their commercial adventures. Their wives went along for the trip, but this was basically a man's holiday, an exercise in commercial machismo. Between jousting over the merits of different fishing grounds and over which line and tackle to use, the two men explored the idea of the new plane. Eventually it came down to a kind of dare, a challenge to the other's daring: "If you build it, I'll buy it," said

Trippe. It was a gauntlet Allen had little choice but to pick up: "If you'll buy it, I'll build it," he replied. Nothing was signed or sealed, but by the time Allen returned to Seattle, there was an understanding that Boeing would build the new plane and Trippe would buy it.

For the Pan Am boss, the Jumbo represented a tremendous risk. No detailed figures had been worked out at this stage, but given that the conception of the plane called for a beast two-and-a-half times the size of a 707, which sold for $7 million each, it did not take long to calculate that the new machine would not come in at less than $20 million. Undeterred, Trippe told Allen that he felt twenty-five of the new planes would be enough for a start; an order worth about $450 million. Big numbers to play with, but 1965 had been a good year for Trippe. Pan Am made $50 million in profits, and with air traffic soaring around the world, half a billion dollars did not seem a huge price for staying ahead of his competitors.

Despite the massive investment involved, Trippe and Allen were unconcerned about the long-term future of their new plane. As far as they could see it did not really have a long-term future. Both were charter members of the "supersonic will conquer the world" school; Trippe had already ordered Concorde, and was buying the SST as well, just as soon as Allen and the U.S. government got around to building it. The Jumbo was a stopgap, a cattle-train to move passengers in bulk before the supersonic era. They believed it would have a relatively short shelf-life as a passenger plane, but in the long term would be useful as a freighter, a market both men believed would explode as giant planes took over from ships to transport bulk goods around the world.

Returning to Seattle, Bill Allen had a customer but no plane. With Boeing, and particularly within the engineering department, the SST was the sexy project to work on, where the brightest engineers were assigned. The new subsonic jet — no name or number had yet been attached to it — was not a glamor project. The task of designing it was passed to the grittiest and least glamorous of the Boeing engineers - Joe Sutter.

Today Sutter is an old man. He still has an office and a secretary at Boeing, in a low-slung concrete building that looks out over the company airstrip running along the bay. He wanders in occasionally, keeping a careful eye on the old firm and dispensing words of wisdom to the attentive younger bloods. Which, for one of the most influential engineers alive, is right and fitting.

In 1965 it was very different. Sutter was relatively junior in the company's engineering hierarchy, and not a man many would have marked out for greatness. Small and solid, with a slow western manner of speech, he came from a Balkan family (their original name was regarded as unpronounceable in America) and had grown up close to the plant where he would make his career.

"The reason I came to work at Boeing was because I lived right up on that hill over there," he recalls, gesturing to the hills on the other side of the bay from the airstrip. "This airport was the only airport in town, and when I was a young child one of our favorite pastimes was to wander down. . .and see what was going on."[2] Many of the schoolkids had hung around on the hills watching the military planes roll off the runways, and Sutter had witnessed the crash of the B-29 prototype, but it did nothing to lessen his enthusiasm for the flying machines he saw every day. "Boeing was an important cog in our community even then. A lot of people living in our neighborhood worked at Boeing, so I became interested in aviation," he recalls. "I thought a career in aeronautical engineering would be an interesting life, which it turned out to be. I am one of the few engineers at Boeing who came from Seattle. When I joined, during the war, there were people coming here from all over the country. And when I came in as a junior aerodynamist, and I looked around at all these people who were five or ten years older than me, I figured I would have to hang in there a long while to get anywhere with that crowd."

Which turned out to be true. Sutter joined the company from the University of Washington, which hardly compared with MIT and the other great technical schools. He began with certification work on the Stratocruiser and went on to work on the 707, 727 and 737. By the time Allen had to make his decision, Sutter had a reputation as a solid and dependable workman, the right man to design this mundane hulk of an aircraft. He took charge of one hundred or so engineers in a block known simply as 1085 Building; at Boeing numbers carry more resonance than names. The 747 team occupied the second floor, equipped with metal drawing desks and strip lighting. The outline of the plane had been discussed only briefly with Pan Am and other airlines interested in the new Jumbo. Boeing was offering anything between a 250-seater and a 350-seater, and consensus was that bigger was better, as it always was in the 1960s. But apart from the fact that it needed to be big, and to be able to carry cargo as well as passengers, Sutter and his colleagues confronted a blank sheet of paper.

One basic configuration for the plane had already been discussed: a doubledecker. The idea was simple: take the existing design of a large plane such as the 707, put one fuselage on top of another, and you have a plane twice the size. Juan Trippe, in particular, loved the idea. A doubledecker plane like the old Stratocruiser winging its way across the Atlantic seemed the perfect vehicle for attracting passengers.

Sutter hated it. Models existed of the two-decker 747, but to Sutter they were all monsters. Apart from anything else, the prospect of evacuating passengers from a two-deck plane in an emergency struck him as a catastrophe in the making. For months, the designers played around with different versions of the doubledecker, but found nothing they liked. However, working with the then-standard approach of six passengers seating abreast, there seemed no way of fitting 350 people into one plane, unless you made it incredibly long or put the people on top of each other — until designers began thinking about the cargo requirements.

In 1965 a new standard for freight containers had been agreed upon, with the cross-section of each box measuring eight by eight feet, designed for uniformity between road, rail and ship transport. These containers would always be too heavy to be carried by air, but it seemed advantageous to the Boeing designers if their freighter plane were constructed to the same shape. Putting two containers side by side, they drew a circle around the space needed, and suddenly they had something that looked like a fuselage.[3] Admittedly, a very wide fuselage — on the passenger deck it would be more than twenty feet across — but the engineers had their breakthrough. The plane would not only be much bigger than any before, it would be much wider and would need only one deck. In retrospect, it seemed a rather obvious idea, but it took that one insight to create the widebody jet.

The widebody was one of two key innovations in design introduced on the 747. The other was the pod sprouting from the top of the machine, like a bruise on the head of a cartoon character. It too resulted from the needs of a cargo plane. It would be easier to load cargo if the front of the plane could be swung open, but that left the problem of where to put the flight deck. One early design for a doubledecker had the flight deck on the lower level, with passengers on the upper floor able to look through windows and see where they were going. The design was dubbed the anteater because of its droopy nose. The idea of shifting the flight deck was revived, but this time it was put on top — the windows rose out of the nose, and the rest of the compartment was swept back to preserve the aerodynamic qualities of the design.

Initially Sutter and his team planned to put radar and other navigational equipment into the space behind the cockpit, but that changed when Juan Trippe saw a mock-up of the plane. Entirely uninterested in mundane matters like navigational equipment, his idea was to use the space as a first-class cocktail lounge. And so the 747's exclusive upper deck was created. Other airlines came up with even odder ideas for the open space created by the new widebodied design. "Some of them wanted downstairs cocktail lounges," recalls Sutter. "They wanted barber shops and hairdressing salons. One joker was even trying to talk to us about a swimming pool. We told him no." The basic design was put in place through 1965: the wide body, the raised hub, the wingspan; once those decisions were made, the rest of the plane fitted in as best it could.

Despite the frantic encouragement of Trippe behind the scenes, Boeing still had the job of selling the plane. Ironically, they had to sell it to Pan Am in particular. As he had done so often in the past, Trippe, in his last great adventure, played the rivals in the aerospace industry against one another. The Europeans were not in the race to build the Jumbo, but Douglas and Lockheed were still very much in the game. Douglas was talking to Pan Am and the rest of the airlines about a 250- to 300-seat tri-jet, which eventually appeared as the DC-10. It found plenty of takers; more than Boeing was finding for the proposed 747. Other airlines were cool on the new giant, figuring they might buy it if it got built, but doing nothing to bring it into existence. Douglas decided to build the tri-jet, believing that Boeing was creating a plane for Pan Am alone, and that no market existed beyond Trippe's fevered imagination.

Lockheed went in the opposite direction, stoking Trippe's gigantesque fantasies; it was never difficult to talk the old man into even more ambitious plans. Lockheed representatives scuttled around the industry talking about a tripledecker plane carrying nine hundred people, trumping Boeing's by a factor of three, and arguing that it was a natural extension of the C-5A program snatched from Boeing. Lockheed turned out to be only kidding. The airlines no more wanted to fly such a monster than

Lockheed wanted to build it, but they kicked up sand around the 747. Robert McNamara believed it was a waste of resources for the country to be building two new giant aircraft at the same time, and argued to that effect within the government: Either the Lockheed or the Boeing plane should be built but not both. Trippe intervened personally to win government support for the 747, though, in truth, there was little to prevent Boeing building the plane if its board was so minded. The issue culminated at a meeting in the Oval Office between Trippe, Bill Allen and President Johnson, where a bemused Johnson gave his personal blessing.

Allen was quiet during the meeting. He was not used to seeking presidential permission for a project, and was not sure he liked the idea. Even without this political meddling, Allen was having a tough time back at the ranch. Within Boeing it had been a traumatic year, designing the basic shape of the 747 and steering it through the government and the airlines. "In those days, Boeing was either going to build that airplane or it was going to give the business to Douglas," Sutter recalls. "And if Douglas had got the business, then Douglas would be what Boeing is today. But that was all one hell of a big gamble. The 747 was two-and-a-half times as big as the 707, and the company literally ran out of money while developing the airplane. It was one of the riskiest decisions ever made. Remember, at that time the Concorde had come out and proved that supersonic travel was delightful, and Douglas was bringing out a stretched DC-8. So the 747 was quite a different animal from what anyone else had conceived. . .a hell of a lot of people were daunted. The question being asked by everybody here was would that big thing even fly?"[4]

Making a plane fly is a delicate balance between design, weight and engine power. Put simply, the heavier the plane, the more engine thrust it needs to take off and fly (actually, to take off, which is when it needs maximum power — cruising through the sky requires much less thrust). At the time the initial contract was signed between Pan Am and Boeing, a plane of 655,000 pounds was envisaged. But by 1968, it was bigger and fatter — up to 710,000 pounds — while the range had fallen to 5000 miles, and the cruising height (which governed the fuel consumption, since a plane consumes less fuel as it climbs higher) to 33,000 feet. There was a real fear that the engines being developed by Pratt & Whitney would not be ready in time, and real doubt they would be powerful enough to lift the monster off the ground.

Trippe, of course, had wanted the biggest engine in the world — the big fan engine being designed by Gerhard Neumann at General Electric for the C-5A. Its development was being bankrolled by the Pentagon, and Trippe was always keen to let the U.S. military pay for his programs. But the G.E. engine had severe problems, one being that it was designed to power the C-5A's much lower cruising speed. Boeing also suspected that the engine would be what the industry calls a "smoker:" a big noisy machine suitable for a military plane but utterly inappropriate to the quiet luxury demanded by the business passengers and tourists who would fill the new Jumbo. Rolls-Royce had lobbied hard for its new RB211 engine for the 747, but Sutter was deeply suspicious of the quantity of sophisticated and untested technology Rolls was throwing into the new machine (suspicions which were justified — the RB211 was the machine that bankrupted Rolls-Royce and prompted a government rescue in the early 1970s). Eventually Pratt & Whitney, despite deep misgivings, agreed to develop a new engine for the plane.

The engines were not alone in posing problems. There was also the sheer size of the building program. The 747 was among the largest industrial products ever built, requiring factory space of a scale and scope never previously seen. If the age of industrial gigantism reached its peak anywhere, it was in the factory that built the 747. Imagine its size, then remember that you need space to hold several at a time, plus the massive cranes and jigs swinging components into a single, completed airplane — and then leave room to drive it through the front door.

The largest building in the world was always going to be a huge engineering feat, and a political hot potato. It would involve truckloads of money — for contractors, for workers, and even as a tourist site (which it became in due course). It would be one of the saltiest pork barrels ever, as Boeing was aware. Politically, Boeing was not the sharpest company in the U.S.; its Northwestern parochialism insulated it to some extent from the rapacious lobbying and backscratching that characterizes American government at its rawest. Yet even these Seattle innocents knew the leverage that the decision on location would give them, and it had long been policy that location decisions were not made without a couple of senators and a clutch of congressmen as part of the price. Though there were strong sentimental attachments, there was no particular reason why the plane had to be built in Seattle. The 747 was, in effect, a new company, with its own workers, suppliers and management. In theory, it could be built anywhere.

Politics suggested California as the most obvious site. It had the strongest aerospace industry and thus the most powerful aerospace lobby. A massive Boeing plant in the region would woo some of the local politicians away from Douglas, then Boeing's major competitor. A site at Walnut Creek, just east of Oakland, was thought suitable. Inside the company there was fierce debate: the more hard-headed proponents of political influence lobbied for California, while the sentimentalists pressed for the company to maintain its traditional allegiance to the Pacific Northwest. The seclusion and isolation of this far corner had been part of the culture of the firm; the purity of its landscape and air, plus the simple values which its farming and logging economy encouraged, were part of the atmosphere that made Boeing special, isolating it from the corrupting influence of bigger cities, and more cosmopolitan states. It was a mawkish view, but one with plenty of followers.

The sentimentalists were not without political acumen. The two veteran senators from Washington State, Warren Magnuson, an old guard member of Roosevelt's New Deal, and Henry ("Scoop") Jackson, had maintained a careful balance between representing the loggers and the farmers as well as the hordes of blue-collar workers employed at the Boeing plants, and representing the industrial and military might of the state's leading company. Both came from Everett, a small working-class town dominated by lumber mills, about thirty miles north of Seattle. As early as June 1966, Boeing had taken an option on land in the town. Other sites were surveyed, creating brief flurries of land speculation despite Boeing's attempts to keep secret its intentions. But Everett had a military runway that could easily be extended, and when the town offered to build new junctions with Interstate 5, which runs through Washington State down to California, the contract was quickly agreed upon.

To build the plant, Bill Allen chose one of the few outsiders ever to penetrate Boeing's ingrown culture, a man named Mel Stamper, who had joined the company four years earlier from General Motors. Stamper had headed up — and sold — the company's lossmaking gas turbine division. Building the largest structure in the world was his next task. The demands of the 747 appeared insatiable: the sides of the building would rise 10 stories from the ground, and the roof would span 63 acres, creating a space inside of 205 million cubic feet. One problem immediately became apparent, a technicality which captured the scale of the project: the building would be so large that it would form its own interior micro-climate. Neither heating nor air-conditioning was likely to be necessary because of its location, but in its open spaces clouds were going to form in certain conditions, floating gently above the workers, and it might even rain. As if these problems were not enough, there was little time. The tight timetable of the 747 project meant the building had to be ready to start manufacturing by 1969.

Within the maze of departmental responsibilities that made up the 747 project, Stamper was only one player. Organization charts revealed little of who was driving the simultaneous parts forward. Sutter, for example, appeared as a director of engineering, just one of ten or so managers in the second tier of the top management of the company. And yet, as he drove the design forward, he emerged as the dominant force within the project, the man who more than any other was identified with the building of the 747. But even as he did so, drawing in more and more designers to finish on time, the company was falling behind on building the machine, and its finances were rapidly worsening. Costs escalated day by day, not just because of the size of the undertaking, but because Trippe demanded that his planes be in service by 1970. As early as 1968, top executives at Boeing realised that the 747, like the Concorde, was accumulating one of the most serious budget overruns endured by a civil airliner.

In the background, as was his wont, Bill Allen adopted a relaxed attitude. The 747 had been his baby and he was aware that he was taking a gamble. But, not himself an airplane man, he was unaware of how great a gamble. Such had been the competence of the Boeing team in the past that planes had rolled out of the design and production departments without much difficulty. He could be forgiven for thinking that the 747 would be the same, only bigger. But as the costs grew and grew, his was a painful education in the logistics of pushing the frontiers of technology.

At its peak, the 747 project employed 12,500 engineers, ironing out the myriad technical problems the plane kept throwing up: an army of people known within the company as Sutter's runaways. They had a profound sense of their specialness, bound up in the adventure of creation. All around them, the company was rapidly going broke, and it was largely their fault.

In 1966, when the undertaking was initiated, the company had been on a roll. New products were pouring off the lines, and the airline industry, in one of its periodic booms, was snapping up aircraft as fast as Boeing could fasten the rivets. As the decade wore on, the sunny optimism gave way to a darker hue. The war in Vietnam was taking an increasing toll on the U.S. (and later the world) economy, pushing up government expenditure, stoking inflation and sucking up purchasing power. The effects were quickly felt by the airlines, which responded, as usual, by cutting their order books. And Boeing was hurting as much as, if not more than, the other players in the industry.

At the beginning of 1968 — the last of the sunny years of expansion — the company had orders for 328 aircraft, worth $2.6 billion. It was a soft and deep cushion, able to bear the tremendous load of the 747. Only twelve months later the cushion was thinner: the order book showed only 164 aircraft, as orders were fulfilled and options cancelled. The line was heading downward, and could be going all the way to zero. Through the first few months of that year, not a single U.S. airline ordered a new plane, nor were any international orders in sight. And the money was flying out the door.

For Boeing, 1969 was the most crucial and traumatic year for the 747, and one that tested the company's fiber in a way it had not been tested since the enforced break-up of the United conglomerate in the early 1930s, more than a generation earlier. Ironically, and painfully for many of the people involved, it was also the year when Bill Allen stepped out of day-to-day involvement in the company.

The old guard — the men who remembered Bill Boeing, and who had shared the rough and dangerous early days of the company — had been slowly departing the scene. In 1966, Clair Egtvedt, who had been president of the company in name at least since 1939, had finally bowed out. From then on, as he passed his seventieth birthday, Allen had pondered retirement and his succession, a subject which exercised the minds of the senior executives almost as much as the 747 and the ill-fated SST. On April 29, 1968 the board appointed Thornton Arnold Wilson — known universally in the industry as T. Wilson — as president, and though Allen remained as chairman the baton had been passed to a younger man.

Allen departed the stage with much of his irrepressible spirit of leadership still intact. In one example, shortly before standing aside, he had visited the nearby home of his overwrought manager Stamper, still wrestling with the mammoth task of completing the Everett plant. It was late, and Stamper was still at the office, so Allen left behind a quotation from one of his boyhood heroes: "Far better to dare mighty things than to take rank with those who live in the grey twilight that knows no victory or defeat."[5]

The quotation was from Teddy Roosevelt, one of the few genuine American imperialists, and a fitting hero for Allen, who had made the company an embodiment of American economic expansionism and one of the main suppliers of its military machine. If there were such a thing as American imperialism, Boeing would rank among its sturdiest troops. But Allen was aware that the times were changing, and that a different spirit was to enter the body of the company.

Allen was never a pilot or a plane builder; Wilson was. Hailing from Missouri, he had migrated to Boeing and spent his career there, working as a technician on the B-47, the Dash 80, the company's first jet, and on the giant B-52. Allen had marked him out by the early fifties, grooming him for higher office by sending him to MIT to learn industrial management. Later he had managed Boeing's Minuteman missile project for the government, a complex task which involved not only difficult technical issues but controlling the sprawling expense of the development. Wilson established his reputation as one of the few who understood both aeronautics and finance — a rare and, by the late 1960s, an increasingly valuable skill. He became vice-president in charge of operations and planning, and from there leapfrogged his rivals to take the presidency of the company.

Allen had realized that Boeing needed someone who could keep a tight rein on the purse strings. But playing his preferred role as the jocular uncle of the company, he gave Wilson only one piece of advice on handing over the top job, "Always wear your hat when you go to New York." Yet it soon became clear that Wilson represented a new style as well as a new face. One of his first actions was to build himself a presidential suite, complete with bathroom and shower, on the same third floor where Allen still kept his modest office. He moved executive salaries more into line with the extravagant rewards American corporate executives were beginning to bestow upon themselves, starting, naturally, with himself. He added $21,000 to his pay, taking it to $130,000, $6,000 more than Allen had ever paid himself and $50,000 more than anyone else in the company.

Some changes were certainly needed. In his last days, Allen had allowed the situation to slip dangerously out of control. On taking command, Wilson became painfully aware, in a way Allen had not been, how slippery Boeing's finances were. Designing a new aircraft does nothing for cashflow: all the big costs are up front — design, testing, plant and tooling costs have to be met immediately. The revenues, meanwhile, are many years behind; the airlines put up small deposits for their orders and options, but they don't pay until the plane is delivered. The cashflow is all one way, and in the case of the 747 it was fast becoming a river.

In addition to the demands of Pan Am that the plane be built in record time, another set of wolves now began howling at the door. Boeing could not have financed the 747 from its own reserves; that would have been impossible. It was being bankrolled by a syndicate of banks, led by First National City Bank of New York (known now as Citicorp), which had put up more than $34 million. As the costs rose, the bankers, who invariably have weak stomachs, became squeamish. They needed to see an actual plane to restore their faith. Roll-out for the 747 was set for 30 September 1968. The plane was by no means ready, but Wilson needed a public display to reassure the outside world that it was being built, and to silence the wolves, at least temporarily. Piecing together the first test plane did not go well. Its translation from paper to metal was never likely to be a precise science, particularly in the days before computers could iron out design wrinkles. Even so, some of the alignments of major sections were out by as much as half an inch.

The plane nearly didn't make it for the appointed day; when the landing gear was being attached, one set of wheels smashed through a wing, causing extensive damage. Bruised and battered, a patched-up version was wheeled out of the newly finished Everett hangar, and there was a celebration. Pompous speeches were made, and the event was widely reported, but all present knew that the plane sitting on the tarmac was in no shape to fly.

It was another six months before a 747 took to the skies; six months during which the money was still draining away. Time was running out fast. Boeing had to get the planes into Pan Am service by early 1970 or incur heavy penalty payments. Worse, the company could not start delivering to other airlines until it had made the first Pan Am deliveries. Before any of that could happen the Jumbo needed a certificate of airworthiness from the Federal Aviation Authority, which had to be by October or November at the latest; the first test flight could not even be contemplated before February 1969. Many voices in the company argued that it could not be done, or not done with the guarantee of a safe airplane. Wilson knew otherwise — it had to be done, or Boeing would be bankrupt.

Early in 1969, the main problem was the engine. Pratt & Whitney had not promised fancy new technology, as had Rolls-Royce, but this was still the most powerful jet engine ever built, and completing it against a tight schedule was no easy task. By mid-1969, there was graphic illustration at the Everett plant of the trouble Pratt & Whitney were causing Boeing. Sixteen built 747s sat on the grey tarmac outside the plant, each with blocks of cement weighing almost 10,000 pounds strapped to the undercarriage of the wings. No engines, just cement. Those planes were worth a fortune — a lost fortune until they could fly — and Boeing executives calculated that the stockpile of engineless, useless Jumbos would have burned their way through the entire net worth of the company before then.

The engine — the JT-9D — was being completed in a year less than what Pratt & Whitney's engineers considered prudent for a new machine. A B-52 was being used to test them; its old Pratt engines were stripped out, and one of the new engines used where two of the old had been, since the 747 was almost as large as a B-52 but was powered by only four engines compared with the B-52's eight. And the early test versions, none of which was ready until 1968, showed a worrying tendency to stall. Not an encouraging feature for a plane carrying 350 passengers. On top of that, Boeing and Pratt & Whitney were still arguing about the thrust; the requirements were creeping upwards as the weight of the 747 increased. It was only late in 1969, a few months before the plane was due to go into service, that Pratt & Whitney engineers came up with a solution: the engines would have a form of water injection to raise the power needed for take-off — a sleight of hand used on military jets. Squirting water into the gas turbines made the air-fuel mixture expand faster, generating more thrust. The snag was that the plane now had to carry water as well, creating more weight. Pan Am accepted this to meet the deadline, but reluctantly and as a temporary solution, to be solved permanently as soon as possible.

The troubles did not end there. The maiden test flight was completed in February 1969, and went smoothly, despite some bitten fingernails around the Boeing plant. Allen, who turned out for the display, warned the test pilot darkly that the future of the company was in his hands. But then disaster struck. The FAA, worried by the sheer size of the 747, and the immense loss of life in any crash, was keeping a very beady eye on the plane. Boeing had expected that, but was unprepared for more than two hundred FAA inspectors to move into Seattle, checking every last detail. Nor was it prepared for the first serious incident. The third test plane was on a simple run from Everett to Renton in Seattle, and coming in to land on the short runway, when the test pilot, Ralph Cokely, misjudged his final descent altitude and brought the plane down on a heap of rocks between the runway and the lake. The rocks ripped off the landing gear, leaving the belly to scratch unprotected along the concrete surface, sparks flying in every direction as the metal tore into the ground. Later, the press office claimed that the wheels had come off, as designed, without puncturing the wing or releasing the thousands of gallons of petrol stored there, but it was scant comfort for a high-profile public disaster. Cokely was promptly fired by Wilson.

Not just the test pilots had their jobs on the line. For Wilson, the technical hitches dragging on through 1969 created a fear that his might be the shortest reign in the company's history. He had good reason to worry — the baying of the bankers was getting louder. The net worth of Boeing in 1969, the book value by which the bankers could measure the security of their loans should the worst happen and the plug have to be pulled, was $796 million. It already owed well over that, and the bankers were worried that they might never be repaid. The company met monthly with its banking syndicate, usually to ask for more money but also to review progress, and the exchanges were becoming colder and shorter as the months progressed.

In a conversation with his deputy Tex Boullioun later that year, Wilson expressed his worries graphically. The two men had worked together for many years, and the president could confide to him his deepest fears. "Tex, we are not getting anywhere," he said. "I'm going to get fired in six months if we don't make some kind of a turnaround." He produced the only solution he could think of: cutting costs in the most savage and direct ways. "The logic is simple. If I don't do it, the board will bring in some ice-water guy from the outside who will . . . I might as well be the ice-water guy. I just want you to know there's only one guy I know for sure that's going before I do, and that's you."[6]

With that threat — particularly stinging to an old colleague — Wilson hauled his most senior executive into a drive to slice costs. In 1969, when the financial pressures were at their apex, 25,576 people were sacked from Boeing, from vice-presidents to office cleaners. One hundred million dollars was stripped from the cost base, staunching but not stopping the bleeding of cash. With staff being whittled away all around them, the project team raced to complete the testing of the 747. Hope of getting its airworthiness certificate by October 1969 had faded, but it had to be in place by November or the deliveries would never reach Pan Am. Almost everything *was* in place by the middle of the month, except for one document, accidentally chucked out in the rush; replacing it caused another two-week delay. In December 1969, with the decade spinning to a close, the FAA came through with certification.

Boeing had been within a whisker of the deadline, but Pan Am had their planes for the first commercial flight. Boeing had some money; not all they had hoped for, but after some $2 billion had been lavished upon it, the 747 was earning money rather than draining it. To a relieved Wilson and other senior executives, their worst nightmares seemed over. In truth, they were just beginning. Building the 747 had been a great achievement, a testament to the drive and genius Allen and Trippe sparked in each other, and praise was lavished on them. "The two people who put the 747 together were Bill Allen and Juan Trippe, and if either of those two people were missing at that time the program may not have happened," Sutter confirmed many years later. But Allen and Trippe were gone by the time the plane was finished, and its future was entrusted to other men, men to whom this extravagant gamble would later seem less visionary and more foolhardy.

It was in many ways fitting that the 747 was completed in the last month of the last year of the 1960s; it was very much a creature of that decade, a symbol of adventurous expansionism. As the 1960s turned into the 1970s, those at Boeing discovered how quickly the idealism of the last decade was transmuted into the sourness of the new.

5

LE DÉFI
AMÉRICAIN

It was quite a day for Roger Beteille, a dapper Frenchman, noted for always wearing a white tie: December 18, 1970, almost a year into the new decade, and eleven months after Boeing had flown its first 747, a dream of sorts had been realized. There was no celebration however, and Beteille could have been forgiven for pinching himself.

In the center of Paris, in a few bare rooms in 160 Avenue de Versailles, were Beteille, the chief executive of the new enterprise, and his chairman, Henri Ziegler. There were secretaries and a few support staff. But that aside, on the day that Airbus Industrie was formally constituted as a *groupement d'intérêt économique* (GIE) under French law, there was nothing. No planes, no plant, little money and precious little support. Nothing really apart from an idea — an extravagant and dangerous idea, shared by Beteille and Ziegler, but by few others: an idea of overcoming the American dominance of the aerospace industry, and restoring the European challenge to pre-eminence. For both men it was an idealistic adventure which would invigorate the entire European economy, revitalize pride among the nations of the European continent, and secure a prosperous future. It was so utopian and unlikely, and the chosen instrument so blunt and tarnished, that both men felt more comfortable keeping it secret. To preserve themselves from ridicule, they revealed as little as possible of their plans. This would be a project which, in its early days, would be best served by being cloaked in as much darkness as possible.

Ziegler, who cropped up earlier as the man who presided over the last and most desperate days of Concorde, had already established himself as the champion of the European aerospace industry as an expression of continental renaissance. He feared for the industry in the wake of Concorde's demise, sensing that the Europeans had bet too heavily on a single technology and in the process had squandered political as well as monetary capital. He realized that this would make its resurrection a far harder and longer task. Which was perhaps why he had mourned Concorde so personally and so bitterly.

Ziegler was a creature of de Gaulle's France. He had been a prominent resistance fighter during the war, one of the general's men, decorated many times for his bravery, and had risen to be chief of staff of the Free French forces in Britain. Defiance in the face of hopeless odds was bred in him, as was the Gaullist notion of national destiny and greatness. At the end of the war he became an official at the French War Ministry, where he angered his seniors by insisting that there was little future for a fragmented European aerospace industry, and in particular for France trying to fly solo. Sacked by the Air Minister, he had moved to private industry and dabbled in politics; he ran the office of Jacques Chaban-Delmas when he was Air Minister in the mid-1950s. Then, on July 31, 1968, when he was considering returning to politics full-time, he was tapped as chairman of Sud Aviation, his brief being to sort out the mess surrounding Concorde. He had made clear that he had been opposed to the project, and insisted that Europe should be concentrating on subsonic aircraft. Nonetheless, a loyal if single-minded *apparatchik* of the French state, he was prepared to do what he could.

Beteille was a younger man, also a product of Gaullist France but influenced by the cosmopolitan, pan-European tide of the post-war continent and less burdened with memories of the war. He had benefited from the conventional training of the French élite and had immersed himself in the twisting fortunes of the European aerospace industry. A graduate of the École Polytechnique, he had worked as an engineer with both Sud-Est and Sud Aviation, and for a spell at De Havillands in Britain on the ill-fated Comet. Working on both sides of the Channel, in what were then the only two European aerospace industries that counted, had given him a unique perspective on the strengths and weaknesses of the industry, and the daunting size of the American giants. He too had digested the European defeats and was determined not to do so again.

As they contemplated the scene from the Avenue de Versailles, Ziegler and Beteille were overwhelmed not just by the slog ahead but by what they had achieved. Getting even those few sparse rooms had been a monumental battle, lasting years, and with many twists and turns along the way.

The idea of a European subsonic consortium had been knocking around the capitals of the Continent for many years. As the 1960s wore on, the overpowering dominance of the American manufacturers was but one visible expression of its dominance of the world economy, which was beginning to irritate the majority of Europeans. In 1967 a polemic by Jean-Jacques Servan-Schreiber became a huge bestseller across Europe. *Le Défi Américain* (*The American Challenge*)[1] succeeded in capturing and stirring the sense of resentment at the humbling of their economies, their livelihoods and their pride beneath the Yankee juggernaut. "American industry spills out across the world primarily because of the energy released by the American corporation," Servan-Schreiber wrote. He attributed that energy not to the American industrialists but to a "highly organized economic system based on large units, financed and guided by national governments." American national and corporate power, in his analysis, were seamlessly woven into an economic battering ram. "Most striking of all is the strategic character of American industrial penetration. One by one, U.S. corporations capture those sectors of the economy with the highest growth rates." He argued that the only way to compete was for Europe to create its own national identity, guided and helped by governments, to challenge the Americans on their own terms. The choice was stark: "Building an independent Europe or letting it become an annex of the United States."

From this populist atmosphere the notion of an Airbus emerged. Aerospace, after all, was one of the key growth industries the Americans were capturing. The notion was raised formally as long ago as 1964, shortly after Britain and France had agreed to build the Concorde together. Sud Aviation put a proposal to the British Aircraft Corporation, and a meeting was held between the two companies in Paris. They were looking at a high-density short-range plane, in the 180-200 seats range, powered by two jet engines, to be in service by the early 1970s. Air France and BEA would be the two key customers, but there might also be potential for sales around the world.

The initial meeting went well, and the two companies agreed to make some preliminary designs. The project was given the working name Galion, and throughout 1965 regular meetings were held to firm up the design and marketing of the new aircraft. During that time, however, Sud Aviation had a change of heart and began thinking about the potential for a 300-seat aircraft, while BAC remained in favor of the 180-200-seat market. In part, each was obeying the whims of their national airlines: Air France was pushing Sud Aviation towards 250 or more seats, while BEA was looking for a new, smaller aircraft. As they had done so often in the past, the European manufacturers were acting as industrial suppliers to their national airlines rather than addressing themselves to the world market. The partners seemed, even to the participants, to be walking down a road they knew led nowhere.

By the time of the 1965 Paris Airshow, the scheme was gathering momentum. While talks were going on between the British and the French, the French also put out feelers to the Germans. Seven German companies came together in an organization known as the Studiengruppe Airbus, to examine what they might contribute to the project and what they might get from it. This was the first time the Germans had become involved in European aerospace cooperation, which was hardly surprising. Although their tradition of aeronautical innovation ranked with any of its rivals, the industry had been devastated during the Second World War, and was only slowly picking itself off the floor.

Until 1955, the Allies prevented Germany from building aircraft of any sort or playing any role in the development of jet planes. After some time, the industry re-established itself on a modest scale, building planes for the German Army. Partly to reduce the cost of supporting a military industry, by the mid-1960s the German government was looking for ways for the industry to expand into civil projects, which they were prepared to underwrite with taxpayers' money, and European collaboration appeared to offer the best, indeed only, way forward. The market was too crowded to contemplate setting up an independent airframe manufacturer.

Political will seemed to exist in all three countries. In November 1965 a Franco-British working party was established to see whether a common specification for a new plane could be hammered out. Over the next two years, different proposals winged their way between the different companies and the different governments. Two compromises emerged: one that it would be a 200-250-seat plane; the other that it would be known as the Airbus.

In May 1967, three years after the proposal had first been mooted, a meeting of ministers was held in Paris to thrash out the details. It was hosted by André Bettencourt, French Foreign Minister, whose presence was intended to indicate how seriously the French took the venture, and that they intended to provide the leadership. At a lesser level, Germany was represented by Johann Schillhorn, a state secretary at the Ministry of Economics, and Britain by John Stonehouse, Labour Minister of State for Technology. At the end of the meeting a document was signed, the first of many, which gave tangible definition to the Airbus.

It was to be a twinjet, with £190 million set aside for developing the airframe; Britain and France would each pay 37.5 percent of that amount, with shares to match; the Germans, still very much the junior partners, would put up the remaining 20 percent. The engines would be supplied by Rolls-Royce, their estimated development cost was £60 million, three-quarters of which would be paid by the British Treasury, with the French and the Germans putting up the rest (in return for which French and German engine makers would receive some of the work). The agreement speculated that 250 of the planes would be sold, speculation backed up by a commitment that all three national airlines would include the plane in their fleets. Beteille was appointed in July 1967 to coordinate the study projects, and in September a formal Memorandum of Understanding between the three countries was signed at Lancaster House in London. It set a target date of one year for the design to be completed; the plane was to be in service with the airlines by the spring of 1973, six years away.

So much for memoranda of understanding. In the complex genesis of the Airbus, as soon as anything was put into a memorandum it was promptly forgotten. In 1968, less than twelve months after the agreement had been signed, doubts were emerging on both sides of the Channel.

In France, disenchantment with the Airbus was swelling. Air France feared that too much would be conceded to BEA, and the aircraft would be too small. At the same time, Dassault was lobbying hard for the Mercure, its own follow-up to the Caravelle, still the champion of the

French industry though it had not been a great commercial success. The Mercure was planned as a 150-seat plane, much smaller than Air France wanted, but at least it was French. To many of the officials it seemed a more glamorous project than the Airbus, which, to the Ministry of Finance in Paris, an institution used to staring into these things, looked like a bottomless pit. At the same time Concorde was in disarray, and doubts about heading down the same path again were justifiable. As it turned out, only Ziegler and a collection of French students saved the Airbus; Ziegler warned that 30,000 jobs would be lost if the Airbus were cancelled, and aircraft workers in Toulouse were the first to join the student strikes in 1968. The French government was tottering and de Gaulle was about to depart the scene: these reasons were sufficient to keep the Airbus temporarily alive.

In Britain, there were no student rebellions, but enthusiasm was ebbing as fast. When the issue was raised at a meeting of Harold Wilson's cabinet in July, ministers seemed to be vying with one another for the pleasure of twisting the knife into the Anglo-French collaboration: "Again there seemed to be a repetition of past mistakes. The price was escalating once again, particularly of the air frame," recorded Richard Crossman in his diaries.[2] "Tony Crosland made the very modest suggestion that we should defer a final decision for five months and go on paying until then. The Chancellor [Roy Jenkins, later, ironically, president of the European Commission] wanted to cut the project now and it was fairly obvious that he was mainly concerned that if we postpone the decision on this we shall find it more difficult to cancel Concorde in December. But I've got a feeling the French won't allow us to cancel Concorde anyway, and we must be content to cancel the Airbus by itself."

The cabinet agreed to carry on for a while longer, but it was increasingly clear that there was little political muscle behind it. There were more pressing concerns: the British had in Rolls-Royce a major aero-engine manufacturer, and were constantly stuck with the dilemma of whether to concentrate on the engines or the airframe side of the industry (they could, of course, have concentrated on both, but conceptual thinking of that sort is way beyond the British mandarins). Rolls-Royce had long been of the view that its best future lay in supplying engines for American aircraft, which it judged would dominate the world market. The company was ready to play along with the Airbus idea — particularly with public funds thrown in — but it really hankered after a deal with a major American manufacturer.

At the time that the Airbus proposal was being developed, Lockheed, which was trying to break back into the civil airliner market, locked Rolls into an exclusive deal to supply engines for its new Tristar. Although that deal did not exclude it from participating in the Airbus, it made the project considerably less attractive to the government, which was committed to financing 70 percent of the cost of developing the RB211 engine for the Lockheed plane. This would take a large chunk of the limited funds available for the aerospace industry. At the same time BAC was lobbying for public funds to be devoted instead to its new plane, the BAC 3-11. Largely at ministerial whim, BAC had been replaced as participant in Airbus by Hawker Siddeley, on the grounds that BAC was the British partner in Concorde, which meant that it was now the other chap's turn. BAC, an influential force, was therefore as hostile to Airbus as it had earlier been in favor.

Early in 1969 the then German Chancellor, Dr. Kiesinger, made a last-ditch effort to keep the British with Airbus, appealing personally to Harold Wilson when they met in Bonn in February. His efforts were of no avail. In March the French and Germans attempted to up the stakes by announcing that they would build Airbus anyway, regardless of whether the British stayed in; the threat of being excluded was thinly veiled. None of this made any difference to the Wilson government, which had made up its mind that it did not care about exclusion from what it saw as pointless European aircraft programs. In April that year, after another round of ministerial meetings, Tony Benn, by now the Minister for Technology, told the House of Commons that Britain would not after all be a participant in the Airbus. Even against some stiff competition, this was without doubt one of the stupidest industrial policy decisions ever made by a British government. Having backed two losers — Concorde and the RB211 for the Tristar — it contrived to miss out on the one potential winner the European aerospace industry offered.

For the remaining two partners in Airbus the British withdrawal created an immediate crisis. The problems were not so much financial; the Germans, after all, had been contributing only 20 percent because it was felt that was all the standing their aerospace industry had; the government of the Federal Republic was more than willing to put up more if needed.

So too were the French, although they were more reluctant and not entirely unsympathetic to the British decision.

The industrial infrastructure posed the problem, and the sudden British exit exacerbated it. Hawker Siddeley had already done most of the design work on the wing and were tooled up to manufacture; dropping out now meant a whole year's work wasted. Against that, to bring the wing into production would cost about £5 million, more than the company felt it could finance were it to carry on as a private partner in the venture. The French and the Germans were also in a dilemma: the wing is the most complex part of an aircraft to design, and there were doubts, particularly in Germany, whether expertise existed outside Britain to make an adequate wing. Either way, it would certainly delay development, and might jeopardize the whole enterprise.

Into this situation stepped Franz-Josef Strauss, the rotund Bavarian leader of the CSU in Germany and then Defense Minister in the German government. (The CSU is the Bavarian wing of the conservative Christian Democratic party; Strauss was its leader for more than two decades, giving him long-term influence in German government, which he used shamelessly to promote the Bavarian aerospace industry. He will emerge, in due course, as a crucial figure in the story of Airbus.) This was his first overt involvement, and he set about solving the dilemma posed by the British withdrawal — by raiding the German Treasury. The French were not willing to lubricate the deal with any more cash for a British company. Strauss was, and he was in a position to whip the Finance Ministry into line. He offered Hawker Siddeley a deal whereby West Germany would finance 60 percent of the development costs of the wing, amounting to an indirect subsidy of DM250 million (more than $150 million). In return, the British company signed a fixed-price contract to supply the wings for the aircraft, a deal which was extremely profitable. For the Germans to start subsidizing a British company was an unlikely act of generosity; in truth, it was probably the only way to keep Airbus alive. Which it achieved. In May 1969, only a month after the British government pulled out, an agreement to establish Airbus Industrie was signed between Germany and France at the Paris Airshow. As a reward for his ingenuity, Strauss became president of Airbus, starting a tradition whereby the presidency goes to a German and the chief executive, until now at least, is French.

Ziegler and Beteille now had a piece of paper, and they had partners, and they had the expertise of a British manufacturer, if not the backing of its government. All they needed was a factory and an airplane, and perhaps some customers. One of the sharpest disagreements between the British and the French had been the best size for the new plane. Beteille had been in close contact with Frank Kolk, technical director of American Airlines, and one of the most influential men in the airline industry. Kolk had long been pressing U.S. manufacturers to come up with a widebodied twin. Boeing considered the idea, but went for the 747 instead. Kolk also talked to McDonnell Douglas, but they went with the DC-10, their big tri-jet. Kolk insisted the twin was what was needed. On high-density short-haul routes between big cities a widebody twin was the only plane that could carry a lot of people at low cost. Few were prepared to listen to him, but the few included Beteille, with whom Kolk shared his plans for the plane he wanted built.

This seemed to Beteille an opportunity staring the Europeans in the face. There was a significant gap in the market, which the American manufacturers had so far failed to fill. There would be no point in Airbus attempting to compete directly with the Americans. It might sell against Boeing and Douglas to Air France and Lufthansa, but never to the U.S. nor probably to other world airlines; offered a choice, they would buy American rather than European. If Airbus were to break out of the trap of being simply a supplier to their partners' national airlines, it had to offer a machine that could compete globally, contending against Boeing and Douglas for orders from every airline in the world. The widebodied twin was a way of sliding into the market. And with the British out of the way, Beteille could pursue that goal more wholeheartedly. The smaller aircraft favored by Britain would have resembled the 737 too closely.

"At the time we launched the A300, the general feeling of the market, and especially the U.S. market, was that there was no way you could fly 200 people with two engines," recalls Bernard Ziegler, technical director of Airbus. "I can remember the U.S. airlines saying to us, 'Fly that many people in a twin? You are mad. Never.' We believed there was no rationale to that, it was purely an emotional view. And from that came the idea of a widebody twin. Boeing failed to understand that. If Boeing had understood that right at the start, they would have cut our throat."

The A300, which Airbus decided to build, was designed as a wide-body twinjet, seating 266 passengers, with a range of 4150 nautical miles. The Americans were not hostile to the new venture initially; there was no throat-cutting, at least not then. Boeing was too wrapped up in the 747 to consider that section of the market, and Douglas too involved in the DC-10, and both thought it too small a market to be of much interest. Both also regarded the Europeans as a bit of a joke, and did not take this new competitor seriously. Important differences did emerge, however, in their attitudes towards their fledgling European cousin; these set a tone between the three companies which persisted over the next two decades. McDonnell Douglas, inadvertently perhaps, were prepared to take a benign, even helpful view. Boeing, while not going for the jugular, wouldn't have hesitated to slice a few of the arteries of the Airbus system.

In the small world of international aerospace, where only a few dozen people really count, the players are well known to one another. Ziegler, a player for many years, used his connections to nurture the new creation. The A300 was a big plane, not in the same league as the 747, but not that far behind, and an expensive machine to bring into being. Time, as ever, was also tight. Ziegler went to see James McDonnell (universally known in the industry as Ol' Mac), who had been running the company since the merger with Douglas almost a decade earlier, to explore whether there was a possibility of collaboration. Airbus was having particular difficulties with the nacelle, the pod that holds the engine to the wing, which, because of the perfect balance that must be achieved between the wing, the engine and the structure holding the two together, is one of the most complex bits of engineering on an aircraft. It might be possible to share development costs with the DC-10, a plane of similar size. McDonnell listened to the proposal and agreed, deaf to the potential competition that might one day be posed by Airbus. He even offered to help them further by letting the Europeans buy fuselages off the shelf from the DC-10, a proposal Airbus turned down because it wanted a hull an inch or so wider. Yet in selling them the nacelle, McDonnell saved the consortium a great deal of time and money, which today the company no doubt regrets.

Boeing was a lot savvier. Under the leadership of T. Wilson, the company had developed a colder, more politicized edge, and though far from taking the Airbus seriously, it was happy to stir up the always murky

European waters. If mud was in the pool already, there was no harm in making it stick. The opportunity came in Italy. T. Wilson had recognized that the insularity of the Seattle company was a potential weakness. Being very American was fine so long as the American market was far and away the world's largest, but the growth of air travel in Europe and elsewhere in the 1960s, coupled with the declining range of the European manufacturers (the Caravelle, Comet and BAC 1-11 were becoming elderly, and no other manufacturers had sprung up outside the U.S., Britain and France), meant that the Americans were now taking more and more of the world market. Indeed, Airbus protagonists are fond of quoting the statistic that by the late 1960s and early 1970s, 90 percent of the airplanes sold worldwide were made in the U.S. It was good business but risky; other nations would not be happy to fill Boeing's bank account forever with dollars that were often hard to come by. If the American hegemony were to be maintained, the spoils had to be shared; not equally, of course, but it had to be more than a one-way flow. The wheels of geo-industrial competition were turning faster now. Wilson was aware of their speed.

The logic implied alliances, tying Europeans in as contractors on Boeing and other American products. Some early discussions were held with Dassault about collaboration on a revamped version of the Mercure, but they came to nothing. Talks were also held, improbably, between Boeing and Sud Aviation, led by Beteille and Jacques Mitterrand, brother of the Socialist Party leader and later President, François Mitterrand. (Jacques Mitterrand was an executive at Sud Aviation and became head of Aérospatiale when the two main French aerospace companies were combined into a single nationalized entity.) The proposal was to create a medium-sized tri-jet, but it too came to nothing. In most people's estimation Boeing was on one of its occasional fishing expeditions.

Beteille was not serious in his talks with Boeing. He too was fishing. But he was serious in his desire to widen the Airbus consortium. Though the British withdrawal had been partly a relief, it had seriously diminished the financial and industrial resources at his disposal and, in the masterplan being stitched together by him and Ziegler, it was crucial to get as many of the European powers involved in Airbus as possible. Only as a strong, united European force could the consortium be a success.

Hence his interest in the Italians. Italy had a small aerospace industry grouped under the wing of the state-owned Aeritalia, a minor but significant piece of the European jigsaw. Beteille wanted it as part of his picture. The Italians had not been involved in the early talks about Airbus, but once it was up and running, discussions indicated a high degree of interest on both sides. This was where Boeing stepped in. Through 1971 and 1972 Boeing was looking at a plane codenamed the QSHA (quiet short-haul airplane). Noise reduction was a hot issue at the turn of the decade, and this was an experiment in designing a machine that made less racket than other planes. Italian engineers had been invited over to Seattle to help work on the project, a privilege for which they were paying Boeing handsomely (the idea being that they would learn from the experience and grow stronger). Wooed by Beteille and Ziegler, the Italians faced a choice of whether to throw in their lot with Airbus instead. The proposal appeared attractive; they would be partners, and would not have to pay for the privilege of working on someone else's plane. Within the Italian government, the Airbus approach — backed strongly by the German and French governments, both partners of Italy in the European Community — sparked a fierce debate about which way to go: Airbus or Boeing? Boeing sweetened the pill. Aeritalia, they said, could be a full partner in building the new plane. Partnership in a Boeing plane looked like a big deal compared with a stake in Airbus, in which few people outside the Avenue de Versailles had much faith. The Italians chose Boeing.

Yet in the geo-industrial cauldron deals are not what they seem. People fake, and companies bluff, and Boeing turned out to be "only kidding." The deal fell apart because, as T. Wilson put it later with brutal candor, Boeing "decided not to build its half [of the plane]."[3] The QSHA never did get built, and probably was never a serious contender for production. The Italians had been gulled; all they finally got out of Boeing was a deal to build some of the trailing sections of the wing and parts of the tail section of the 767, less than 10 percent of its skin. "[The Italians] got very sore about it," joked Wilson.[4] But the paper plane, and the paper deal with the Italians, had served a temporary and cynical purpose: it kept the Italians out of Airbus, and hampered Beteille's efforts to put together a pan-European consortium.

The loss of the Italians was not the only setback in those early days. There were also the Dutch. Although a small country, through Fokker the Dutch had always been a marginal player in the world industry. Unlike most small European manufacturers, such as Saab of Sweden, Fokker has always been a civil as well as a military producer, and the civil side, concentrated in small jets and turboprops, has accounted for 70-80 percent of its output. Both the company and the Dutch government were keen on international collaboration, and talks were held with the Americans and with Airbus in the early 1970s. The Dutch were wary of the Airbus structure, fearing they would be lost between the Germans and the French. Instead, they became an associate member, supplying pans and with a voice, but far from full members. The same compromise solution was extended to the Belgians, who joined as associates through Belairbus, a grouping of their own small manufacturers.

With those two deals Beteille had succeeded in tying in most of the significant countries among the six founders of the European Community. He had steered the early politics of the consortium soundly, and the initial structure of Airbus was at last in place.

Ziegler, still overseeing the French side of Concorde, was anxious not to see Airbus repeat the pattern of expense and delay of its unloved parent. Concorde had never really been a commercial operation. It had been an exercise in inter-governmental collaboration between two governments that did not get on very well. Though the British were no longer there, none of the Airbus partners wanted to wind up in the same situation. Airbus was a collaboration between companies, but because those companies were either state-owned or partially state-owned, the distinction was finer in reality than it appeared on paper.

Airbus was a *groupement d'intérêt économique,* a form of commercial partnership established in French law in the mid-1960s, which was mainly intended to help wine growers. A GIE, as it is known, is a flexible and user-friendly form of corporate structure, although it tends to baffle Anglo-Saxons — and Americans in particular — used to the rigid structure of the limited company. A GIE is not a company, and escapes many of the obligations of a company. For example, it does not have to publish accounts nor does it have to pay taxes, unless it chooses to do so (a choice Airbus, unsurprisingly, has not yet made). It simply pools the capital contributed by its members, and its results are taken on to the books of its member companies in proportion to their share of the enterprise. To Americans this has always looked like a neat — read devious European — device for disguising subsidies and losses. But, for Beteille and his colleagues, it fitted their conception of Airbus; to have given it separate corporate existence would have suggested it was distinct from its members — a distortion of the reality.

The members of the consortium were, however, subject to some tight restrictions. They were not allowed to produce any plane that competed with the Airbus product range. And although they were free to leave, they remained responsible for the financial commitments they had already entered into: once they were in they were in, and it would be very difficult to get out.

Through 1970 and 1971, the skeleton of the production system was laid out. Because it was largely a chimera, it drew heavily on the support and expertise of its members. The sections were to be designed and built by the members, as well as the wings, which were to be completed by Hawker Siddeley. The French and German governments stumped up initially the entire cost of the A300, but the funds were funnelled through Aérospatiale and Deutsche Airbus (as the German grouping of companies became known) rather than going directly to Airbus. The consortium had only two tasks: one was assembling the planes into a finished product, the other was selling them. Both would be carried out by headquarters staff, who at first were drafted in temporarily.

With the launch date for the A300 scheduled for 1974, time was scarce. As the leaders of the consortium — and the most experienced partners — the French insisted that final assembly be on French soil. For convenience, a plant was chosen in Toulouse, close to the airport and across the road from the massive Aérospatiale headquarters and factories which were the dominant force in French aerospace (the headquarters of Airbus Industrie followed, moving from Paris to an office block visible from the runway at Toulouse airport).

Initially parts of the A300 were being constructed in three different countries: wings in Britain; the forward and rear fuselage in Germany, as well as the upper center fuselage and parts of the tail surfaces; while Aerospatiale took responsibility for the nose section, including the flight deck, the lower part of the center fuselage, and the engine pylons. A system for putting it all together was designed by Felix Kracht, a German engineer, and this led to the creation of one of the symbols of the consortium — the SuperGuppy, an unsightly, souped-up propeller-driven plane (actually a Boeing) with a massively raised roof which flies the prefabricated parts to Toulouse for final assembly. SuperGuppies still land every day at the assembly plant to deliver their offerings, although the fleet is gradually being phased out, to be replaced, more appropriately, with a fleet of modified A300s.

Kracht was responsible, too, for another innovation. He insisted that while any language was acceptable for in-house communications, anything written by the consortium had to be in English. On the Concorde project, by contrast, nothing was formally decided until it was written down in both English and French. Airbus quickly adopted a language which insiders refer to as "Boeing slang."

Unlike the Concorde, and confounding the many skeptical voices heard at its launch, the A300 was delivered on time and on budget. It was expensive, but no more than had been forecast. The prototype made its first flight on October 28, 1972, thirty-three days ahead of the schedule stipulated in the original agreement. The first plane in service flew between Paris and London under the Air France colors on May 23, 1974, dead on schedule.

Building the plane was one thing; selling it another altogether. Though the A300 had been planned as a commercial airplane, that did not guarantee an easy or warm reception among the airlines. It was competing mainly with the DC-10 and the Lockheed L-1011 Tristar, but it was smaller than both, and cheaper. At launch the A300 cost $24 million (although the price was always negotiable), compared with around $30 million each for the American planes.

One customer came in very early. Six options on A300s were taken in September 1970, three months before the consortium was even in formal existence but, since the customer was Air France, that was no great surprise. A year later those options were converted into firm orders, and options for six more taken out, but it would still have been strange if Air France, state-owned and slavishly loyal to its government, had not come in immediately. Other partner countries also chipped in. Lufthansa followed Air France, but waited until May 1973 to place its order — even then it was only for three firm, plus four options, about the minimum it could decently get away with. That made a total of nine firm, and ten options. The estimated break-even point was 360 planes: there was some way to go.

A sure way of increasing sales was to rope more countries into the consortium, a key part of Beteille's strategy for creating a pan-European approach. Negotiations with the Spanish in 1971 showed how fruitful this could be. The local manufacturer Construcciones Aeronauticas SA (known as CASA) had been approached and showed considerable interest, but Airbus was not going to accept this junior partner without drawing a little blood. Beteille and his colleagues insisted that the Spanish airline Iberia place an order for A300s as a sign of goodwill. Though the airline was reluctant, the Spanish government, then still under Franco, ensured that the order was placed. In January 1972 it was announced that CASA would take a 4.2 percent share in Airbus, becoming the third full member of the consortium, while Iberia signed a contract for four A300s, plus options on eight more. The deal did not survive, however. In 1974, invoking a minor clause in the contract, which stated that it could be cancelled if sales of the A300 did not reach fifty planes, Iberia wriggled out of its commitment — a decision which caused a lot of ill-feeling in Toulouse. So once again sales were confined to the two core member countries, and there were no signs of the nations on the periphery of the consortium chipping in with support. KLM did not show interest, nor, despite the involvement of Hawker Siddeley, did the British, which the French saw as yet another mark of treachery.

The view from Toulouse was beginning to look bleak. Beteille and his team had built their plane, delivered it, calculated the market, attacked it, and the A300 was turning out to be a dog. The gloomy predictions about Airbus might turn out to be true. If they were, this final disaster would probably trigger the death of the European aerospace industry. There were one or two bright spots. In September 1974, Korean Airlines placed an order, and a few others raised the temperature by placing options, only to cancel them a few months later. With the plane in service, and the assembly lines geared to manufacture four A300s a month, by the end of 1974 there were no customers but Air France, Lufthansa and Korean Airlines.

Things did look up a little in the following year. Air Inter, the regional French airline, came in with some orders, as did Indian Airlines and South African Airways. During 1975, Airbus received 33 firm orders, and another 22 options; by year's end there were eight aircraft in service with four different airlines. But spats with the Americans had also started. At one stage the Airbus salesmen thought they had secured a sale of two A300s to TransBrasil, which would have been financed in dollars. Airbus had put together a financing deal involving Crédit Lyonnais and Dresdner

Bank, but Boeing (so Airbus personnel alleged) got Washington to stop the export of the necessary currency, on the grounds that the Brazilians were already too heavily in hock to American banks. Boeing picked up the order instead.

Early in 1975, Henri Ziegler retired, and his place was taken by Bernard Lathière, another former Aérospatiale man, who was steeped in the tortuous history of European competition with the Americans. Lathière had been born in Calcutta in 1929, where his father was a salesman for the Michelin tire company. He graduated from the élite ENA and joined the civil service, and after spells as an adviser to ministers, was appointed in 1968 as Directeur Adjoint de l'Aviation Civile, masterminding state aid for the aircraft industry, which gave him overall responsibility for both the Airbus and Concorde programs. With a reputation for enjoying good food, wine and cigars, he fitted neatly into the freewheeling style of the consortium, and enjoyed baiting the men from Seattle: he liked to describe Airbus as the Little Red Riding Hood of the industry who bit the Big Bad Wolf of Boeing. Lathière began his reign in robust style, promising to build fifty-four planes that year, even though there were only twenty orders in the pipeline at the time. "Airbus is a political symbol of what Europeans can do when they are united," he said early in his régime. "These are countries that have been trying to kill each other for centuries." But for all the talk, the Seattle wolves were not feeling the bites.

In 1975 Lathière chose to make public the strategy that Beteille and Ziegler had hatched five years earlier. Both men had realized that one European plane was neither here nor there — the key to success lay in building a family of planes, of different sizes, but sharing common characteristics. Airlines could then stock their fleets from a single supplier, reducing the need for engineers and pilots trained in handling several different makes. Common features among the planes would reduce design and engineering costs for the manufacturer. It was a strategy used by Douglas and then by Boeing, with stunning success, but one the Europeans, through lack of financial and industrial muscle and possibly inability to see the point of it, had so far ignored. The Airbus consortium set itself two explicit goals: it would create a family of planes, and it would target a 30 percent share of the aerospace market. The supervisory board approved a strategic outline to capture a third of the market, which involved building a new small jet, and two larger jets.

"Even at the time the A300 entered service, we were saying to ourselves that in a free market, if you want to have any influence you must have a share of the business that is no less than half of that of the dominant player," recalls Adam Brown, head of planning at Airbus and the consortium's chief strategist. "That led to a sort of arithmetical conclusion that if Airbus was going to have any control over the terms of business in this market, we would have to have something like a 30 percent share. In heroically simple terms we saw a situation where Boeing would have about 60 percent, we would have 30 percent and the rest would have 10 percent. We then very quickly realized that if we were going to have 30 percent of the business, we were not going to be able to do that with a single plane."

Though the strategy had been implicit from the start, and openly talked about in Toulouse, it was probably wise not to have talked openly about it in 1970, when building the A300 still seemed a wild and foolhardy idea. Building a whole family of planes would have been regarded as industrial fantasy, an idea so deranged and expensive that it would have gorged on public subsidies for decades to come.

Now, in 1975, with the A300 sliding towards huge losses, it was necessary to talk up the spirits of the consortium, to suggest there was something worth pursuing. Yet Lathière was about to preside over the darkest and most demoralizing period in Airbus's development, at least since the breakdown of relations with the British. Although 1975 had been passable, by 1976 fears for the future of Airbus were returning with a vengeance. Despite aggressive selling to every airline in the world, the months wore on without any new orders. And planes were still being produced at the Toulouse assembly line. It was during this year that the term "whitetails" became part of industry jargon: when Airbus finished a plane for which it had no customer, and therefore could not paint in the livery of any airline, it would paint the machine white, and park it on the Toulouse lot. As 1976 dragged on, there was a growing queue of whitetails on the tarmac.

A whole year went by without a single sale. There were plenty of reasons and explanations for the failure. The A300 was still relatively new, and Airbus was an unknown quantity. Airlines were cautious about buying Airbus. They could not be sure the organization would be around through the twenty- to thirty-year life of the plane to service it and supply spare parts; given the track record of European aerospace ventures they could be forgiven their skepticism. But no matter how often it was rationalized, the performance was bitterly disappointing. The A300 was not that new any more; it had been on sale for six years, and was already coming up against paper airplanes hawked by the other manufacturers. Boeing and McDonnell Douglas salesmen told airlines that they would be better advised not to buy the A300 because their airlines would shortly be announcing new aircraft in a similar category — only much better. It was an old trick but effective.

By the turn of 1977, however, there was new hope. Lathière and Beteille had plans for breaking into the American market, the original target of the A300. News leaked out that Western Airlines, based in California, was interested in ten planes. Negotiations were going well and the airline seemed close to signing. Then, in a cruel twist of fate, the deal slid away. At the end of January, the French government released a known Palestinian Liberation Organization terrorist, provoking a wave of anger across the United States. Western balked at becoming the first American airline to buy what was widely perceived as a French plane. It pulled out, splitting its order between DC-10s and Boeing 727s. Yet another promising lead had swirled down the plughole, and the mood in Toulouse went from desperation to near-despair. "Don't miss the last train out of Toulouse," became an ironic saying in the consortium's headquarters.

Failure in the U.S. was the most painful aspect of the saga. The U.S was not only the biggest market in the world, it was the most influential. If the Americans could be seen to be buying the planes against competition from Boeing and McDonnell Douglas, other airlines around the world would take more interest. But the consortium was getting nowhere. It needed help. Beteille and Lathière resolved to make one more bold push across the Atlantic. The Western Airlines episode had proved that A300 was not a nonstarter. Airbus Industrie set up a New York office, and persuaded George Warde, a former president of American Airlines, to become vice-president in charge of its U.S. operations. Warde was a big hitter in American aviation circles, and Airbus immediately won some credibility in the American market. Warde could open a lot of doors for the Europeans — or so they hoped.

The first door he squeezed ajar was that of Eastern Airlines, one of the giants of the American industry, and a far bigger fish than Western.

Along with United, American and TWA, Eastern was one of the big four domestic and international carriers in the U.S. In 1975 it had been taken over by Frank Borman, a former astronaut, a hard man who was determined to squeeze greater efficiency from the airline. Among other things, that meant squeezing better terms out of the manufacturers, since the capital costs of acquiring a fleet are, after fuel, an airline's major outlay.

Within weeks of taking over the U.S. operation, Warde made a presentation of the virtues of the A300 to Borman and the senior managers at Eastern. They were impressed, but not impressed enough to buy, being concerned about the servicing and support Airbus could provide in the U.S. How about Airbus letting Eastern have a few planes for a period to see how they went, suggested Borman. Quickly dubbed "fly before you buy," this was a novel sales technique. Boeing, Douglas and Lockheed had been hungry for sales many times, but had never been reduced to lending their planes out. Beteille and Lathière were desperate men, though, and this was better than nothing. There was not much to lose and a great deal to be gained. Without promising anything, Borman made it clear that if the tests went well a substantial sale would be the next step.

A deal was arranged: Eastern would pay about $7 million to train its crews to fly the A300s, but Airbus would pay all costs of maintenance and of getting certification in the U.S. Eastern decided to try the planes out on the toughest routes on its flight schedule: Miami to New York and Miami to Montreal. Both involved big changes in temperature en route, which would test the reliability and quality of any airplane. This was to be the A300's most stringent test yet, with perhaps its entire future riding on how well it performed. Three months into the trial, the figures looked promising: The planes flew flawlessly, landing and turning around with hardly a glitch. Fuel consumption, which sometimes differs widely between promise and performance, came in at 3 percent less than Airbus had promised. Borman was impressed: here was a plane which flew above specifications, flew cheaper, and was cheap to buy. In April 1977, Borman began negotiating a massive order: 23 A300s right away, and options on another nine, plus 25 of the upgraded model Airbus was planning. The deal was worth $778 million.

It was agreed in principle, but there were two obstacles to be cleared before it could be finalized. One was technical. The heavy undercarriage of the A300 suggested it might put unbearable stress on sections of the runway at New York's La Guardia airport, and the runway might crack. Unless that could be sorted out the plane might not get landing rights. A way was found of reinenforcing the undercarriage and modifying the landing gear. It was expensive, but well worth it for a deal this size. The other problem was financial. Eastern wanted the airplanes, but it didn't actually have the money to pay for them. Deregulation in American aviation had begun and fares were being cut. That, combined with the effects of the Borman takeover of the airline, had left Eastern in hock to the tune of $1.3 billion. It had cashflow but not the upfront cash, and its credit rating was not looking too healthy.

To Boeing and McDonnell Douglas, a customer without money was hardly a customer at all. Lathière and Beteille decided not to look at it that way.They needed customers, American customers, whether they had money or not. To resolve the situation they brought in the financial engineers. The A300 was not a very innovative plane in terms of aeronautical engineering, and was never intended to be; in terms of financial engineering, however (like all subsequent Airbus planes), it was one of the most innovative machines ever built.

The basic proposition was simple. The customer needed the planes and the money to pay for them. Airbus could supply the planes. If it could supply the money as well, the loop could be closed and a deal struck. The package was put together by Warde and Beteille. It began with the Bank of America, which put up $522 million at the generous interest of 3.5 percent a year, fixed for fifteen years. Two of the most friendly banks to the Airbus cause, Crédit Lyonnais and Dresdner Bank, advanced another $250 million in the form of export credits. Airbus itself provided another $96 million in loans, while General Electric, which was to supply the engines for the planes, chipped in $45 million, also as a loan.

Borman had already squeezed blood, but he wanted more. He complained that he really wanted a plane with only 170 seats, not the larger A300, which he was far from sure he could fill. This had the look of a deal-breaker, but Beteille and his team pondered it, and came back with an amazing answer. Okay, Beteille offered, you pay us for 170 seats only, and if you use more, you pay us extra.[5] It was an offer that could not be refused: Airbus was offering to underwrite all the risks to Eastern of operating the plane. It had only to fill the two-thirds it paid for, and had extra capacity should demand pick up. The deal was struck.

For the people in Toulouse it was a triumph, their first sale in the heartland of the aviation industry, and the first European planes to be sold in the U.S. since the Comet and the Caravelle two decades earlier. Perhaps, just perhaps, the dream of a full range of Airbus aircraft was not to be a fantasy after all.

On the other side of the Atlantic, the manufacturers were starting to worry. The Eastern deal was only one sale, but it was an omen. Boeing and McDonnell Douglas were not happy to see the Europeans creeping into their market, especially with such a sneaky set of sales tactics. Eastern rubbed salt into the wounds by launching a massive advertising campaign to mark the debut of their new European planes. Their publicists dubbed it the "Whisper Jet," introducing the virtues of the A300 to the American public. Competition had arrived.

Competition — more of it — was precisely what the two U.S. manufacturers did not need, and they were not about to take this Old World impudence lying down. Both Boeing and McDonnell Douglas complained bitterly about the financing techniques deployed to close the deal, whipping up support in Congress to bolster their position. Charles Vanik, a member of the powerful Ways and Means Committee of the House of Representatives, argued their case. The Eastern sale, he told the House, raised a "serious question of unfair trade practices and excessive export subsidies"; a subcommittee set up an inquiry to examine the "financial trickery" alleged to have surrounded the transaction.

Airbus discovered, and discovered quickly, that selling to the U.S. involved more than convincing the airlines of a credible product. It involved convincing the politicians and the public that there was nothing underhanded or unsavory about its sales techniques. The arena was hostile, and the lobbying firepower of the American aerospace industry immense. Airbus rustled up counter-propaganda to compete. It pointed out that Boeing had used leasing techniques in the past, although only over some hydrofoil ferryboats it had been trying to unload. George Warde was wheeled out to explain that a large part of the content of each Airbus was of American origin; almost a quarter if you counted the General Electric engines. But the stout defense of the deal came unstuck when Frank Borman, a man of little tact or sensitivity, made a speech to an assembly of his staff praising the deal struck with Airbus. Elated by the terms he had achieved, his rhetoric ran ahead of him: "If you don't kiss the French flag every time you see it, at least salute it. The export financing on our Airbus deal subsidized this airline by more than $100 million."[6]

Airbus had indeed made a remarkably generous deal with Borman and Eastern. But these were desperate times, and called for desperate measures. With the Eastern deal wrapped up, the spring of 1977 seemed more promising in Toulouse than any year since the consortium was conceived. The Eastern deal was announced by Borman on May 2, 1977. At the same time, Thai Airlines announced an order for four A300s. Later that summer, Egyptair followed Eastern's lead in a leasing deal for the A300.

In the original methods of financing, Airbus struck a rich seam, and one that it was to exploit ruthlessly. It had made a breakthrough, and sold planes in places that no European manufacturer had previously penetrated. The costs were high and it was far from clear how Airbus would earn a profit from its leasing arrangements. And there was a political cost, a sharp foretaste of the determination of the consortium to bludgeon its way into the market using whatever means necessary. This would pave the way for one of the fiercest battles of the geo-industrial conflict between the Old World and the New that was now becoming overt.

But that was in the future. For now, the clouds were lifting, and the fantasy, hatched in those empty rooms in the center of Paris seven years earlier, was turning into reality. The specter of another European failure was about to be lifted. And the sentence of death passed on the European aerospace industry in the wake of Concorde had been postponed.

6

DARK DAYS
IN SEATTLE

In the middle of 1971, a little over a year after the 747 had gone into service with Pan Am, a Seattle real estate man, with a humor and intelligence for which that profession is not noted, rented a billboard on the I-5 which runs through the outskirts of Seattle and twists close to the Boeing plant. His spot was carefully chosen, close to the airport, where the Boeing people were bound to see it, probably every day as they drove to and from work. On it, he put a poster with a picture of a single light bulb and the line, "Will the last person leaving Seattle please put out the lights?" [1]

The joke was popular, despite its undertow, and the anger that lay behind it was understandable. Real estate values in the city and its sprawling suburbs had fallen by 40 percent in that year alone, a catastrophic collapse, and the industry was suffering as bad a downturn as had been known anywhere. The same was true of retailing, construction, the bars, the auto lots — everything. Seattle registered unemployment of 17 percent that year, the highest of any city in the United States. What had been a boom town was falling apart even faster than it had risen. Everybody was hurting, and everybody was blaming the same person: T. Wilson, the new president of the Boeing Company.

The rout of 1969, when Wilson had begun to make cutbacks at the company to keep the bankers at bay and to find the money to complete the work on the 747, had been a foretaste of even more bitter days to come. The 747 had been finished, and had worked, and was now starting to generate cash, but nowhere near enough to cover the enormous debts Boeing had taken on board. Nor were the sales anything like as good as had been forecast for the new Jumbo.

The timing was unfortunate. The 747 had been conceived during a period of great optimism, but in the seventies, when it was finally launched, the climate was different. Inflation, sparked by the Vietnam war, had led to a downturn in the economy, and the strains on the dollar had precipitated the crack-up of the Bretton Woods system which had brought some stability to the world's currencies. The great oil price shock that followed the Middle East war of 1973, quadrupling the price of the airlines' life blood, hurtled the world economy even deeper into recession. All this was bad news for the airlines, and for the manufacturers who supplied them. Ever since the dawn of the jet age, the demand for fast, efficient travel had been a rising curve, one that was assumed would rise forever. The 747 was built for a world where more people would be travelling farther and faster than ever before. Yet now that it was here, the assumptions on which it had been built were disappearing. The Jumbo seemed like a beached whale, a bloated relic of a more prosperous time.

The first and most immediate effects were on the airlines. Taking their lead from Juan Trippe and Pan Am, they had rushed to place their orders for the 747 throughout the late 1960s. By 1969, when the prototypes were flying and being demonstrated, 196 Jumbos had been sold to thirty-one different airlines around the world, a tremendous figure for a plane which was not yet operational. And Boeing was committed to rolling eight a month off the Everett production line once it was in full swing. Yet many of the Jumbos were soon flying almost empty, chugging across the Atlantic and the Pacific, a few passengers dotted in their vast empty spaces. The losses were horrific, and Pan Am, as the first airline in, with the biggest order, was the first to feel the pain.

Juan Trippe had bowed out before the full consequences of his last great adventure hit home. At the end of 1968 he retired from the company he had built up over forty years, to be replaced by Harold Gray, who was already dying of cancer when he became president. He was followed by Najeeb Halaby, a lawyer and former test pilot who had only joined the company in 1965 and who found himself quickly bested by the problems of a fleet of empty 747s. Financing alone was costing over $120 million a year and, despite efforts to play hardball with Boeing on price and rebates, Halaby was a trapped man: "[Pan Am is] locked in a shrinking box, with the top, bottom and sides all closing in at once," was how he described the predicament.2 Halaby was ousted by the board in 1972; the losses continued.

The box was indeed shrinking. Other airlines took notice of what was happening at Pan Am, and had no desire to be trapped as they were. Of the near 200 747s ordered, some were options and many of those were cancelled, even when it meant loss of deposits. Where airlines had to take the planes, they did, but with little grace, and little idea of how to use them. Above all, in this climate they were not interested in buying any more of a model they now began to regard as a financial as well as a physical monster. In 1970, one of the worst years Boeing has ever suffered, the company failed to win a single order for a new plane in the U.S., its key domestic market, and booked only $716 million in sales in the rest of the world. In the following year, the government-funded SST project was cancelled, drying up another source of immediate funds and future reve-nues, and creating another 5000 surplus workers despite that one congres-sional vote. The 747, conceived of as a stopgap until the SST took over, would now have to be the long-term future of the company, and nobody was buying. At this rate, and with its overheads, Boeing was not going to be in business much longer.

For Wilson there was only one solution. He was a frugal man by nature and (despite having pushed up his own salary) lived frugally; he drove to work in a cheap Chevrolet and lived in the ranch house in southwest Seattle he had bought while still a young engineer at the company. Austerity came naturally to him, and his natural response was to start swinging the axe even more savagely.

The workload of producing the 747 and building the Everett plant had led to a tremendous build-up in the Boeing labor force. At its peak in 1968, the company employed 142,200, one in five of the entire Seattle labor force, and many more were dependent upon it for ancillary services. It was a company town, and Boeing had been a generous and sometimes sloppy employer (in Seattle it was known as the Lazy B). Twenty-five thousand were axed in 1969, but it was in 1970 that the real massacre began; another 41,000 people picked up their cards, leaving only 79,100 still employed. Through 1971, the carnage continued unabated. Another 22,600 jobs were terminated. Over the three years, 86,000 employees had been fired, more than 60 percent of the 1968 figure.

These were not just blue-collar jobs. Only 30,000 of the firings were on the production line. Wilson went through the entire organization, putting a generation of company managers and staffers to the knife. The corporate headquarters staff, which had numbered more than 1700, fell to 200. Eleven of the vice-presidents disappeared during the three-year cull, and even the research laboratory was done away with (partly because NASA was canceling research contracts which often went to Boeing). Not just the headcount was reduced; standards fell. Every effort was made to cut costs to the bone; building renewals were scrapped, the flowerbeds around the offices and factories were untended. The process of internal cheese-paring came to a halt only when an outbreak of fungus on the lavatory floors exposed the decision to save money on cleaners (a janitor was rehired to fix the problem).[3]

The impact on the staff was shattering, on all levels. "I can clearly remember, those of us who were young at the time were just disillusioned by what was happening," recalls Ron Woodward, then a young engineer and now head of the company's Renton division. "We could not believe that this bubble had burst. We believed that we had been doing all the right things. And then when, among the other things, the SST project was cancelled, we felt violated by our own government. A lot of the people whom I had started at the company left, left Seattle, and moved back east or whatever. We were all fighting for our survival. There were rumors, every day, about whether the banks were going to take us over. We knew how threatened we were."[4]

The threat was real and tangible. The debts were certainly high enough for the banks to foreclose if they judged that the best way of getting their money back. They stayed their hand, judging that the organization was worth more intact than broken up. But they were pushing for more revenue. In one particularly bizarre episode, Wilson and his team hatched a plan to sell the entire 737 program to the Japanese, whose economy was then embarking on the miracle of its post-war years and who were keen to enter the aerospace business. A consortium of Kawasaki, Mitsubishi and Fuji — three of the most powerful companies that dominate Japanese commerce — had started making inroads, producing military planes for the Japanese air force and a commercial Kawasaki turbo-prop, which made little headway in the market.

A relationship had already developed on the 747, for which the Japanese were making the wing-flaps. A proposal was considered to sell them the 737; they could manufacture and market it, and the deal would bring an infusion of cash to Boeing. Tentative discussions were held, but did not progress very far; for Boeing it was too radical and too desperate a step, because it would have shattered their integrated family of aircraft, probably forever. For the Japanese, as well, it was probably a step too far, too soon. Never mind the political implications, which, even in the early seventies, long before anti-Japanese hysteria engulfed America, would have been mind-boggling. All the same, the fact that it surfaced at all was an indication of how deep into the bone Wilson was prepared to cut.

Wilson then turned to a solution that only Bill Boeing himself, in the darkest of days after the First World War, had contemplated. Then it had been furniture; now Wilson set up a committee called the Office of Corporate and Business Development, a team of eleven people whose task was to come up with areas of diversification to reduce dependence on the cycles of the aircraft business. They came up with a mish-mash of ideas: light rail transport, commercial hydrofoils, energy systems, urban planning, waste-water purification, desalination systems, even property development. None came to much (although all were tried), but their significance lay not in their success or otherwise, but in what they said about the mood of the company. For the first time in half a century, Boeing seemed to be losing faith in the aircraft industry and its ability to dominate it.

Faith was in short supply in those dark days, not just for Boeing, but for the entire American aerospace industry. Douglas, the great competitor of Boeing, fell on hard times even sooner. Donald Douglas became an increasingly remote and eccentric figure, spending more and more time with his mistress, Peggy Tucker, who rose to ever more prominent positions within the company, ending up in charge of all transportation and food supply contracts. Tucker controlled access to Douglas, and became in many ways the most important person in the company. Unless you were in her good books, you couldn't get to see the top man. By the mid-1960s, the company was racking up huge losses and was effectively taken over by McDonnell, a St. Louis company best known for its weapons business (Douglas stayed on the board until his death from cancer in 1981). The combined company re-entered the commercial aircraft fray with the DC-10, an ambitious three-engined widebody, as did Lockheed, which having kept out of the commercial business for a decade or more, came back with the Tristar.

The DC-10 and the Tristar were very similar planes, both looking to sell in the same market. Although both enjoyed reasonable success. they were carving up a limited market, undercutting each other savagely on price and winding up with half the business either could have achieved on its own. Indeed, so intense was the pressure on Lockheed, caused by the Tristar and by the cost of the Galaxy program it had snatched from Boeing, that the company had to be bailed out with a $250 million loan from the U.S. government (approved in the Senate by only one vote). Both planes were marked by tragedy of different sorts.

On March 3, 1973, a Turkish Airlines DC-10 took off from Orly Airport in Paris and crashed into the woods to the north of the city, killing all 346 passengers. It was the worst disaster in aviation history (and the reason, incidentally, why Airbus won its early order from South African Airways). Other crashes cemented its reputation of being a fundamentally unsafe aircraft, and more than unkind: fate was involved. The Paris crash was traced to a faulty design of the mechanism controlling the rear cargo door. The fault was already known; indeed the FAA had wanted to ground all DC-10s until the problem was fixed, but McDonnell Douglas had persuaded the regulators that it was routine work which did not merit the damage a grounding order would do. The modifications demanded had not been carried out on the Turkish Airlines plane, despite initial claims from the company that they had. In essence, the people died unnecessarily, dealing a blow to its reputation from which the company never fully recovered.

Lockheed, meanwhile, established a reputation for corrupt dealing, igniting an orgy of self-recrimination within the American aerospace industry which burned all its players, and which, in the opinion of many, left the industry permanently handicapped as it strove to compete in a more cynical world. The myriad details of the Lockheed scandal are beyond our scope here, but elements of it are relevant insofar as they touch upon the embattled atmosphere in Seattle in the 1970s. The Watergate scandal of 1973, culminating in the resignation of President Nixon, sparked one of the bouts of inquisitorial introspection in which America indulges every now and then. The bare outlines of the story are this. Responding to an endless stream of allegations and revelations about Lockheed sales practices, particularly with the Tristar, the Securities and Exchange Commission, the U.S. financial regulator, started its own investigation. In the summer of 1975, it reported that the company had been bribing officials in overseas markets on a massive scale for many years. Its report sparked a series of Senate hearings, under the chairmanship of Frank Church.

Lockheed denied the allegations, protesting, to the general skepticism of everybody outside the company, that its hands were clean. As the evidence became overwhelming and the company admitted having made payoffs of $22 million to foreign countries and officials in return for aircraft orders, it went on to claim payoffs were necessary if it was to match the inducements offered by the competition. In one particularly dramatic incident, the company admitted that its president, Carl Kotchian, had spent seventy days holed up in a Tokyo hotel room waiting to see if $3.5 million in bribes could land an order for twenty-one Tristars from All Nippon Airways, despite the fact that the company had already ordered DC-10s. The money was well spent. Lockheed snatched the order from Douglas, but that confession led to the resignation of Japanese Prime Minister Kakuei Tanaka, whose office had benefited handsomely from Lockheed's generosity.

In the end, after an investigation by the Justice Department, Lockheed pleaded guilty to four felony charges of wire fraud, four counts of having made misleading statements to the U.S. government, and two violations of U.S. customs law. It paid heavy fines, and was never again a serious player in the civil aerospace business. But its defense that it was merely matching the competition, playing by the rules of the game, inevitably focused attention on the two other big players in the U.S. industry. Lockheed as good as fingered the opposition. "Some call it extortion, some call it grease. Some call it bribery," Kotchian told the New York *Times*. "I look at these payments as necessary to sell a product."

McDonnell Douglas was the first to fall under the spotlight. During the Senate hearings the company admitted that between 1970 and 1975 it had paid out roughly $2.5 million in fees to consultants, commissions and so on. Later, the SEC brought charges alleging that $15.6 million had been paid out illegally to secure sales in foreign countries. The figure went up to $21.57 million, and four top executives were personally charged with crimes including fraud, conspiracy and making false statements to a government agency. McDonnell Douglas agreed to settle out of court, neither admitting or denying the allegations, but promising not to repeat the crimes, and to appoint an internal investigative panel.

Boeing inevitably came under the microscope as well. Despite numerous internal codes of conduct which prevented such things, and even prevented employees receiving gifts from customers, its hands also turned out not to be clean. T. Wilson was called to testify before the Church Committee hearings, an experience he personally found uncomfortable. In its 1975 report and accounts, the company had attempted to puncture any investigation by admitting that it had retained sales consultants in overseas countries, and that some of those consultants might indeed have been people who held positions in the governments of those countries. But it went on to claim that none of them was in a position to influence decisions about buying aircraft, which, to stockholders, might have raised a question about why they were on the Boeing payroll in the first place.

The denials were fervently maintained, and the company also claimed that it had no firm knowledge of the corruption to which Lockheed had confessed; officials conceded that they had heard rumors of such things, but nothing precise. Yet as the investigations continued, the company appeared to know more than it had been prepared to admit. In 1978, under pressure from the SEC, the company reached an out-of-court settlement, which — while neither admitting nor denying guilt — came clean about foreign payments. Boeing had made payments totalling $54 million — more than either Lockheed or McDonnell Douglas had admitted — which related to airplane sales worth $943 million in eighteen different countries. The company claimed that these were legitimate consulting fees. A committee of directors was appointed to carry out an internal inquiry which, after much checking, felt able to conclude, "The Boeing company has made a complete disclosure of payments to foreign officials, and no further investigations are required."

Unfortunately they were. The SEC was satisfied, but the Justice Department was not, and it pursued the case. In July 1982, it reported that Boeing had withheld material facts from the SEC. Boeing then pleaded guilty to a charge of concealing that it had made $7.38 million in "questionable payments" involving the sale of airplanes in Spain,

Honduras, the Dominican Republic, and Lebanon, places where bribery is not unknown. The company passed the buck down the line, shielding the board from blame. It protested that despite its strict internal codes a few middle managers and sales agents appeared to have been too enthusiastic in striving to meet their targets — the traditional defense of a corporation caught red-handed.

It was an embarrassing period for the company and for the entire U.S. industry, and dragged on for the best part of a decade, diverting time, attention and resources, and sullying the reputations of the planemakers. When coupled with the mounting difficulties in the market, it contributed mightily to the gloom and despondency that engulfed Seattle during the first years of that decade — although the crippling blow to Lockheed did at least mean that another competitor was taken out. Yet as well as tarnishing Boeing's reputation, the corruption scandals had immediate and practical knock-on effects on the whole of the American industry. In the wake of the scandal, the Carter Administration passed the Foreign Corrupt Practices Act, a very American piece of moralistic legislation, which made it illegal for citizens of the United States to bribe overseas officials. It also imposed heavy fines, or a prison sentence of up to five years, for any individual or company found guilty of passing backhanders. Although the law levelled the playing field between the major American manufacturers who then dominated the world and were all in the same boat, it did not apply to manufacturers based outside the United States. In particular it did not affect the Europeans, who have always taken what Americans regard as a more cynical and Europeans regard as a more mature approach to matters of this sort.

In a demoralized Seattle, meanwhile, there were fresh challenges to be faced — and fresh opportunities. Though the 747 was still a new plane, the rest of the line were looking a little elderly. The 727 and the 737 both stretched back to the early 1960s, and both had clocked up a decade and a half of service. By the time a new plane was in service both would be more than two decades old. The 727 was the most pressing issue. Aeronautics had moved on since it was designed. Newer, bigger engines were now available, lighter materials could be used, and the old 727 was rapidly becoming an inefficient and unacceptable machine, particularly to many of the American airlines. With passengers growing used to the increased comfort of widebody aircraft, the narrow, cramped space of the 727 on the

shorn and less densely travelled routes was seen as increasingly unattrac-
tive. Sales of the plane were ebbing fast through the early years of the
1970s, adding to the financial woes of the company.

Boeing was unsure what to do, and reluctant to spend the money
involved in the design of a new plane. Since the start of the jet age it had
always been out in front: with the 707 reaching the end of its natural life,
Allen had trumped it with the 747, three times its size, and revolutionary
in every way. This time Boeing's approach was more cautious. T. Wilson
was attracted to the idea of derivatives as a way of squeezing the maximum
return out of an investment; a philosophy which was becoming popular
within the company. The engineers were set to work to spruce up the 727
so that it would look better alongside the widebodies.

They came up with a package which involved adapting the spacious
look of the 747 to the 727, essentially by redesigning the interior to make
the cabin appear squarer, and less like the inside of a tube. Boeing was
happy with the designs, which the company believed would give them a
product to compete with the DC-10, and even with the A300 (if that needed
to be competed with, which the Seattle people were still not sure about).
The plane would have a faster cruising speed than either; true, its operating
costs would be 30 percent higher, because of the older engines and older
materials, but Boeing would sell it for about 25-30 percent less than its
rivals. The airlines would pay more to fly it, but the capital and financing
costs would be less, so, on balance, ticket prices and profit margins should
be about the same.

The airlines didn't see it that way. Unlike the more freewheeling Allen
days, when a plane could be launched on the back of a hunch and some
harassment from Juan Trippe, pre-marketing studies were now the order of
the day. A design would be chewed over extensively with the customers; here,
the airlines chewed over the revamped 727 and spat it out. "We looked at
what it would do for our earnings potential, and said no, this is not what we
want," commented a senior United Airlines official.[5] The verdict from the
rest of the industry was much the same. Although Boeing may have been able
to tart up the 727 a little, few airlines were happy to contemplate buying a
plane of early 1960s vintage which they would still have to be flying in the
early years of the twenty-first century.

Boeing went back to the drawing board. The company would have
to consider a new plane, but what sort of new plane? And how were they

to pay for it? These were questions crucial to the future of the company and dominated strategic thinking in Seattle for the next few years. One option had been the QSHA, to be produced with Aeritalia, but Boeing had pulled away from that concept, leaving their Italian partners flattened. By the mid-1970s other ideas were coming to the fore. Design work started in earnest on a plane dubbed the 7X7; the X was put into the name because Wilson did not want to commit the company to a specific aircraft. For a long time a three-engined plane with 180 to 200 seats was the front-runner. Though twinjets were increasingly popular, because of their cheaper running costs, many of the airlines were still very dubious about them. The problem was this: if an engine fails on a three- or four-engined plane, the plane can keep going, though not so fast; if an engine goes on a twinjet, the plane has to land — and quickly. To fly in a twin jet over the Atlantic, or over the Rockies, as many American airlines do, you need to be pretty confident about your engines.

Between 1975 and 1976, the airlines decided they were confident enough to buy a twin jet for this segment of the market. One major influence was the decision by Eastern to buy the A300 in 1975, the first signal that twin jets were becoming acceptable in the American market, and that the Europeans were in the competition. The tri-jet designs were junked, and Boeing began working on a twin. At the same time they decided that what was needed was not one new plane but two: the 7X7 for the 180-200-seat market, and an aircraft dubbed the 7N7 for the 150-seat market, both occupying the slots between the 737 and the 747. Over the year a compromise of sorts emerged. The 7N7, later the 767, would be a twin-aisle widebodied plane, but with seven-abreast seating rather than the eight abreast format used on the big planes, and also on the Airbus A300. That would give it slightly less drag than a true widebody, and so improve fuel efficiency, while allowing the airlines two-three-two seating configurations, which gives maximum window or aisle seats. Its sister plane, the 7N7, now to be the 757, would be a single-aisle narrowbody, with a new design, even though it still looked like a spruced-up 727. From close discussions with the airlines, Boeing figured it could slot United in as the launch customer for the 767, and Eastern and British Airways were figured for the 757.

That British Airways, now a nationalized airline, appeared to be a willing customer for the 757 sparked an idea in Seattle which was both outrageous and simple, and which seemed a neat solution to many of the most pressing problems the company faced. For starters, there was money. Boeing was still hurting financially, and the launch of two new aircraft programs simultaneously was going to be expensive, very expensive. Estimates in Seattle ran into billions of dollars. If a way could be found to defray some of these costs, the financial pain could be dulled. On top of that, there was the nagging worry of the impact the Airbus consortium might eventually have on the market. The sale to Eastern of the A300s had already had an influence on the 767 decision, and the interest shown by carriers such as Western was also of concern. So too was the fact that many American airlines had been converted to the twin jet concept, clearly influenced by the A300, even if they had not yet seriously considered buying the European planes.

If a way could be found of easing the financial burden of the 757/767 program, while thwarting the aspirations of Beteille and his European pirates, that would be quite a coup. With that simple, though devious logic began one of the great escapades in the geo-industrial conflict, a game which was to have profound consequences for the players on both sides of the battle lines. Boeing had made an early attempt with the French. During the discussions leading up to the 767, talks were held with Jacques Mitterrand, now running Aérospatiale, about collaboration on building a wing for the new plane; improbably, there had been talks with Airbus Industrie about a joint venture on a medium-sized plane. Once again, these looked like fishing expeditions, and there was little serious chance of prising the French from the European consortium of which they had been the major instigators.

The key, as before, was the British. They are semi-detached Europeans, separated from the rest of the continent not just by a strip of water but by a gulf of aspiration and identity. If any nation could be worked loose from the rest of Europe, it was the British. The aerospace industry in the U.K. had now been consolidated and nationalized into British Aerospace, a state-owned entity which included the old British Aircraft Corporation and Hawker Siddeley, who were was still making the wings for the A300. Nationalization had been bitterly opposed, not only by the Conservative Party but by the companies involved; they particularly objected to the leftwing rhetoric of the nationalization bill, such as a clause making worker participation in management compulsory. By the end of 1976, with the two companies thrown together, the new British Aerospace was in a state of disarray.

Boeing was aware that there had been renewed contacts between Toulouse and London. Airbus was putting together plans for its second plane, a smaller version of the A300 called the A310, which would represent the consortium's first step out on the road to a family of planes. Inevitably, creating the second plane would put a heavy load on its financial and industrial resources, of which Airbus was, as usual, chronically short. In 1976 tentative talks had been held between Lord Beswick, the new chairman of British Aerospace, and Jacques Mitterrand about British participation in the A310; whether just in building the wing under contract, or rejoining the consortium, was still in the air. Yet the fact that they were talking indicated that moves might be afoot.

In Seattle, the prospect of the British rejoining Airbus was viewed with real fear. Not only would such a move puncture the prospect of European collaboration on new Boeing planes, it would make the consortium much more powerful. Yet Boeing could see why the British were talking. British Aerospace had a major defense business, supplying the British Army and other armies around the world. But in the civil markets it was going nowhere, particularly with Concorde, for which it was now responsible; building big new planes such as the BAC 1-11 was now too expensive to contemplate alone. It could have some future in small, regional jets such as the 146, but in the mainstream civil market its future looked bleak. Wilson could see that a deal had almost certainly to be struck somewhere. The question was, would it be with the Americans or the Europeans?

Wilson naturally wanted the British with him rather than with Beteille and Lathière, and he began putting together some bait. That it should involve the new planes was self-evident — that was where Boeing had work available. The second obvious thought was that it should involve the wings of the plane, since the great expertise of the British lay in wing design and manufacture. The third was that it should involve the engines. Aside from British Aerospace, Rolls-Royce (now also state-owned, having been nationalized after it went bankrupt in 1973) was the other major participant in the British aerospace industry. The government was likely to be at least as influenced by the interests of Rolls as of British Aerospace.

The deal Wilson put together went like this: British Aerospace would build the wings on the 757 on a fixed-price contract, much like the Hawker

Siddeley deal with Airbus on the A300. At the same time Rolls engines would be one of the launch engines for the new plane. Airlines could choose other engines if they wanted to, but making Rolls-Royce's available at the start of the program would give the British company an advantage. Relations with Rolls had improved anyway; their engines had just been made available for the 747 for the first time, and the proposed deal would give them another powerful boost. Wilson now introduced a third element: British Airways was already likely to be a launch customer for the 757. With the wings being built by British Aerospace, and the engines by Rolls-Royce, the airline would effectively be the key to launching a plane which would be around 50 percent British. It could effectively be presented as a British plane — but with a Boeing badge, and all the reputation, prestige and back-up that badge implied. To the people in Seattle this seemed a generous offer, certainly more generous than anything they had offered to the Italians.

It seemed that way to many people in Britain as well. Sir Kenneth Keith, then chairman of Rolls-Royce, was particularly tempted. Rolls had decided long before that supplying the American industry was what it wanted, and nothing happening in Toulouse had brought about a change of mind. The ill-fated deal with Lockheed over Tristar had been driven by that desire; here was a chance to collaborate with the most powerful rather than the weakest of the U.S. giants. Engines for the 757, if it were as successful as other Boeing planes, would be a goldmine which could probably dig Rolls out of its financial problems. Keith had no problems — Rolls was in, and would use its considerable lobbying power to bring the others on board.

British Airways was similarly impressed. Its internal management had always been attracted by the Boeing range, and had wanted to buy more of its planes in the past; it had bought 1-11s and Tridents only because the government insisted. The airline had already decided it wanted a narrowbody plane to re-equip its short-haul fleet, which ruled out both the 767 and A310. The 757 was the natural choice, particularly if the company could persuade its political masters it was buying a British rather than an American (or indeed French) plane. They too were in.

Wilson now had two of the most powerful players in the British aviation industry on board. All he had to do was convince British Aerospace, and he was home and dry; the government was unlikely to overrule the opinion of all three. British Aerospace, however, was not so keen on the bait from Seattle. Formal talks between the two companies were initiated early in 1977, and lasted throughout the year, culminating in an offer being tabled for the British company in February 1978. Its essence was a fixed-price contract to supply the wings for the 757. In Aerospace there were doubts and unease about the terms of the contract. For example, Boeing would make little allowance for wage inflation, which could make the contract unprofitable. But the doubts went deeper than that. The 757 struck British Aerospace, as it had many others, as a revamped 727; the fuselage was much the same, and only the wings were to be new. It seemed to British Aerospace that they were being asked to do the hard work on the new aircraft as no more than subcontractors. Boeing were adamant that the British company could not be a partner, simply a supplier. Worse, after the 757, there was no guarantee that they would have a role in other Boeing planes. The contract might be profitable in the short-term, but by taking it British Aerospace might be jeopardizing the company's long-term future in the civil aircraft industry.

To many of the players in this escapade, those questions did not matter too much. Britain was gripped by an almost pathological defeatism in the 1970s, and nowhere more so than among its commercial and political élite. Pessimism was the ruling philosophy, with good reason. A generation had come to power whose lives had coincided with the slide of the country from the world's strongest military and industrial power to a nearly bankrupt bit player on the world stage. Defeat was what they knew best, and they believed it was unstoppable; "managed decline," to use a phrase popular at the time, was the best that could be hoped for. The Boeing proposal fitted perfectly into that mindset. It was managed decline in microcosm; the managed decline of the once-great British aircraft industry.

For that reason the proposal was attractive to many of the strongholds of pessimism, in particular to the Treasury, which was adamant that the Boeing deal was the best available, and that rejoining Airbus would cost money. The Department of Trade and Industry was more ambivalent, its mandarins tending to sympathize more with Aerospace's point of view, and the Foreign Office was keen to see the company rejoin Airbus: it was worried, as always, by the Franco-German axis within the European Community, and wanted Britain in Airbus to strengthen the U.K.'s position in the Community. But the Foreign Office advocacy was potentially counter-productive, because to the Treasury and other skeptics their position confirmed the view that the Airbus consortium existed for political rather than industrial purposes.

The political dimension was by now paramount, however. Both the German and the French governments were keen to see the British back in the Airbus fold, and were not reluctant to use their influence at the highest levels to secure that objective. Both Helmut Schmidt, the West German Chancellor, and Valery Giscard d'Estaing, the French President, were pressing Prime Minister James Callaghan. Callaghan knew Schmidt reasonably well, and was open to his suggestions, although the Germans were content to leave detailed negotiations to the French. But the involvement of two European leaders was an indication of how seriously the issue was taken on the Continent, and how seriously it would have to be taken in Britain. "The situation was intensely political," recalled Callaghan later. "Had we not gone into Airbus, it would have been interpreted as a political act. Giscard would have used it against us and Schmidt [would have] drawn a similar conclusion." It seemed that Callaghan himself would have to decide the issue; he was learning what many in aerospace had long known. "Heads of government must interest themselves in this industry," he said. "There is a lot of politics in it."6

However, as Callaghan's long political career had demonstrated, he was not a decisive man, and was fazed by having to make a choice. His advisers were leaning towards Boeing; the essence of their position was that Airbus was certain to fail, and that British Aerospace would therefore be better off with the Americans, however humble their role might be. Against that, he had to placate his European allies and consider the interests of a management who had recently been through the trauma of nationalization. A choice had to be made. Unless, of course, a way out could be found.

An escape hatch briefly appeared, in the predictable shape of McDonnell Douglas. The California company was in trouble, but it was talking about plans to build a new 180-seat plane, and was known to be interested in partnerships, perhaps with the Europeans. Why not strike a deal with McDonnell Douglas to build the plane in collaboration with an Airbus consortium expanded to include the British? This looked to Callaghan like a way of squaring the circle. Not only would he get a deal with the Europeans, he would get a tie-in with a major American manufacturer. Though a fudge and a compromise, it might keep everybody happy.

A decision was becoming pressing. It was three months since Boeing had tabled its formal proposal, and Seattle was getting impatient. Airbus was waiting to announce a decision on the A310, and had started to look around for someone else to build the wings should the British decide not to climb aboard. It was also being hinted that the wing contract on the A300 would be cancelled if the British did not rejoin Airbus, a none too subtle ploy to step up the pressure on London.

On the weekend of June 24, Callaghan flew to Washington to see if he could resolve the situation. He first had lunch with Frank Borman, head of Eastern, and he sought assurances that the airline would buy the 757 with Rolls-Royce engines. Borman was happy to do so and also to provide a slightly different view of Airbus from the line peddled by Callaghan's advisers in London. Borman was now one of Airbus's major customers and said they were good planes which airlines were happy to buy. This was news to Callaghan. Two more meetings were scheduled, and these took him to the heart of the issue. The stakes had been upped by a public announcement from the French government of what had been known privately for some time: if the British rejoined Airbus, British Airways would have to buy European rather than American planes. The French were aware of the meetings in Washington, and could see no harm in rattling the British cage.

That evening Callaghan had dinner with the Boeing men: T. Wilson and his sidekick, Tex Boullioun. The questions were blunt. Callaghan wanted to know if the company were serious about building the 757, or whether it was simply an attempt to sabotage a renewed relationship with the Europeans. T. Wilson told him that the 757 was a serious plane, and Boeing would go ahead whether the British were involved or not (which, of course, turned out to be true). As the evening wore on, though, tempers became frayed. On the issue of wider collaboration, Wilson was less cooperative. The truth was that Boeing saw the British in an essentially subordinate role, a fact difficult to disguise. Wilson was non-committal on whether the 757 collaboration would lead to other deals in the future, for the simple reason that there was nothing to commit to. The British were to be subcontractors; anything else would have to be looked at on a case-by-case basis. Neither side warmed to the other.

The following night, Callaghan had dinner with Sanford McDonnell, then president of McDonnell Douglas. This was Callaghan's chance to explore his idea for the three-way British Aerospace, Airbus, McDonnell Douglas consortium to create a new medium-sized plane. McDonnell had no objections to the deal in principle; his company needed to keep up with Boeing by building a new plane, but he was short of funds. Callaghan suggested that he could swing the Germans and the French into line, and proposed a fifty-fifty deal: McDonnell Douglas would put up half the money, and own half the resulting alliance; the Europeans would put up the rest, although the precise share between British Aerospace and Airbus was left deliberately vague. McDonnell did not like the sound of the numbers: half the cost was probably too big a commitment for his company. How about a third?

McDonnell Douglas had shown interest, but lacked the appetite to close the deal. The three-way consortium was attractive, but it was probably too late to start a lengthy set of negotiations. The Boeing and Airbus proposals remained the options and Callaghan was now convinced that the European commitment offered the best future for British Aerospace. T. Wilson, it appeared, had been unable to veil his intentions and had blown the deal.

Though the British were now leaning towards the Airbus solution, there were still tricky problems to overcome. Most pressing were the precise terms on which the British would rejoin the consortium. The proposal was that British Aerospace would take a 20 percent stake, with the Germans and the French taking their shares down to 37.9 percent each. The Spanish would stick on 4.2 percent. To ensure a balance of power it was agreed that the majority needed for major decisions would be lifted from 75 to 80 percent, which meant that no decision could be taken without the approval of either the British or the Spanish (a clause which calmed fears that the U.K. would have to pay for the ambitions of the French and Germans). Money was also involved, and it was agreed that £50 million would be available to British Aerospace initially to fund their investment, with the prospect of more when the consortium expanded its program. The Treasury was still doggedly fighting a rearguard action against the deal, but Chancellor Denis Healey did not feel it was a major issue. He formally opposed it, but the financial mandarins could do nothing to stop it or to prevent the subsidy of public money. Airbus was a state-owned consortium, and could not be expected to raise funds privately, even if bankers could be found to bankroll so risky a venture.

The major problem was British Airways, which was determined to buy Boeing rather than Airbus planes. It had lined up the support of its unions, and the government did not feel in a position to overrule the decision. The plan was still to fit Rolls-Royce engines on to the 757, and scrapping the BA order would have jeopardized that relationship. It could even have led to the cancellation of the 757 program, since the only other airline interested at that stage was Eastern. Treading carefully through the conflicting desires of British Aerospace and Rolls-Royce, the government felt that it could not concede to the demands of the planemakers without giving something to the engine manufacturers. British Airways would buy Boeing planes, and British Aerospace would join Airbus.

The French found this difficult to believe. Though the British insisted that the government had no influence over what British Airways did or did not buy, this was certainly not the way things were done in France. To the French, and to Giscard in particular, it was a matter of faith. They had been irritated for eight years by the refusal of the British to buy Airbus, even though the wings were made in the U.K. and the Germans had bankrolled a lot of the development work. If the English could not bring themselves to buy the planes now, when the country was on the brink of rejoining the consortium and the national airline was on the point of making a major purchase, what chance was there of selling to Britain in the future? Giscard knew that the success of Airbus still demanded massive political and industrial will, and the consortium could ill afford a partner not prepared to pull its weight. And, if Airbus could not even sell to the countries paying to build them, what hope was there of selling elsewhere in the world? The public relations impact would be deadly, and Giscard dug in his heels: the British had to buy some planes or the deal would be junked.

For a time, it looked as though the deal was indeed off. No compromise appeared possible, until, at the last moment, an unlikely maverick stepped into the frame. Sir Freddie Laker was one of those irrepressible entrepreneurs the country throws up from time to time, who operate on the fringes of the establishment. Laker had built up a business flying charter airlines and, in 1977, after a long battle with the government, got a license to fly from London to New York. His Skytrain, a no-frills service offering flights for £99, was a tremendous hit, threatening to break up the cozy cartel between the state-run or state-backed airlines, which still monopolized air travel in the 1970s and which charged monopoly prices. Laker offered an early glimpse of the tidal wave of deregulation later to engulf the airline business, and amid intense competition for the North Atlantic traffic Laker later went bankrupt (allowing the receivers to sue British Airways successfully for unfair competition). But in 1978 he was riding a wave, and moved suddenly to place an order for ten Airbus planes. This puzzled the Boeing salesmen in the U.K.; they knew Sir Freddie well, and he had not contacted them to say he was considering a major order or to inquire what terms Boeing might offer. However, they discovered that Laker had filed an application under the Treaty of Rome to start flying routes in Europe, and hinted darkly that the two events might be connected.

Whether they were or not, his order was neatly timed, giving the British and the French a chance to get off the hook. Giscard had been told by Beteille that the search for an alternative source of wings for their planes (should the British not rejoin Airbus) was not going well, and the French President was now ready for compromise. The Laker order was portrayed as a British buy, even though it was a private company, and the French had initially insisted that British Airways buy the planes. After Callaghan had been in touch once more with Giscard and Schmidt, the French agreed: the Laker deal was enough.

The British were now to rejoin Airbus. By October 24, 1978, after more than a year of delicate negotiations, and almost a decade after they had decided to quit the original consortium, British readmission to the European challenge was formally announced. The terms were not as good as if they had stayed in all along — and it was hard to see what had been gained by spending eight years on the sidelines — but for Airbus Industrie it was powerful support for a united European front to combat American dominance of the aerospace industry.

For T. Wilson and his colleagues in Seattle, the British decision was a painful blow, and confirmation that, when it came to playing European politics, they were not the equals of their competitors in Toulouse. Making big planes, not geo-industrial politics, was the skill they had been raised in. In retrospect, insiders reckoned Boeing wasn't prepared to go far enough to capture its prey. "In the end, they just did not trust us enough," one official said much later. Boeing had not been prepared to compromise the one hundred percent control the company maintains of all its projects; it wanted serfs, not partners. And despite the best efforts of a powerful lobby within the commercial and political establishment, the British were not quite far enough along the curve of decline to accept serfdom as the best they could shoot for. The reflexive imperialism of the giant American corporation had on this occasion been its undoing.

The reckoning for Boeing was still some way off, though its near-bankruptcy in the early 1970s, followed by the revelations of bribery, followed by its European defeats, had scarred its image. By the end of the decade the wounds were healing, and Boeing was emerging, on the surface at least, bigger and stronger than ever. The maneuverings in Europe behind it, the 757 and the 767 did get launched as American planes (although the Italians did a small amount of work on the 767, as did the Japanese).

The decision to launch the two models was finally taken in the summer of 1978, with British Airways and Eastern as the launch customers for the 757, and United, the key airline in the U.S. and the carrier it had been designed for, as the launch customer for the 767. The United deal was particularly critical; it had been thinking hard about buying Airbuses, but in July committed itself to buying thirty planes from Boeing at a cost of $1.2 billion. In November, its lead was followed by American Airlines and Delta, bringing orders for the plane to eighty, and a month later TWA booked ten. The 767 was forging ahead. Canadian carriers bought the plane the next year, as did All Nippon Airlines, bringing orders to 135 in the first year of its launch: one of the fastest and most complete successes of any Boeing plane. The 757 did not make rapid headway. After British Airways and Eastern, it was two years before the Boeing salesmen found another buyer, but it was still a derivative of the 727 and was not costing nearly so much to produce.

The clouds were starting to lift. That year, the company booked orders for 461 planes, a new record for any twelve-month period and more than twice the combined total achieved by all the other airframe manufacturers. Profits were looking good as well: 5.9 percent on sales, topping the Fortune 500 in total returns, and recording the highest profit margin since 1941, when returns had been boosted by the easy money made from selling war planes. The 747 was also beginning to come good: in 1978, 83 of the monsters were sold around the world, up fourfold from the last three years, and the plane was approaching breakeven. The massive Everett plant was churning out two Jumbos a week (up from one a fortnight at the company's low point), and any further sales represented money in the bank.

Bill Allen's great gamble was beginning to reap rewards for his inheritors. The transformation in travel which Allen and Trippe had forecast for the 747 had been realized: the new plane drove down ticket prices, opened up new routes and created a market for mass long-distance travel that had not previously existed. Airlines had to have them, and a small country was not complete without its national airline's Jumbo on the tarmac as a symbol of nationhood. It was also a symbol of the new world where borders and oceans, barriers which had divided people and continents for centuries, melted beneath the roaring steel hulk of the 747. As much as the great ocean liners of an earlier era, the plane was the definitive mode of transport of its time, different only in that it was better suited to a more egalitarian age; each Jumbo carried more people than the liners, there were more of them, and each could make two flights a day, disgorging teeming masses into crowded airports. Just as the great shipbuilders of the last century had been the builders and the beneficiaries of the pax Britannica, so the planemakers were the builders and beneficiaries of the pax Americana. The 747 was creating a market which no other company could share; it had achieved the greatest of all industrial fantasies — a monopoly.

Just as American planes were consolidating their grip on world civil aviation, so Boeing was consolidating its hold on the American industry. The Turkish Airlines crash of 1973 had been a terrible setback for McDonnell Douglas, but it paled beside the crash in May 1979, when an American Airlines DC-10 lost an engine during take-off from Chicago and crashed, killing the 273 people on board. This was the third fatal crash during the nine years the DC-10 had been in production, and the FAA now issued a grounding order, stopping all flights around the world. Sales slowed to a trickle; the jinxed reputation of the aircraft was widely touted, and few airlines felt comfortable offering it to their passengers. It stayed in production — once a plane is in production, there is little to be gained by cancelling — but by 1988, when the last DC-10 rolled off the Californian production lines, only 446 had been sold, well short of breakeven level. McDonnell Douglas were financially weakened and technologically stymied.

Over at Lockheed matters were even worse. The bribery scandal had wounded the company, and the Tristar, by the end of the decade, was clearly a failed project. Lockheed had hoped to break even on sales of 300 planes, but rising production costs lifted that figure to more like 500. It had not sold enough to meet even its initial targets; only 244 sales were made. Losing $150 million a year by keeping the plane in production, the company resolved to kill the program in December 1981, stopping all production and taking a $400 million write-off. Over the thirteen years of its existence, Tristar had cost the company $2.5 billion, enough to scare it away from the civil aerospace business. With the cancellation of Tristar, Lockheed was out of the industry, this time for keeps.

The wounds suffered by both McDonnell Douglas and Lockheed left Boeing master of all it surveyed. Through its long history, the company had struggled for dominance and appeared to have achieved its goal as the 1970s closed. Its American competitors had been smashed, and the company was pre-eminent in the world's largest market. Through being bolder than its rivals, and surviving greater risks, it had achieved leadership, sewing up more than 60 percent of the world industry. Civil aerospace was looking increasingly like a Boeing fiefdom.

And yet its failures in Europe still rankled, as well they might. It still seemed possible that Boeing's victory might be a shadow, a fleeting triumph. In allowing Airbus to emerge united, the company was about to face a competitor which had learnt from its achievements and was prepared to challenge it with the same tools Boeing had used over the past decades — taking chances and playing rough.

7

THE SILK ROUTE

Late in April 1991, Jean Pierson, new managing director of Airbus Industrie, gave a lecture at the Cranfield management school in Britain. An honorary fellow of the school, he took the opportunity to wax philosophical about the reinvigoration of European industry, and the role of Airbus within it. In that year, with the imminent integration of the single European market, the continent had acquired a new sense of vigor. Its aspirations, which a decade earlier had been blighted by Eurosclerosis, had been reignited; the dream of Beteille, Lathière and others of challenging the Americans in the aerospace industry had been transformed into the wider belief in economic challenge to the world under the banner of pan-European collaboration; a banner first unfurled and most enthusiastically carried by Airbus Industrie.

"Aviation has changed the way we live, the way we do business. Aviation has allowed us to consider mankind for the first time in the context of a truly global village. And the European contribution to this has been significant," Pierson began, warming to his theme of European renaissance. "Airbus Industrie is often singled out as an example of a successful European venture, as an ambitious, extraordinary experiment in cooperation. It has become a model for such ventures in the aerospace industry and other capital-intensive activities. The Airbus experience could also have paved the way, as 1992 approaches, for the European company concept. In the span of twenty years, a short time in our industry, Airbus Industrie has managed to restore European civil aircraft manufacturing to its proper place in the market. Let us go back to 1970 for one minute. Imagine if I had gone then to a bank and said, 'I have just started a management team from various European countries. I intend to make large aircraft to compete with Boeing. Will you lend me $1 billion? You may lose all of it. Or you may start to make some money twenty years from now.' I leave to your imagination the welcome I would have had. No financial institution would have taken on such a risk, or if it had the interest rates would have been simply prohibitive. It was therefore up to the governments of each of the countries participating in Airbus Industrie to substitute themselves for the bankers and assume such risks."

Hitting his stride, Pierson launched into a hymn to European achievement that Servan-Schreiber would have been proud of. "Airbus Industrie stands as a symbol of what Europe can accomplish when it combines its forces around a common project. A forerunner of the concept of globalization in the aircraft industry, Airbus Industrie has spurred a large number of projects in cooperation across a broad spectrum of the industry. It stands, today, as the only recourse against a monopoly of the civil aerospace industry by U.S. manufacturers. Our products come in over one hundred different colors — the colors of our customers around the world. That is the real commercial power that is now back in European hands.

"It has taken us twenty years to generate our first operating surplus. Those years have not been smooth all the way. Airbus Industrie has had more than its fair share of turbulence since its creation. Sure, at times there were temptations to weigh short-term individualistic considerations against long-term collective interests. Sure, at times there was tension, dissent and debate within the partnership; but at no time has the unity of the partnership been at risk. With much patience, our partners chose to invest in what they know to be a very long-term business activity and accepted fully that it would take a while before they saw a return on their investment. In doing so they generated wealth in Europe, the wealth that comes from skills retention, employment and career opportunities, import substitution, export earnings. The determination of the partners to keep the damaging old demons of intra-European rivalry at bay was a key factor in the success of Airbus Industrie. It is in the interests of Europe that this determination should prevail. If there could be one lesson. . .to be learned from the Airbus Industrie experience, it would be that cooperation is the key to prosperity and that there simply is room no more for narrow, nationalistic endeavors."

The veil was now lifted. Airbus was no longer claiming simply to be an ad hoc coalition to produce a single jet. It was claiming openly to be an experiment in European industrial regeneration; the pretorian guard in athe geo-industrial battle between competing powers. That Pierson could talk so frankly, and lay out such an ambitious vision without fear of ridicule, was a reflection of what had been a remarkable decade for Airbus. He was talking at a time when the fortunes of the industry were at a high point. A few weeks earlier, he had announced that the consortium had made its first operating profit. A few months later he was able to announce that Airbus had sold 50 planes, plus another 50 options, to United Airlines, in a deal worth $3 billion — a deal that took it into the heart of the U.S. market and confirmed its stature as a major player in the industry.

For those with long memories, sensitive to the ghosts and spirits that haunt the aerospace business, the United decision to join the Airbus camp had a particular resonance. United was not just the operator of the world's largest fleet of aircraft, it was a part of the Boeing family. The two companies had been members of Bill Boeing's aeronautical conglomerate of the 1930s and, though that had been split, the planemaker and the plane operator had remained close ever since. Airbus had knocked on its door many times, had talked and chatted on the steps, but had each time been turned away. That United was now buying Airbus planes was an indication of how far the European consortium had travelled. In fifteen years, it had turned itself from a bit player, meddling in the fringes, into the mainstream competitor to the might of Boeing. But, as Pierson had hinted, it had been a long and difficult march, which at times had seemed as likely to end in defeat.

United has been a player in this story at several stages. Back in 1978, when the European consortium was a delicate fledgling, United had played a critical role in the launch of its second aircraft. The management in Toulouse, and Beteille in particular, had decided that being the manufacturer of a single plane was a recipe for commercial humiliation. A family had to be developed, and the sooner the better. The A300 had been designed as an aircraft which could be produced in several different versions. The first to be considered after the A300 was a slightly smaller plane, originally known as the B10, but soon redesignated the A310, with a shorter fuselage, seating 218 passengers in a standard two-class layout. Unlike previous European aircraft launches, and unlike the A300, this launch was to take place with firm orders in the bag. This was another example of stealing a strategic leaf from the Boeing book; the American company always had airlines signed up prelaunch, whereas the Europeans tended to build the planes in the hope that a purchaser would turn up sooner or later. Two airlines were found to sign up to the A310, and both were close to home: Lufthansa and Swissair. With those in the bag, and the British now back on board, bringing money and increased production capacity, the consortium's partners felt sufficiently emboldened to give the go-ahead to the second program, allowing a formal announcement to be made on July 6, 1978.

But it was in the United States that Beteille and his colleague hoped to make real progress. It was there, the enemy's territory, that they needed to succeed. Four U.S. airlines were then deciding on replacements for the medium-range fleets, and it was with an awareness of those upcoming orders that Airbus had been so keen to push ahead with the launch of the A310. The airlines were Delta, American, TWA and United, all giants of the airline industry. Delta had decided against buying a European plane more or less on principle, and the consortium received short shrift there. At United and American the Europeans received a more friendly reception. Both invited Airbus to give detailed presentations on their machines, initiating a contest between Boeing and Airbus for the orders. Both regarded the emergence of Airbus as a useful weapon in their negotiations with Boeing over price, and it was one they were prepared to use aggressively. At United the management went so far as to prepare the board for the political flak that would result from buying European rather than American (the board was reminded that United had included a few French planes — the Caravelle — in its fleet in the past). In the event, both airlines stuck with what they knew, deciding to buy the new 767s rather than the new A310s.

At TWA, Airbus came closer to success. Negotiations dragged on through much of 1979, with both sides making detailed presentations on the respective virtues of their product. Towards the end of the year, it seemed that TWA were leaning towards Airbus, largely because of the liberal financial terms the Europeans were able to offer as part of their package, but also because of the superiority in fuel performance claimed for the A310 over the 767. The TWA board was due to meet in mid-December to reach a final decision. The night before, Tex Boullioun from Boeing turned up to meet TWA's management, and proposed a bet. If the 767 did not consume less fuel than the A310 once it was in service, Boeing would compensate TWA for the difference in performance. In effect, he was offering a guaranteed performance level and removing uncertainty from their quandary. He also offered to bring the financial package from Boeing into line with the Airbus offer, which meant that Boeing and Pratt & Whitney, the engine supplier on the deal, would be supplying around half the funds needed. The terms offered by the two sides had thus been levelled, and, all else being equal, the board decided to stick with a known American supplier rather than risk the terms offered by a relatively unknown European.

From four potentially large deals in the U.S., Airbus had walked away empty-handed. Yet it had demonstrated two things: it could at least capture the ears of the American airlines, and it could inflict severe financial pain on Boeing. Officials at the Seattle company later conceded that the United deal — worth a total of $1.2 billion — cost about $1 million per plane in price concessions, twice what they would have conceded had the carrier not been threatening to order from Airbus instead. The TWA deal was expensive for precisely the same reason. From these experiences, the Toulouse salesmen carried away an important lesson: the American carriers would use them as a tool to get better terms from their manufacturers, but were not yet prepared to buy Airbus planes. A long and expensive war of attrition, it became clear, was beginning.

Though disappointed, the partners in the consortium did not have to worry unduly about the refusal of the Americans to sign in 1978 and 1979. Plenty of other airlines around the world were converting into customers. The A300 had been designed as a fuel-efficient aircraft at a time when the price of fuel was still relatively low. Airlines could see the point of saving money on energy, but it was not the paramount consideration that it was to become. Nor, at the time the program was launched, was it enough to allay fears about the safety of a twin-engined aircraft.

The first oil price shock of 1973-4 had given one boost to its fortunes, which was to become yet more powerful a factor in 1979, when further turmoil in the Middle East doubled the price again. Coupled with this, the A300 had now been in service with airlines for close on five years, with no crashes and no lives lost. The more they saw of the twins in service, the more the airlines became convinced that they were safe. And the fact that Boeing had now decided to make its own medium-range twin, the 767, vindicated the technology. If even Boeing was making them, surely it was time to concede that the twin jets were an option.

Giving Airbus a boost in the marketplace had not been part of Boeing's thinking in launching the 767, but it was the unintended consequence. The airlines could go to Seattle and order as many 767s as they liked, but they could not fly one away. The program had just been launched and several years would elapse before they began rolling off the production line. Airbus, by contrast, had some bright, white A300s sitting on the tarmac. If you wanted a widebody twin jet right away, you had to go to Toulouse. And, with the price of oil rocketing, amid dire predictions of a worldwide shortage pushing the price ever higher, many airlines did want them — and right away.

The years 1978 and 1979 were a phenomenon in the story of the consortium. After selling only thirty-eight planes in the first eight years of its existence, it made a remarkable breakthrough. By the end of 1979 orders had risen to 256 planes for 32 different airlines; in 1979 alone it had sold 133 firm and booked 88 options; it sold more widebodied aircraft (the only sector in which it was competing) than any other manufacturer, Boeing included, and took, in dollar terms, a 26 percent share of the market for civil aircraft. From almost nothing, the European consortium had arrived formidably on the world stage.

Airbus had the oil sheiks of the Middle East to thank for hiking the price, and the same people to thank for recycling millions of those petrodollars back into the Western economy via Toulouse. Their purchases were not the result of any concern about putting back some of the money, they were the result of a coldly calculated and executed strategy. In the mid-1970s, Beteille, Lathière and their American Airbus representative George Warde had put together a strategy which they called the "silk route." It was in many ways a very European strategy, its name harking back to the traditional trade routes through which luxury goods had flowed from the Orient to Europe and back again, over millennia, and it summoned up the myriad connections and influences Europe had built throughout the East over centuries.

The main planks of the strategy were, however, rooted firmly in the modern characteristics of the industry. One of the features of the aircraft business is that no carrier likes to be or to become an "orphan airline," where an airline is alone in flying a particular jet in its region. Should emergency spare parts or maintenance work be needed it might face a problem, because the parts could be thousands of miles away. It would prefer to know that it could, if necessary, borrow the bits from a neighboring airline. It follows that if you can sell a plane to one country, the next country along is quite likely to follow suit. And if a national airline can be encircled by a set of carriers all flying a particular jet, the surrounded airline is likely to conform. It is the commercial equivalent of the domino theory; once one falls, the rest will follow.

For Beteille, Lathière and Warde, the region to set the dominoes tumbling was the East. America was going to be tough, being the home market for Boeing and McDonnell Douglas. And they knew their way around Europe. But the East was virgin territory; a Boeing fiefdom until now, but not firmly in that camp. With effort, it could be prised loose. On top of that, it was starting to emerge economically as the fastest growing region in the world, and growing economies gobble new transport at a tremendous rate. It was a region, moreover, not served by railways and roads, where newly prosperous countries were likely to leapfrog a stage of development, going for air routes instead of surface transport. The capital involved in building an air route, consisting only of planes and airports, is much less than that required for surface routes and in many East Asian countries aircraft are literally buses.

So the silk route strategy was devised. Airbus would expand to the East, knocking down one country after another in a line stretching from the edges of the Mediterranean as far as Japan and Korea. Airlines in the Far East came first; through 1978 and 1979, the consortium made sales in the Philippines, Malaysia and Indonesia and, slightly closer to home, in Pakistan and Iran. In 1979, one A300 was sold in Egypt, and by the following year, much of the booming Middle East was sewn up, with sales in Kuwait, the Lebanon and Saudi Arabia.

In the three Middle East sales of 1980, the A300 had triumphed after a direct head-to-head fight between Airbus and Boeing. Those orders, much to the annoyance of Boeing, demonstrated how clearly Airbus had learnt the rules of the geo-industrial game, and how ready it was to fire all bullets in its chamber. At the turn of the decade, the Americans were unpopular in the Middle East, largely because of their support for Israel throughout the conflicts of the 1970s. There was nothing new in that; what was new was the readiness of the consortium to convert geo-political strategies into geo-industrial strengths, to give the latter precedence over the former.

In March 1980, the French President Valéry Giscard d'Estaing made a tour of the Middle East states. His trip just happened to be at a time when three of the region's airlines were making decisions about re-equipping their fleets. While he was in Kuwait, Giscard announced a joint venture with France to build a petrochemical plant in the country while opening the way for Kuwaiti property investment in Paris. More significantly, Giscard made a series of speeches urging the Israelis to withdraw from the occupied territories and supporting the rights of the Palestinians to self-determination, the first upfront support for the Palestinian and Arab cause voiced by a senior Western leader. While he was there, the U.N. Security Council passed a resolution calling for Israel to remove Jewish settlements in the occupied territories — a vote the U.S. at first supported but changed its mind on, angering the Arab nations once again.

While the politics of the region were being played out in the background, within Kuwait Airlines a smaller drama was developing. The board of the airline was known to have opted for the 767 over the A300 but the decision had to be approved by the government.[1] The Kuwait government was strongly pro- Palestinian, so it was no surprise to the people in Toulouse when the decision was made public a few days later: Airbus had won. Although no open deals had been done, and it was doubtful that there was even any quid pro quo in private, the Boeing salespeople complained bitterly that they had been outwitted by Giscard's diplomatic salesmanship. (There was rich irony in a successor of de Gaulle, who had once described a visiting Japanese premier as "a little transistor salesman," becoming an enthusiastic airplane salesman.) Their bitterness increased as the other orders fell to Airbus. In the Lebanon, Middle East Airlines asked for sealed tender bids from the competing manufacturers, designed to stop the allegations of corruption which had dogged the airline. When the bids were opened, Airbus turned out to be the lowest, but only after the arbitrary figure of $2.6 million (it was revealed later) had been added to the price of every Boeing plane. By the time the sales teams moved to Saudi Arabia, the Boeing team were sadly demoralized; the company never got close enough to the Saudi royal family, also strong Palestinian supporters, to put their case. By December 1980, that sale too had gone to Airbus.

The triumphs along the silk route had given a powerful boost to Airbus, strengthening its position in the marketplace and giving it a swath of territory where it could claim to be Boeing's equal. Its successes in the region meant it chalked up more impressive results: in 1981 as the Middle East coups were logged into the order books, it was again the world's top manufacturer of widebodied aircraft, pushing Boeing into second place and the other two American manufacturers into third and fourth in a league of four (reduced to three after Lockheed dropped out that year). Emboldened by their success, Beteille and his colleagues began to believe that the moment was ripe for further moves. It was time to expand.

Within the consortium plans for more aircraft had been floating around for many years. As early as 1975, the supervisory board had approved the building of a family to compete with Boeing. After the A300 and A310 — essentially different versions of the same plane — the question was: which segment of the market do we attack next? As was often the case within Airbus, the resolution of such issues was neither smooth nor quick; the consortium was too unwieldy, and there were too many competing interests, for major issues to be resolved easily.

Since the mid-1970s a proposal for a second joint European venture had been in the air. It was known as the Joint European Transport, and would be a consortium similar to Airbus, but this time to build a small single-aisle aircraft to compete with the Boeing 737 and the DC-9, as well as to replace ageing Caravelles and BAC 1-11s. Strangely, in retrospect, the proposal had been to push this in parallel with Airbus, with the same national partners (although potentially with some new members), but as an entirely separate venture, based on new agreements and a new structure. That such an idea was floated reflected the divergent views of Airbus Industrie at the time. Though those in Toulouse saw themselves as the hub of a new aerospace conglomerate challenging Boeing, the four partners, who guarded jealously their distinct national identities, saw it as an ad hoc marketing vehicle charged with selling the A300.

The success in the marketplace in the early 1980s convinced the partners that in Airbus they had a workable structure, one not to be casually tossed aside. Arguing for the family concept, Beteille and the staff at Toulouse lobbied hard for their banner to carry the new project. They succeeded. The Joint European Transport proposal was dropped, and the new small jet, it was decided, would be made by Airbus. But in Toulouse there was little agreement about whether the new jet should be a small plane at all. Other ambitions lurked. There were ideas for a long-range jet to capitalize on the success of the A300/A310 program, an even larger twin-engined jet known as the B9, and a very long-range four-engined aircraft, known as the B11. After internal argument, it was decided that the market was not ready for another big Airbus plane, and the decision was made for the single-aisle option. In another self-conscious piece of mimicry, the partners followed the Boeing practice of naming each new plane ten digits along the scale, so the new plane would be known as the A320 — one more reminder of the real target of this venture.

In a move that struck the rest of the industry as showing indecent enthusiasm to please its major shareholder, Air France stepped in with an order in June 1981 before a formal decision had even been made to build it (something of a first for the industry). Yet, even when a decision had been made that the A320 would be the next project, the issue of how it was going to be paid for remained: Air France's francs alone would not be sufficient. The A300/A310 programs had essentially been bankrolled by the German and French governments, although Airbus had given I.O.U.'s to repay the money as and when sales allowed. For the A320, the four governments now involved were not prepared to be so generous. Over the next two years, amid much background haggling, the elements of a package were worked out.

In West Germany, the government agreed to meet 90 percent of the development costs for Deutsche Airbus, DM 1.5 billion (about $750 million). In return, Deutsche Airbus would repay about DM 2.5 million for every A320 sold, up to the first 600, allowing the government to recoup its money (just) if the plane sold well, but without much interest. If 600 were not sold, the West German taxpayers would not get their money back, meaning that they, rather than the company, were taking the risk.

The British government, not surprisingly, was less generous towards British Aerospace, and the negotiations were held up by sniping from

London about the consortium's tactics. Norman Lamont, then a junior Industry Minister, and later a much-disliked Chancellor, voiced public criticisms that Airbus should concentrate less on making sales at any price and more on making a profit, which struck the strategists in Toulouse as missing the point about market penetration. British Aerospace had been given a handout of £50 million on rejoining Airbus; for the A320, it was given a loan from the government of £250 million, to cover development costs through 1984 to 1988. Of that, £50 million would have to be repaid in the early 1990s, regardless of what happened to the plane, while the rest would be recouped from a levy on each sale, as and when it was made. Additionally, the company had to find £200 million from its own resources, meaning in effect that half its total investment of £500 million was at risk if the plane did not succeed.

The French were not in a mood to be generous either; the ill-judged socialist experiments with the economy that followed the election of François Mitterrand as President had put a strain on public finances. For Aérospatiale's share of the project, the government agreed to meet 75 percent of the development costs; however, after the program was formally launched, it persuaded Paribas and a consortium of French banks to lend Aérospatiale FF 380 million towards the cost of the plane, with repayments to be made only when the plane started selling, and with no interest due until the A320 was in the air — more generous terms than French bankers are usually prepared to offer.

The governments involved in the project were not giving money away for nothing. Negotiations over the launch of the A320 were held up by disputes over distribution of the work on the new aircraftt. Politicians want to see jobs in return for money, and they want them among their own electorate. The Germans were pressing for an increased share of the work, to reflect their huge financial contribution to the consortium; at one stage they argued for 40 percent of the plane to be built in Germany. The British suggested that there should be a different division of the cake on the A320, claiming that it was against the interest of the partners to specialize too narrowly on one part of the plane; this time, BAe said, they should build the nose and the fuselage, and the final assembly and flight-testing of the plane should be in Britain. The French hated this idea. Final assembly accounts for only a small proportion of the value of the plane — about 6 percent — and involves only 250 jobs. But issues of national honor were at stake. Assembly in Toulouse gave Airbus the appearance of being a French plane; every time an Airbus is sold it shows up as a plus on the French balance of trade statistics, even though only a small proportion of its value is French.

At Airbus headquarters, Beteille was fighting a rearguard action against what he termed "musical sub-assemblies."[2] The Airbus production system, spread over four countries, was not the most efficient, he argued, and stopping the partners from specializing in sections could only make the consortium less efficient. After more than a year of wrangling, the British were blocked by a simple French maneuver. Increasing their role to the degree BAe was demanding would imply that the Treasury would bankroll a greater proportion of the development costs, an inference which soon sent the BAe executives skulking back to their kennels. After more than a year of haggling, a compromise was reached: the work on the A320 would be shared out along broadly the same lines as the A300/A310. Though prolonged, the internal wrangling strengthened Airbus as a more permanent entity, with national divisions, and less of an ad hoc coalition between four competing companies.

It was still a coalition between four competing countries, however, and the wrangling over the financing and work-sharing was a reflection of deeper national anxieties. Until there was clear evidence that it could make its way in the marketplace, Britain and Germany were not prepared to approve the project, which meant that until they could find some more airlines to sign up for the A320, the money would not be handed over.

Air France had already committed itself to the new plane, but another launch customer was needed. Surprisingly, Airbus found it in Britain. When British Airways had bought 757s rather than A300s, they had promised to consider Airbus planes in the future. With the airline about to re-equip its fleet of small planes, the consortium tried to make BA keep its promise. British Airways did look at the A320, but insisted that it needed planes right away; it could not wait for the new aircraft to be designed and built. Airbus offered to lease a set of Boeing 737s to tide BA over until the A320 was ready. Even this was not good enough. BA obstinately decided to lease 737s itself.

As in 1978, Airbus had greater success with the independent British airlines. British Caledonian had been built up by Sir Adam Thompson as the second force in British aviation, trading on its Scottishness to win landing rights, although it was mainly based at Gatwick, London's second airport (but the stewardesses did wear tartan). After a long battle with Boeing, lasting almost two years, Airbus clinched an order for seven A320s, with options on another ten, but only after two important concessions. One was that they install at considerable extra cost another fuel tank, giving it greater range. Airbus offered to meet the cost of re-equipping the older planes in British Caledonian's fleet to meet new noise restrictions, and produced a financial package whereby a group of banks would buy the A320s, then lease them to the airline once they were built and in service. Once again, by supplying the financing as well as the planes, a sale had been made. Thompson signed up; ironically, his airline was soon to be taken over by British Airways, which, much to its distaste, inherited the A320s, the only Airbus planes ever to fly under its colors. Beteille claimed that the decision by an independent airline, with no state involvement, proved there was a place for the A320.

Sir Adam Thompson was one of the commercial heroes lauded by Margaret Thatcher. He was not quite such a hero as Lord King, chairman of British Airways, but his decision to buy the Airbus plane did lessen her antipathy to a European project which consumed vast amounts of public money (public expenditure and Europe were two of the things Mrs. Thatcher disliked most, which made Airbus something of a demon figure). It also swayed Norman Tebbit, Secretary of State for Industry. At a briefing with Thatcher and Tebbit, Sir Austin Pearce, chairman of British Aerospace, argued that the money for the A320 was neither a subsidy nor a gift: it was simply a case of the impossibility of finding commercial funding, and if the British government was not prepared to put up the £250 million he needed, he would have no choice but to take Britain out of the Airbus consortium yet again. Pearce stressed that there had been talks with Canada, Australia and Japan, any one of which might step in as partners if the British would not back the new plane.

Pearce was playing a game of high-level brinkmanship. A second withdrawal would not only have been disastrous for Britain's reputation in Europe, it would have spelled the end of her civil aerospace industry. His brinkmanship found echoes in Germany, where the minister most directly responsible for Airbus, Martin Gruner, Federal Aerospace Policy Coordinator. expressed doubts publicly about the commercial viability of the project. He suggested the consortium needed closer to eighty pre-launch orders before his government could feel comfortable about providing the money. Within the Kohl administration, he was countered by the bouncing figure of Franz-Josef Strauss, still chairman of Airbus's supervisory board, and on the boards of Lufthansa and several German banks. He warned that not going ahead with the A320 would increase rising levels of unemployment in West Germany, which he was ready to use his influence in the Christian Democratic party to prevent. Despite this, late in 1983 both the British and the German governments deferred their final decisions, a nasty warning that agreement had still not been reached. The future of Airbus lay in the balance.

With its two main partners wobbling, the French intervened to keep the A320 afloat. There appeared to be some signs of a coordinated effort between Jacques Mitterrand, head of Aérospatiale, and his brother François, now President of the Fifth Republic, to railroad the British and the Germans into a decision. Earlier in 1983, Jacques Mitterrand had leaked a letter accusing the British and the Germans of not being sufficiently supportive of Airbus given its successes in the marketplace, and singling out their lack of cooperation on the A320 as particularly irksome. Later in the year, François Mitterrand threw the full weight of his office behind the new plane. "The A320 will be built," he told journalists, "and I am its number one salesman."[3] It was a rare moment of candor about his role for the Toulouse planemakers.

Mitterrand was true to his word. At a European Community summit early in 1984 he discussed the issue at length with both Kohl and Thatcher. Kohl had been turned around by Strauss's lobbying, not about German unemployment only but about the need to maintain a European aerospace industry as well as the Franco-German alliance which had been such a consistent feature of post-war German foreign policy. There were dark hints that any more wobbling from Germany might provoke a major political rift with the French. Thatcher was still doubtful, but Mitterrand persuaded her. Despite their political differences, the two enjoyed an excellent personal relationship. By the end of the summit, word was quietly relayed to Toulouse that Britain and Germany would find the money for the A320, and the pieces of the jigsaw came into place. The new program was launched on March 4, 1984. Ten years after the launch of the A300, the family was finally taking shape.

With the A320, Airbus took a technological leap. The A300 had distinguished itself by being the first widebodied twin into the market. The A320 did not occupy such an obvious niche. Both the DC9 and the 737 (particularly Boeing's revamped version, the 737-300) competed for sales of medium-range single-aisle planes, and both were better known and better established. Coming from behind, Airbus had to build a plane different from the Boeing and McDonnell Douglas products; it would do so by addressing the issue that airlines really cared about in an era of increased competition and deregulation — cost.

The A300 had been cheaper to fly because it used two engines instead of three; one engine was not a possibility. Instead, Airbus looked to the savings that could be made in crew numbers and training. The A320 introduced the technological innovation for which Airbus has become best known — fly-by-wire. Traditionally aircraft have been flown by a serious of pulleys and wires connecting the controls in the cockpit to the flaps that control the aircraft in flight. The A320 dispensed with the metal wires, controlling the plane instead through a set of electronic computer systems. One result was that the pilot would fly the plane using a single joystick (something like playing a computer game), rather than through a set of levers. Another effect was a saving in weight; electronics are much lighter than mechanical controls. And the layout developed the trend towards a two-man rather than a three-man crew, while allowing more common identity among planes in the Airbus range: they are all much the same to fly electronically, whereas mechanically controlled planes are different in their handling requirements.

Fly-by-wire is not new technology. It was used on military jets for many years, and, indeed, had been used on the Concorde. But it was new on mainstream civil jets, and was to prove controversial. Pilots' unions hated it, since it meant fewer jobs; the French pilots' unions in particular (and unpatriotically) complained bitterly about the system, suggesting, among other gripes, that it was unsafe. Boeing, which was to delay introducing fly-by-wire systems for more than a decade, muttered darkly about the safety implications of flying with a joystick. "I would never put a sidestick controller on any commercial aircraft," commented Joe Sutter. "Airbus is not going to sell a lot of airplanes by touting technology."[4]

The Airbus designers were not especially interested in technological breakthroughs. They wanted something their salesmen could use to shift aircraft out of the hangars in Toulouse. "Our bet with the A320 was that fly-by-wire was on its way to becoming a mature technology," recalls Bernard Ziegler, the technical director, "and that we could create a family of aircraft in which the computers would feel the same in all the planes. That was a very exciting idea for us. It was not our intention to promote technology but to discover how to use it to make a better product for the customer. We have always been minded not to be conservative. We were not fascinated by technology, we were just being open-minded and seeing what could be built with the technology. . .already available on the shelf." Yet, in introducing the fly-by-wire system on the A320, the Airbus designers, drawn from all four consortium members, faced a mini-version of the conflicts taking place elsewhere on the program. "The first reaction of the four technical directors ... was to tell me that I was crazy," recalls Ziegler. "We had to convince them step by step."[5]

Despite being offered what they believed was a superior product, which could be flown more cheaply than the planes offered by Airbus's rivals, the airlines were not initially impressed. They had been buying A300/A310s largely because they had to, not because they had an affection for the European planes. In the wake of the A320 launch, the aircraft industry slipped into one of its periodic downturns, and it looked as though the skepticism of Thatcher and Kohl was to be justified. Airbus was hit in both the widebody and the single-aisle sectors of the market. In 1982 and 1983 respectively, only 69 and 48 widebodied aircraft were ordered around the world, compared with 115 in 1980. The Airbus share in that falling market was just 7.2 percent in 1982 and 12.5 percent in 1983, a far cry from the leadership it had been hoping to establish.

The A320 did not distinguish itself either. In 1984 and 1985, the two years after it was launched, it achieved market shares in the single-aisle sector of 14.7 and 7.3 percent, and was soundly trounced not only by the Boeing range of aircraft, but by the elderly DC-9 — not an auspicious debut. During those two years the consortium was also hit by cancellations from airlines which had already placed firm orders and options, dragging down its sales totals, pushing break-even further into the distance and increasing the stockpile of whitetails now queuing again on the tarmac in Toulouse.

The crisis in the marketplace bubbled into a bitter internal feud which split the consortium down the middle. The story began with the whitetails sitting on the tarmac, and the attempts by Lathière and his team to shift them. Working alongside the two older men at this time was a heavyweight Frenchman named Pierre Pailleret. A former consultant with McKinsey, Pailleret had joined the Airbus staff in 1975, and, by 1981, at the age of just thirty-six, had risen to become head of sales. Like many Airbus staffers, his love of good food and wine was reflected in his waistline; Pailleret weighted in at 225 pounds, porky even by Airbus standards. He also brought a streak of chuzump to the task, which endeared him to his superiors. During negotiations over airplane sales he regularly sent recalcitrant customers cans of "anti B.S." spray, each one lovingly wrapped in a case lined with velvet.

Lathière and Pailleret were desperate to shift the whitetails on the Toulouse tarmac; they were costing around £20 million a year in finance charges. After hawking them around the industry with little success, word filtered through that Pan Am was looking to reequip. Pailleret was determined they would buy his planes, and no one else's. Pan Am was by now a shadow of Juan Trippe's proud creation, spluttering through one of the most prolonged deathbed scenes in commercial history. Over six months, a team of forty Airbus salesmen cloistered themselves with the Pan Am board in a last-ditch effort to shift the planes. Boeing was pitching for the order as well: Pan Am had long been one of its best customers and still had a prestigious name around the world.

Late in 1984, Pailleret, who had spent months shuttling to and fro across the Atlantic, clinched the deal. Pan Am placed an order for twenty-eight A300s worth around $1 billion, plus options worth another $1 billion. But he had won this skirmish at a high price; even by Airbus standards the financing of the deal was convoluted. Nor were the full details ever released. The fact that Pan Am had run up losses of $564 million in the past three years, and that its balance sheet showed $1.2 billion of debts against $314 million equity, indicated that the airline had little money to pay for new aircraft. And the terms of the deal, leases which kept the planes entirely off the Pan Am balance sheet, hinted that Pailleret had not been asking much for them. "We are dealing with a company that fixes prices without regard to costs and that builds planes without receiving an order," growled the president of Boeing, Dean Thornton, soon after the deal was announced. "We love it when they accuse us of dumping," needled Pailleret in response, "it is free PR."

In Europe, however, it appeared that the partners were more prepared to sympathize with Thornton than with Pailleret. Though the Pan Am deal emptied the tarmac, and created invaluable publicity in the American market, the British and the Germans were horrified by the terms on which the planes had been sold. It was time, they felt, to remind the consortium that Airbus was not an employment scheme, nor was it just a way of needling the Americans. It was a business that had to make money and, on terms like these, profits would never materialize.

Behind the scenes they wanted Lathière's blood. Beteille was already approaching retirement age and, with failing health, had told the partners he did not want to carry on. Lathière would reach the end of his second five-year term on February 4, 1985, and would have been content to sign for another five years. A few days before that date, Franz-Josef Strauss, on a private visit to France, visited Laurent Fabius, the Socialist Prime Minister, in Paris, and their discussions centerd on the future of Airbus and of Lathière in particular. Strauss told Fabius that freewheeling marketing antics — selling planes without cost control and manufacturing without demand — were no longer acceptable. Late that evening Strauss announced that there would he no third term. Little explanation was given. Lathière had been sacked.

In the immediate aftermath it was announced that Beteille would stand in as a temporary managing director while a replacement for Lathiere was found. Soon afterwards, the French Transport Minister, Jean Auroux, announced that Lathière's successor would be Jean Pierson, the forty-four-year-old head of the aircraft division at Aérospatiale. The French government thought it was within its rights in making the announcement: the top job at Airbus, as they understood it, was reserved for the French, and the choice of a replacement was essentially a decision for the French government — the announcement a mere formality. The other partners were not so sure. The day Auroux made his announcement, the supervisory board was meeting in Toulouse, and at the end of its session said that no successor had yet been selected. The Germans and the British had resisted the assumption that the top job was to be the gift of the French government. Behind the scenes, simmering jealousies were bubbling to the surface.

With space created at the top, the Germans were angling to win a greater share. Though Strauss often began Airbus board meetings with lectures about the need for greater unity among the peoples of Europe, he still pushed German interests and he nominated Johann Schaeffler, a key figure in Deutsche Airbus, for the job. The Germans wanted a German; the French a Frenchman; the British began to wonder if perhaps one of them might be best suited for the role. While the three battled over the succession, the top job lay vacant for eight months — a dangerous vacuum at the center of the consortium. Finally a compromise was reached: a Frenchman would have the top job, with a German number two working closely alongside him. Power-sharing would be the new order of the day.

Pierson, the original choice of the French government, had got the job, amid much ill-feeling among the partners, ill-feeling which he was not the man to mollify. Born in 1940, in Tunisia, the son of an army officer, Pierson was well educated; in his case at the École Nationale Supérieure de l'Aéronautique. In 1963, he joined Sud Aviation as an engineer in the production department. He rose fast to become production manager on the French side of Concorde, a hard school in which to learn his trade but one where he was well trained in the politics of the European aerospace industry and in the disasters awaiting multinational collaboration. When he moved into Airbus from Aérospatiale, there were suspicions among the other partners that he would favor his old employers. He denied this then and denies it now, and still claims to treat the French company more harshly than the other three partners, a claim that is not treated as strictly credible elsewhere.

Pierson brought a rougher, more abrasive style to the consortium. He is known in the organization as the Pyrenees Bear, and indeed he has many bearlike qualities. He is hugely fat, chainsmokes, and regularly loses his temper, rowing with allies and enemies with equal enthusiasm. In one significant way he is an outsider among the French industrial élite. An engineer by training, he did not go through the charm schools that give the French establishment so much of its polish. At the lavish meals in the Airbus dining club, he smokes between courses, sometimes even between mouthfuls, and a waiter is on hand to deliver fresh packs of opened Gitanes on a silver tray, a packet of matches neatly by their side. He waves his arms when he speaks, surrounding himself in a fog of smoke and food. To other Europeans he seems almost a caricature Frenchman. Colleagues within Airbus suspect that in private he might well exchange his silk suit for a striped jersey and beret, shoulder a string of onions and cycle off.

Though verging on parody, Pierson is a ruthless and remorseless executive. He digs deep into every aspect of the consortium's activities, but reserves his greatest efforts for selling planes — an activity, all concede, at which he really excels. There are few airline chiefs around the world who have not had the alarming experience of being schmoozed by Monsieur Pierson. It is an emotional performance; each sales campaign, and each step forwards or backwards, is acted in vivid colors, and Pierson takes each defeat and victory personally. The first victim of his roughness was his German number two, Johann Schaeffler. Six months into the double-headed regime, Pierson told the German, "There's no room at the top for two people. I am it, and you are not." Which turned out to be true. In less than a year, Schaeffler had gone. The German attempt to win a greater share of power at the center of Airbus had been jostled aside by the French, and it was the best part of a decade before they played their hand strongly again. Pierson's controversial arrival led to the departure of many key staff; Pailleret, who had been hoping for the top job himself, departed within two years.

Working alongside Pierson was not easy and only the loyal would survive. But the new managing director had some early success to arm him against sniping from his enemies. It was probably a coincidence, but soon after Pierson arrived in Toulouse, sales of the airplanes began to move. In 1985 the A300/A310 captured 44.5 percent of the widebody market, less than Boeing but wiping the floor with McDonnell Douglas, which had only 2.5 percent. The following year, the A320 began to carve into the market for narrowbody planes, selling over 100, again pushing McDonnell Douglas into third place. Overall, Pierson's team sold more Airbus planes in twenty-four months than his predecessors had achieved in the first fifteen years of the consortium's life. In the arena that counted — market share — the new man made an impressive debut.

Airbus now began to make inroads into the U.S. Since the Eastern Airlines order, America had been barren territory, and one of Pierson's first moves was to reorganize the U.S. sales office.

George Warde had left in 1983 (to run Continental Airlines), and was replaced as U.S. chairman by another heavy hitter — Alan Boyd, tempted into the consortium by a salary of around $500,000. Boyd had served as Transport Secretary under Lyndon Johnson, and as a civil aerospace negotiator for President Carter. He had also run Amtrak and knew his way around both government and the airline industry. For his first two years, however, Boyd was reined in by the leash Pailleret kept on the U.S. operations. All pricing decisions, for example, had to be agreed upon by the four partners, in writing, and the sales teams were secondees from the partners, who did not know their way around America or the U.S. aerospace industry. In one incident, a French Airbus salesman was dining with executives from Northwest Airlines when he asked the waitress for a large rubber (to erase some calculations he was making). The Northwest men collapsed with laughter, and the talks came to an end. They weren't about to buy planes from someone who didn't know what a rubber was.

Pierson gave Boyd authority to clear out the Europeans and staff the office with Americans who knew their industry. New men came in, and Boyd moved the offices from a plush suite in New York to a modest building in Herndon, Virginia: he was sensitive to the American impression of Airbus as a bunch of European plutocrats living high on taxpayers' money. The effects were dramatic — one of his first successes, ironically, was with Northwest. The airline was led by Steven Rothmeier, a career executive who moved into the top job in 1985, soon after Northwest's takeover of Republic had made it one of the giants of the industry. Rothmeier was already acquainted with Strauss, and was still close enough to his German ancestry to be interested by the efforts Airbus was making to crack the American market. After Boyd had made the introductions, Pierson dealt with Rothmeier one-to-one, wrapping him in his bearish charm. The Northwest boss was taken on tours of the Toulouse and Hamburg production sites, and submitted to the full Airbus treatment. "It was really a first-class operation. It was like buying a Mercedes-Benz or a BMW," he said later.[6] In October 1986, Northwest signed up for ten A320s to be delivered in 1990 and 1991, with a further ninety to be delivered in blocks of fifteen at a time. The order was worth $3.2 billion, and Airbus had not given a great deal away: Rothmeier claimed that the Boeing 737 or McDonnell Douglas planes would have worked out cheaper, but the better operating costs of the A320 made it a more economic choice in the long run. The Pan Am sale had been made through financing which caused internal uproar at headquarters; the Northwest deal, by contrast, showed that the consortium were selling aircraft on their merits. "Northwest was a very tough customer, and very Midwest," commented an Airbus insider with evident satisfaction. "We had finally broken through the mom-and-apple-pie barrier."

Boyd and his team had prepared the way for the Northwest deal; a year earlier, they had achieved their first sale with American Airlines, another of the giants, and one which had earlier turned down the A300/A310. In 1985 the carrier took fifteen A320s, after a hard-fought battle with Boeing which saw another Airbus financial innovation. American was squeezing Boeing and Airbus against each other to see how much juice they could extract. Airbus, naturally, would give some, while Boeing held back. American wanted the planes but it did not want the debts associated with re-equipping its fleet to show on its balance sheet. It came up with what is now known as a "walkaway lease." The airline takes the plane but can return it at any time with only thirty days' notice; in effect, it is renting from the manufacturer, rather than buying, and since there is no long-term financial commitment, the transaction does not appear as a liability on the balance sheet.

Airbus was enthusiastic about the proposal and met American's demands. It cared little about accounting. Airbus had no balance sheet, so there was no worry about the liabilities showing on its books instead of American's. Boeing was more ambivalent, eventually agreeing to the terms but only for a limited number of planes; it had books to balance. Eventually the order was split, with Boeing and Airbus each picking up a slice. The terms did not matter too much to Boyd and his team. What mattered was that they had sold to one of the largest American carriers and would be serious contenders whenever American was in the market for additions to its fleet. "We dumped the foreign accents, took off the gloves and got the deals done," said John Leahy, president of the Airbus North American subsidiary. "Nothing underhand, we just learned to play as tough as the next guy."

With serious successes in the crucial U.S. market, and the A320 on its way to being commercially viable, the staffers in Toulouse began pondering the next extension to their empire. Beteille and Ziegler were gone, but Pierson was a true believer in their original vision. Creating a family of aircraft to challenge Boeing at every point in the market was still the ultimate ambition — one that was not yet realized. Airbus had a small and a medium-sized aircraft; it was time to move into the big jets.

As early as 1975, it had been part of the Airbus strategy to scale up the family. Before building the A320, there had been a debate about whether to build a small or a large aircraft. Now that program was underway, there was little question where Airbus Industrie would go next. But what type of big jet should it build? Two proposals had been around for many years: a higher capacity twin jet, similar to the A310, but larger; or a long-range, four-engined aircraft. The twin jet would have around 330 seats in a normal two-class layout or up to 440 in economy; the four-engined plane would seat around 300 but with much greater distance capability. Both projects had their protagonists. "There was a fierce battle about whether to go for a twin or a long-range jet," recalls Bernard Ziegler. "People were not talking to each other in the corridors." The tension was punctured by technology: an idea of startling simplicity emerged; building both planes together, in different versions. There was nothing to stop Airbus building one fuselage and one set of wings, and fitting two engines for the twin and four engines for the long-range plane, creating two aircraft for little more than the price of developing one. "It was complicated, but we could do it," Ziegler recalls. "It was a simple idea to express, but very difficult to compute. You could not have done it twenty years ago, but with modern design it was possible."[7]

For the strategists at Airbus, the designers' solution had immediate appeal. It avoided a bruising row within the consortium over where to go next, and they could push ahead with the challenge to Boeing much faster if they did not have to wait for two programs to be launched. This time around money was much easier. The A320 was selling well, and the view of Airbus as a financial black hole was receding. Ministers agreed that the program would once again have to be bankrolled by government funding, but only 65 percent would be paid for by the taxpayers, a much lower proportion than on the previous developments. The French government contributed FF6 billion via Aérospatiale; the British government £450 million via British Aerospace, with all repayments contingent on sales of the aircraft; and the German government coughed up DM3 billion, although no details of the repayment terms have been made public. Once again, Airbus was being funded generously by European taxpayers — this time with little resistance.

The drama surrounding the launch of the A330/A340 revolved around the prospect of collaboration. Since the epic battle of 1978, there had been few formal contacts between European and American manufacturers. The two sides had battled in the marketplace, not over a table.

Almost a decade later the issue re-emerged, in a very different shape. There was awareness that moving into big jets would take the consortium into an even more bitter confrontation with the American industry; this was their home territory, where they still enjoyed a profitable monopoly, and there would inevitably be a fierce backlash. Airbus thought it would be interesting to try the same tactics Boeing had attempted in Europe: divide and rule. Or, if not rule, at least weaken.

McDonnell Douglas was already weak and struggling. The DC-10 program was being wound down, but the company was still putting a brave face on its predicament, looking at a new three-engined plane, the MD-11. In many ways it was a revamped DC-10, but bigger and more modern, which might give it a chance to re-enter the market successfully. Airbus thought the MD-11 could be a challenger to its A330/A340 program — it also looked like a chance to split the American industry. Their proposal, essentially political, had the strong support of the four governments behind Airbus. Early in 1987 John McDonnell, chairman of McDonnell Douglas, had swung through the European capitals on a lightning visit; he met the government ministers responsible for Airbus in each of the partner countries, and pressed the case for a tie-up between American and European manufacturers. In his seductive Midwestern drawl he made the case for forming an entity able "to go after that big bear in Seattle."

Going after the big bear had always been the main temptation for the Europeans, and in March 1987, at a meeting of ministers held in Paris, a mandate was issued to Airbus Industrie to negotiate a collaboration with McDonnell Douglas. The communiqué said the ministers hoped to see a deal struck as soon as feasible. The two sides had been talking for months, and some of the elements of a deal were already in place. Voices within the partnership had proposed a full-scale merger between McDonnell Douglas and Airbus; indeed, during the lengthy negotiations every possible combination was mulled over. There were clear attractions for both sides: competition between the two would stop, and start directly with Boeing; a merger would mean that the governments which had bankrolled Airbus would feel more confident of getting their money back; and long-standing objections of American airlines to buying a plane not made in the U.S. could be laid to rest.

Cooperation across the whole product range raised a host of thorny issues, however. The firmest proposal to emerge was for a machine known provisionally as the AM 300; with an MD-11 fuselage and the high-technology wing of the A330, it would be a three-engined plane to compete directly with the Boeing 747, but modern, more fuel efficient, and much cheaper to run than the Jumbo. Using features from existing programs, it would also be relatively cheap to develop: probably no more than $2 billion, according to internal estimates prepared by both sides.

But the idea of the plane was not enough; the most pressing problem was how to sell it. It would have to compete with the MD-11 and the A330/A340, and it was difficult to see how the collaboration could proceed without tighter relations between the two companies. At one stage Sir Raymond Lygo, chief executive of British Aerospace, flew to the McDonnell Douglas headquarters in St. Louis to see if he could move the negotiations along, an incident which led to a massive row with Strauss, who accused the British of bypassing the other partners, and had a motion passed preventing contact between the partners and McDonnell Douglas except through Airbus.[8]

As the negotiations dragged on, a number of obstacles emerged. Airbus officials were worried that the AM300 would not look like an Airbus. The three engines, in particular, would make it look like a Douglas. From the McDonnell Douglas viewpoint, the new plane would not have much in common with the rest of their range, it resembled the rest of the Airbus family, and would make their other planes look obsolete. Despite these difficulties, the two sides did reach the basis of an agreement: a draft proposal by which McDonnell Douglas would have a share in broader collaboration across the range.

The final confrontation came over the size of the share. Airbus were looking at no more than 35 percent for the Americans, which, it pointed out, would make them the largest partner in the reorganized consortium. John McDonnell balked at that. If his company were to get no more than 35 percent, he told Adam Brown, Airbus strategy director, there was no point in talking any more. After more than a year of circling around each other the talks broke down. They had collapsed for the same reason that Boeing's earlier attempts to woo European manufacturers had failed: nobody on one side of the Atlantic would accept being subordinate to the other side. "I spent eighteen months of my life trying to work with those guys," Brown reflected some years later. "Maybe history will show that a window of opportunity was lost. The fact is that Airbus offered them a lifeline which they in their wisdom rejected. I think that window is now closed."[9]

The closing of the window shut out any prospect of a compromise between the European and American industries. Competition with the Americans would now be more intense than ever. There were some brief talks with Lockheed, but they too came to nothing. In June 1987, the A330/340 program was formally launched, taking the Airbus family into a new sector of the market. At the time of launch ten airlines had made commitments or placed options on the planes, for a total of 130 aircraft. Airbus was still on a roll. In 1987, it bested Boeing again in the widebody sector of the market, taking a 47.9 percent share, a feat it repeated in 1989 when it took 49 percent and production in factories around Europe was stepped up to meet demand. That year, the consortium announced that, when firm orders and options were added together, it had sold more than 1000 planes, an achievement once considered impossible. The consortium had come of age.

The A320 had been rolled out in Toulouse on February 14, 1987, an occasion marked by the razzmatazz for which the consortium was becoming famous: laser beams, dry ice and a taped chorus of angel voices smothered the tarmac as Princess Diana swung champagne to christen the new plane. In a speech to the assembled royals, ministers and airline officials, the French Prime Minister Jacques Chirac praised the consortium, and issued dark warnings about allowing the Americans to meddle in the European renaissance of one of its most important industries. Chirac led the Gaullist party, and his fighting talk would have pleased the general. "The Airbus consortium will not be daunted by the Americans who killed off the Concorde," he fumed. "The A320 has already been a spectacular success. We will fight any trade war blow-for-blow as the future of the aeronautical industry and the employment it brings are at stake."

His remarks were a foretaste of the battle to come. With collaboration no longer an option, continued and relentless confrontation seemed the only alternative. While Airbus had been chalking up success after success, extending its range and penetrating the American market, the reaction in the United States — and in Seattle in particular — had not been friendly. Previous attempts to silence the European guns had failed, and Airbus had become a substantial challenger to their power. The cold war between the two industries was about to turn hot.

8

THE
TRANSATLANTIC
BATTLE

Just after 11 p.m. on December 14, 1993, the phone rang at the home near Toulouse of Michel Dechelotte, director of international affairs at Airbus Industrie. Dechelotte, a thin, wiry man with a sly sense of humor, was tired, but took the call; this was an important night, when years of negotiations on the latest GATT round would reach a climax. On the line was an aide from the office of Sir Leon Brittan, European Commissioner handling the trade negotiations for the Community countries. The aide explained that a deal was close, but he needed to check some details. "Go ahead," replied Dechelotte. The text was read over the line. "The foot-notes?" questioned the Airbus executive. "Yes," came the reply, the footnotes were intact. "Then we can live with that," said Dechelotte.

By four o'clock that morning a deal was completed, and the Uruguay round, which had hung in the balance because of disagreements between the U.S. and Europe over agriculture, films and aircraft, was completed. The papers were full of headlines about a historic accord, and stock markets surged as the threat of a fullscale international trade war was deflated. For Dechelotte and his colleagues there was another emotion: the prospect of a trade war had not worried them unduly but, with this agreement, they believed they had fended off a concerted attempt by the American aerospace industry to put an end to the grand Airbus adventure.

The phone call demonstrated the extraordinary closeness between the management of Airbus and the European Community negotiators battling with the Americans on their behalf. This was reflected across the Atlantic. American negotiators had squared their positions with Boeing and McDonnell Douglas; though in the U.S.A., which is less of a corporate state than any of the European nations or even the EC, the lines were less direct, and more likely to get crossed. The gloves had long ago been cast aside in the battle between the two industries. What had begun as commercial competition between manufacturers of airframes had, in the past few years, escalated into an open battle between the economies of two continents.

Lying behind that phone call was a twisted and complex set of negotiations between Europe and the United States which stretched back over more than a decade. Since 1947 the rules of international trade have been governed by the General Agreement on Tariffs and Trade, better known as the GATT, which was set up to create an open multilateral trading system. It was a response to the trade wars of the 1930s which, in the opinion of many, had contributed to the long, dark world depression of those years. The basic principles of the GATT were very simple: tariffs would be kept to a minimum, and major economic powers would not cut special deals with one another. It was meant to create a trading system both open and fair, allowing small powers the same access to the system as the strong, and in some measure it succeeded.

But because the GATT governs the global trading system, it was inevitable that the escalating dispute between the United States and Europe over the aerospace issue had to be resolved through its mediation. The agreement, initially, had little to say about aircraft. That was one of the many difficult issues the negotiators had not yet considered, and with the industry so dominated by a single country there was little need to do so. By the 1970s, the rise of Airbus began to change the situation. Both sides felt they had something to complain about. The Europeans were concerned about the tariffs the Americans imposed on imported civil airplanes; despite the manufacturers outside the U.S. being puny compared with the domestic giants, foreign planes sold in the U.S. still carried a duty of 6 percent. The Americans were worried about two things: the levels of state subsidy to manufacturers in Europe, and what they saw as government pressure on airlines in Europe to buy European rather than American equipment. In 1979, an Agreement on Trade in Civil Aircraft was signed by the U.S. and the EC which attempted to bring some order to the rules governing the industry. It brought aircraft into the GATT framework, and included some phrases about airlines not being subjected to unreasonable pressure and limitations on the extent of state aid.

The Europeans were cynical about the agreement, concluding that it would not have much effect. The Americans took it more seriously. A Committee on Trade in Civil Aircraft was formed, supposedly to govern disputes. But the U.S. quickly discovered that it was without teeth; as soon as any cases of what they regarded as unfair competition were brought, the committee promptly dismissed them. It was soon apparent that the agreement did not outlaw anything. The Americans had been gulled by some skilled drafting.

None of that need have mattered had it not been that the American manufacturers were now facing real competition, and that something needed to be done about it. In January 1983, representatives of the big airframe and engine manufacturers held a meeting in Washington with the Secretary of Commerce in the Reagan Administration, Malcolm Baldridge. The delegation was led by T. Wilson, the most senior man in the U.S. industry and leader of its biggest company. The aerospace men asked for more assistance from the U.S. government in promoting their cause. They cautioned against protectionism, warning that obvious trade barriers might prompt retaliation, but suggested the government use political leverage where possible to open markets, and asked for a joint task force of government and the industry to take these proposals further. They also wanted a cabinet working party to issue a draft U.S. trade policy on aerospace issues. Baldridge replied sympathetically, saying all that could be done would be done, and he lived up to his word. The U.S. government began taking a much closer interest in the industry. Its long campaign to crack down on European subsidies was about to begin.

Action was slow at first. There were unofficial contacts between Europe and America, but the Americans did not get very far. The Europeans were happy to stonewall, reasoning that any attempt to monitor and control subsidies was a veiled attack on Airbus, whose interests would best be served by delay and procrastination — two skills EC bureaucrats have polished over the years. The U.S. manufacturers were keeping a watchful eye on Airbus, ready to pounce, and quite quickly a pattern emerged. When Airbus penetration of the market rose, so did concern in Washington; when it fell, so did lobbying on the subsidies issue. Early European efforts to break into the civil aerospace business made little stir in the U.S., despite the massive levels of state support by the British and the French for the Concorde and other planes. Nor did the early Airbus efforts arouse any reaction, but their success in selling aircraft to Eastern Airlines bred the first GATT negotiations. The breakthroughs of 1985 and 1986, with sales to Pan Am, American and Northwest, raised American temperatures to a point where they were ready to contemplate ugly retaliation.

In 1985, Clayton Yeutter was appointed Trade Ambassador in the Reagan Administration, with a mandate to crack down on what Americans were beginning to perceive as unfair trade practices among many of their international competitors. Insiders to the long negotiations on the aerospace issue between Europe and the U.S. concede that the Reagan Administration practiced a trade policy which was essentially schizophrenic: the President had been elected on a free market ticket, and the instincts of its officials were for open competition, but when confronted by a particular trade issue, they ended up with a solution remarkably like managed trade. One of the first issues in Reagan's presidency had been the automobile industry, where an agreement was reached limiting Japan's car imports with the U.S. to a fixed number per year. Similar arrangements had been reached on semiconductors, steel and textiles. The European negotiators thus knew that although they were talking to a regime which claimed to favor free trade, its preference would always be for managed trade, with controlled and protected markets.

"Perhaps we should have done something to nip this whole thing in the bud way back, in 1978 or earlier," says Ray Waldman, director of government affairs at Boeing, and a veteran of U.S. trade policy, having served under Nixon, Kissinger and Reagan. "It was only really in the early eighties that there were meetings to urge the U.S. government to pay attention to the industrial targeting of this industry. Then, in the fall of 1985, when the President was looking for targets for an unfair trade strike force, Airbus was singled out as a manifestation of industrial targeting in Europe that was causing harm in the U.S. There was a great deal of concern in the U.S. about the deteriorating trade balance, and . . . about the future of the aircraft industry . . . if Airbus was not checked."[1]

The concern was real, and in many ways understandable. The days of Boeing's youth were the days of unrivalled American economic supremacy, when the country could feel secure in the knowledge that it was not just the strongest power in the world but the richest. Their workers could take for granted the best wages, the best careers and the most comfortable living standards the world had to offer. By the mid-1980s, however, those days and that confidence were little more than distant memories.

The U.S. economy had taken a terrible beating. From a time in the 1950s when U.S. GNP accounted for half the output of the entire world, the proportion had declined to around 20 percent and was still falling. American GNP per head, far the highest in the world in the 1950s and 1960s, had been overtaken by the Japanese and by European countries such as Germany, Switzerland and Sweden. The decline had broken many of the country's major industries — electronics, textiles, steel, automobiles had all been crushed, or were wobbling badly, under the onslaught of foreign competition. A sense of national decline began to grip the U.S. For the first time, many Americans were feeling badly about themselves and their country.

The mood of national pessimism had not left Boeing unscarred: "We had grown up at a time after World War Two when we thought the U.S. could go forever as the dominant economic power in the world," reflects Ron Woodward, who runs the Renton division of the company. "And we really did not believe there was a lot of competition out there. In the sixties, everything American was the biggest and the best in the world. General Motors ruled the world, along with IBM, Westinghouse, and General Electric, and so on, and we thought we were mainly competing with other U.S. rivals."[2]

In Boeing's Seattle headquarters, two thoughts preyed on the minds of executives. They were aware that in the world outside the Pacific Northwest, U.S. economic power was declining, and they shared the national sense of unease. At the same time they had seen how foreign competitors had targeted industries where American companies had been dominant; they had seen the giants being taken apart, systematically, piece by piece, and they did not want it to happen to them. "We had seen the willingness of Airbus to discount airplanes in the U.S. market, and we had seen the successes they were having in the Middle East and along the silk route," Waldman recalls. "That was a bit of a wake-up call. There was also a realization that Airbus was not going to stick with its original strategy of building a medium-sized plane only, and it was starting to look like a company that was going to build a full range of aircraft and go after the same markets as Boeing."

In the mood of national self-doubt, insecurity and unease, the natural inclination in Washington was to believe what the people from Seattle and the rest of the American aerospace industry were telling them: that the Europeans were targeting their industry and would do untold harm unless they were stopped. The bureaucrats had good reason to be concerned; a combination of Boeing's extraordinary success and the decline of other major American industries had made the Seattle company America's single largest exporter, and aerospace contributed more to the American balance of payments than any other industry (a graphic illustration of that came later in the decade when workers at the Boeing plant downed tools briefly, which caused the trade balance to widen sharply for the month when their lines were silent). The only other industry that came close to aerospace in the league table of American exports was movies and entertainment, and there was no sign of foreign competition eating into that dominance. So it seemed only natural for the government to do all it could to protect Boeing and other aerospace manufacturers; if not this industry, which would it protect?

In many ways the concern was exaggerated. The early 1980s had been kind to Boeing, and much of the rest of the decade would be equally sweet. The major competitors in the U.S. market — McDonnell Douglas and Lockheed, against which Boeing had battled all its life — had dropped out of the race after weakening themselves almost beyond repair. In 1985, the year of greatest concern about the threat from Europe, 252 of the 737-300 range had been sold, a record for a single model in a single year — Boeing was hardly a company facing imminent extinction. But 1985 also saw the first moves towards a change of authority in the company, and that too had an effect. T. Wilson was ageing fast and almost fifteen years at the helm had taken its toll. A new man, Frank Shrontz, was named president, and within two years would be both president and chairman of Boeing when Wilson stood down from the second of his two positions.

Shrontz — stockily built, with black hair greying around the edges, thick glasses and a thin impenetrable smile — was not an airman or an engineer by training. Like Bill Allen, he was a lawyer by profession but, unlike Allen, he had not cast away the rules of his profession on joining the aircraft company. Allen had re-invented himself at Boeing, driving the company to the limits of its tolerance in an unlawyer-like way. Shrontz retained a legalistic frame of mind: cautious, careful, moving by calculated but small steps, always as conscious of the downside as the up, and aware of the virtues of cutting one's losses. When it came to running the company, Shrontz was essentially a plea-bargainer, and the strategy of using a legal attack on Airbus struck him as particularly attractive.

Shrontz had graduated with a law degree from the University of Idaho in 1954, followed by a spell at Harvard, where he gained an MBA. He joined Boeing in 1958, as a contract coordinator, and rose quietly and patiently through the back rooms of the organization. By 1967 he was assistant to the vice-president for contracts and marketing. In 1973 he left the company for a spell in government in the Air Force and Defense Departments before returning to Seattle in 1977 as corporate vice-president for contract administration and planning, when he used his government contacts to increase the company's already substantial military business. By the early 1980s, he was in charge of sales and marketing, a key position, and one where he gained Wilson's favor by being one of the principal advocates of wringing more and more from Boeing's existing range of aircraft, creating revamped derivatives rather than risking large amounts of capital on new aircraft programs. Wilson was essentially cautious, and liked to surround himself with other cautious men.

The Boeing Company Shrontz inherited was powerful and strong in a way it had never been before, and, had he wished, the new president would have been able to rest for some years on laurels other men had earned. Certainly, for the first few years, it seemed that nothing could go wrong. In 1987, the year he became chairman and took total control, the company's fortunes hit a record peak. Sales were more than $15 billion, having tripled over the decade, and the backlog of orders was more than $33 billion, another record. The company was sitting on a cash mountain of $3.4 billion, its first really comfortable cushion since the 747 started draining cash away. Employment had picked up again, with 136,000 on the payroll. Both the 747 and the 737, the two mature lines in its range, had reached the stage where their development costs had long since been paid off and they were generating substantial profits; indeed, although

these figures are never hinted at in the accounts, informal industry estimates suggested Boeing was booking profits of around $30 million on
every sale of a 747. To preserve that lucrative inflow, the company was
designing the 747-400, the newest and biggest of the Jumbos, which would
have the range to fly from Europe to the Far East, or Japan to the East
Coast of the U.S., a non-stop twelve-hour flight, and a plane for which the
world's airlines were already lining up. Since the all-important business
travellers put more of a premium on non-stop flights than any other single
factor, a minor battle was looming among the airlines to be the first to
bring the new plane into service.

Things could only, and would only, get better. In 1988 sales started
going crazy. The company's salesmen managed to persuade the airlines
— although in truth little persuasion was involved — to book orders for
636 planes, yet another record: sales reached $30.1 billion, with a backlog
of more than $46 billion. In 1989, All Nippon Airways snapped up twenty
of the new 747-400s for $3.15 billion. GPA, the Irish aircraft leasing
company that had come from nowhere (and unceremoniously went bankrupt a little later after trying to list on the London and New York stock
exchanges) ordered 182 planes, giving Boeing the lion's share of a $17
billion commitment to all three manufacturers. United Airlines trumped
all previous comers by ordering 370 Boeing planes for $15.7 billion. When
a company can book orders worth over $15 billion from one customer, it
seems as if little can be wrong with the organization or its circumstances.

Even the military side of the business was booming, riding on the
wave of defense spending the Reagan Administration unleashed in the
1980s. The company had won contracts to build short-range missiles,
avionics for an anti-submarine plane, a mobile launcher for inter-conti-
nental ballistic missiles, and modules for a space station NASA was
preparing to build, taking it back into the business of exploring outer space.
Its renewed strength in the military field led to contracts to produce
avionics for the Stealth fighter, the new pride of the U.S. Air Force, and
three AWACS surveillance planes.

In addition to the sales successes in civil and military machinery,
there was a small triumph in international relations. Just as a decade earlier
Boeing had been trying to keep the Europeans out of the business, now it
was equally concerned about the Japanese. Japan's Ministry of International Trade (MITI) had long harbored ambitions to take Japan into the

aerospace industry, and Boeing was equally keen to keep them out; fear of Japanese competition in U.S. business circles already bordered on paranoia. Early in 1984, Boeing announced an agreement with Japan for the co-development of a new 150-seat plane, a successor to the 737, known as the 7J7. This deal went far beyond the limited work-sharing agreed for the 767. The Japanese would have a share in the equity and participation in all phases of the development and manufacture of the plane. The J in 7J7 stood for Japan, and the company seemed to have made a successful start with a cooperative venture in the East (they had offered considerably more to the Japanese than they had to the British). That move, which meant a new $3 billion program, seemed to shore up the company's Eastern flank, even if its Western flank was still exposed. With a treasury awash with money, fighting on one front did not pose impenetrable problems.

Yet, just while the surface was glimmering brightly and the sales figures soaring day by day, the waters beneath the surface began to grow dark and cold. The company was benefiting from two factors: a huge boom in the market for the whole industry, but Boeing most of all, as the largest and the most powerful; and the cash cascading in on airplanes already created. It had taken great gambles and won; now it was cashing in its chips. Sooner or later it was likely to hit a losing streak.

An early sign of trouble came with the 7J7 program. Boeing had recognized, as Airbus had, that there was a demand in the market for an improved small plane to replace the ageing fleets of gas-guzzling jets most airlines possessed. The company had staged an impressive rearguard action to prevent the Europeans entering the market. In 1983, at the Paris Airshow, Joe Sutter, father of the world's most profitable aircraft, warned, "We are just sounding a note of caution for people looking at airplanes like the A320, because time marches on and technology marches on. Structure, aerodynamics, systems, and engines are constantly improving." He was followed by Tex Boullioun, who, while talking up the prospects of the 7J7, told journalists in 1984: "The A320 is absolutely impossible economically. It's going to be tough for anybody to come up with a new, small airplane that makes any money."[3] These notes of caution were not intended as friendly pieces of advice to the planemakers in Toulouse or to the European governments that bankrolled them. They were an effort to scare the four governments away from funding the A320 — an effort which came close to success.

In truth, it was Boeing that was having trouble making the numbers add up on a new small aircraft. As the A320 chalked up sales successes around the world, a launch date of early 1988 for the 7J7 began to look less and less attractive. By this stage it had become a wildly ambitious project, with Boeing engineers working on a new propulsion system — a propeller-driven jet engine which promised to revolutionize the economics of commercial flight as radically as had the original jets. Initial estimates suggested that it could slash fuel costs of a small jet by half, rendering everything else in the market obsolete.

Salesmen were told to find launch customers to enable the company to bring it off the drawing board and into the factories. But by the middle of 1987, it was uncertain whether enough customers would sign up to make a launch viable. Allen might have gone ahead anyway, with one order in the bag, but Shrontz was different: he announced a postponement, explaining that the performance figures they were looking at for the 7J7 were unlikely to justify the development money needed. Instead, Boeing would go ahead with the 737-400, yet another revamp of the 1960s stalwart, and the Japanese would have to wait for their chance to participate in a major Boeing program. "A consensus just did not develop around that plane," commented Phil Condit, a later president of the company.

There were other worrying signs. In 1985, the worst crash in aviation history happened to a Boeing plane. Five hundred twenty lives were lost when a Japan Air Lines 747 came down, and Boeing conceded that faulty repair work might have been a factor. They agreed to share compensation costs with the airline. In 1989 the company faced a strike as workers sought to take advantage of its booming order book and profits to improve their wages. Only a little earlier, a major review had been initiated to tackle what senior executives deemed rampant waste and inefficiency within the company.[4]

None of these setbacks seemed to rattle the Boeing management very much. The real drama was developing elsewhere in the U.S. — and was soon to touch Boeing. Through the 1980s, the giants of American industry had been cut to shreds by aggressive young investment bankers and junk-bond merchants of Wall Street who had taken it upon themselves to revitalize what they considered the tired, struggling dinosaurs of the country's commercial establishment. For a time Boeing management thought it was invulnerable as one of the largest and most successful companies in America; surely they were too big, too prestigious and too profitable to be attacked by these barbarians? Yet, having taken comfort in that line of reasoning, Shrontz and his colleagues were shaken from their complacency in the middle of 1987.

In June, Shrontz received the kind of news that had already sent shivers down the spines of a series of chief executives. The corporate raider T. Boone Pickens formally notified Boeing that his Mesa Partnership was seeking government clearance to buy a 15 percent stake in the company. His move could be interpreted in only two ways: Pickens was planning a raid on the business, taking it over lock, stock and barrel, or else he was indulging in greenmail — a 1980s technique where a raider bought a sizeable stake in a company, threatened to take it over, and forced the company to pay him a fat premium for his shares. Probably Pickens was not even sure which way he would go; he would make the play and see which route would yield the easiest profits. Either way, this looked like being a vicious and expensive experience for Boeing.

Shrontz moved quickly; he got the board to approve a shareholder-rights plan which the executives could trigger once a raider took more than 25 percent of the business — in effect, a poison pill. Then, late on July 27, he released to the stockmarket the news of Pickens's request to the government — a move his Wall Street advisers insisted on because the news would inevitably drive up the share price, making the company that much more expensive to take over. The next morning a feeding frenzy began among the traders. Anticipating a takeover battle of epic proportions, the arbitrageurs moved in, buying every Boeing share they could lay hands on, to sell to whomever made the highest bid for the company. More than $300 million of Boeing stock changed hands that day and the price leapt more than $7 a share, to close at $53.

Later that day, Pickens received his approval from the government to buy up to 15 percent of Boeing. Washington officials no doubt disapproved of the move but legally their hands were tied. The raider was acting lawfully, and would sue if they tried to stop him. On Wall Street, the analysts at the stockbroking firms began picking over the bones of Boeing, figuring out how much its carcass might be worth. "Some Wall Street executives say Boeing's characteristics make it a particularly good candidate for a recapitalization that could yield a bonanza for shareholders," reported the *Wall Street Journal*. "Its stock price is well below the $75 to

$100 a share analysts believe the company is worth." To the stockbrokers the argument was simple: Boeing was sitting on a pile of cash — about $3 billion — which it had set aside for developing new planes. A raider could take over the company, pocket the $3 billion and still meet the payments on the debt leveraged for the takeover out of the proceeds from plane and spares sales. Sure, Boeing would have to forget about new models, but in the short term the profits would be fat and easy.

Shrontz, who could figure out the numbers, was appalled. Not only was Pickens threatening and the arbs snapping up the shares, the company was being openly talked about as "in play," a Wall Street term which (roughly translated) meant that the company was dead and the argument was over who would inherit the family silver. Already Ford was rumored to be eyeing a takeover bid, feeding the frenzy of speculation yet further. Within the Seattle headquarters a number of strategic defenses were considered. Some of the spare $3 billion could be used to buy back its own shares; an expensive and curious maneuver for a cash-hungry firm, but this would at least push up the share price and quieten the wolves howling outside its doors. Or Boeing could itself take over another company — a move that would make it harder and more expensive to raid; the Singer sewing machine company was, bizarrely, one candidate considered.

Shrontz mulled over his options, and resolved for the interim to fight Pickens politically rather than financially. On July 30, 1987, three days after the drama had broken, a meeting was held between Boeing executives and Washington State legislators. The state agreed to erect additional barriers, making it harder for any company within its borders to be taken over by a hostile raider. The new laws applied only to companies with more than 20,000 employees in the state, of which, by coincidence, there was only one. At the same time Shrontz lined up support in Washington D.C., threatening to rouse maximum congressional opposition to any takeover attempt; the company was owed plenty of favors in the capital and was ready to call them in. By the end of the summer it seemed as if Shrontz had done enough. Pickens moved on to new pastures, selling his Boeing shares at a substantial profit, and all he'd had to do was file a request with the government at the cost of a few thousand dollars in legal fees.

The scare had been short-lived but real enough, and it had proved to Shrontz and his colleagues that they would have to be more careful. Soon afterwards the company scaled back its ambitions on the 7J7, a sign that it did not want to inflame Wall Street by spending on new products.

Back in Toulouse, they could hardly believe their luck. For a few days it had seemed that their mightiest competitor would fall into the hands of a Texan oilman, a man who knew nothing of the aircraft business and cared less. While stripping the company, he would have been happy to let Airbus make the running on new models. Nor would he have engaged Airbus in cutthroat competition. Their way would have been clearer. But even without a Pickens bid, the Texan had done them a valuable service. The Boeing management was looking nervously over its shoulders before it made a decision, and could only become more cautious and more financially conservative. The excesses of the American financial system — excesses which the Europeans were thankfully spared — had made their ambitions seem less fanciful. It was all nightmare stuff for Boeing: hints of trouble rather than concrete evidence, but enough to trouble Shrontz and his board, and enough to goad Washington into action to protect what was by now the country's most valuable company. The takeover scare died, but the challenge from Airbus did not, and Boeing was now in a weaker position from which to fight.

In response to the pleadings of the manufacturers, Clayton Yeutter, U.S. Trade Ambassador, took up the cudgels enthusiastically. Boeing had already tried to talk the Europeans out of building the A320, to no great effect, and would try again to scotch the A330/A340 program, which was already on the drawing board. This time the approach would be a little more subtle. It would frame its advice through the U.S. government representative, who might appear more credible. In a letter to his counterparts in the four European countries, Yeutter wrote, "Our own preliminary economic analyses do not persuade us that there is a solid economic basis for providing government aid to launch these aircraft programs. The market potential appears too small to allow for recoupment of such government aid, including interest charges, in a manner consistent with the. . .GATT Aircraft Agreement."[5]

The replies he received were not encouraging. Michel Noir, the French Trade Minister, who was one of the four recipients of the American advice, sent the sharpest riposte: Yeutter's advice was appreciated, but in all frankness the U.S. Trade Ambassador should mind his own business,

because whether the Europeans gave assistance to their aircraft manufacturers was for the European governments and their electorates to decide.
Gentle — even ungentle — persuasion was not going to get the Americans
anywhere; a tougher stance was needed.

Dark hints began to be dropped about retaliation the U.S. could
consider if no concessions were forthcoming from the Europeans. In
essence, they could do three things. The U.S. government, if so minded,
could impose countervailing duties on Airbus planes sold in America; it
could take anti-dumping measures to block access or force up the price of
the aircraft; or it could use a Super 301 action, a broad-brush piece of
protectionist legislation which allows sweeping retaliation against anything Congress perceives as unfair trade. (For example, the U.S. could hit
back at German aerospace subsidies by banning or putting duties on sales
of Mercedes and BMW cars in the U.S., which would frighten the German
government far more than action against Airbus.)

"We were looking for arguments and threats," says Waldman of the
U.S. stance. "The threat . . .was not only that the GATT would find against
Airbus, but that a U.S. trade action would also hurt the European consortium. Countervailing duties were probably the easiest action, but anti-
dumping duties were also quite easy — it was quite clear that the airplanes
were sold in the U.S. at below cost. So there were three domestic legal
tools that could have been used."[6]

The threat of retaliatory action was enough to bring the Europeans
to the negotiating table. To lose the U.S. market would wound the
consortium, and a 301 action could inflict real pain on the entire European
economy. Any action by the U.S. would be countered by retaliation by
the European Community, escalating the dispute into a trade war. Talking
was the best way to deal with the American complaints. So began a long
and complex series of negotiations between Europe and America which
consumed enormous amounts of time over the next seven years. Those
negotiations were bitter, with each side appearing to gain the upper hand
at different points. To track them in detail would only recreate the tedium
the negotiators lived through. So, briefly, two issues were in dispute: how
great was the Airbus subsidy from the four governments, and whether
could the governments hope to see a viable future return (if not, it would
count as a distortion of trade, and be ruled illegal under GATT); and how
far was political influence and dirty tricks used by Airbus to win aircraft

sales around the world. Both issues raised acrimonious and heated arguments, and both merit examination.

Nobody had ever denied that Airbus had benefited from government subsidies; it was clear anyway from the regular disagreements among the four governments about contributions. The question was: how much? for how long? and for what purposes?

A brutal vivisection of the finances of Airbus Industrie was carried out by Gellman Research Associates, consultants paid for by the U.S. government, and presented to the Department of Commerce in September 1990. The report acknowledged the achievement of the European governments in establishing Airbus: "The large size of the investment required, the limited number of units sold each year, the difficulty of liquidating assets in the event of financial difficulty and the learning curve effect [which means that costs falls as the number of planes produced rises] make the aircraft manufacturing industry both risky and oligopolistic. By creating and sustaining AI, the governments of the AI member countries have ensured that at least one of the limited number of civil aircraft manufacturers will be European," it said.

The purpose of the report was to puncture not to praise, however. In calculating the total level of government aid, the consultants came up with a picture of devastating expense. Tracing only the support provided, either directly in aid for new programs or indirectly through support for the member companies, the report specified that by 1989 Britain, Germany and France had given Airbus $13.5 billion, measured in 1990 dollars.7 Of that, Germany had contributed by far the most; the breakdown was 58.9 percent from Germany, 25.1 percent from France and 16 percent from Britain. It went on to calculate the worth of those funds by assessing their value had the money been borrowed by the governments: just over $19 billion. Then it calculated the value had Airbus borrowed at normal market rates, as most commercial companies do: that took the value up to $25.8 billion. Of this massive total, it considered that only $500 million had been repaid by the end of 1990. "It can be concluded that AI was able to enter and remain in the commercial aircraft industry only through substantial amounts of government support."

An examination of the prospective profits on the Airbus range of planes was equally damaging. By examining the prices airlines were paying for the machines, and adding in estimates of the commercial cost of capital, the American analysts felt able to assert that none of the Airbus planes was commercially viable. It did detect some differences between the programs. The A300 had "sustained significant negative cash flows even with the provision of government launch aid. These losses have been compensated for, in part, by additional government support in the form of production subsidies and equity infusions to AI member companies." Its derivative, the A300-600/A310 program, would, even before including interest charges, generate a loss of $12.9 billion from launch through to 2008, measured in 1990 dollars. The A320/A321 program, over the same period, would rack up losses of $4.9 billion, again in 1990 dollars. The A330/A340 was expected to do a little better: profits of $3.2 billion by 2008 (disputing Yeutter's confident assertion that there was no economic basis for the program). Gellman cautioned, however, that if interest were added in at commercial rates, the program would make a loss: "No Airbus aircraft program is likely to be commercially viable," the report concluded confidently. On neither the A300 nor A320 programs was the launch aid likely to be repaid; it might on the A330/A340 program, but the aircraft would not generate a satisfactory commercial rate of return.

So much for the financial viability of Airbus. On the likely impact of the consortium on the American aerospace industry — the real meat of the report — the picture was stark and ugly. "Assuming AI continues to sell at prices below those necessary to sustain a commercial rate of return, the expected profits for U.S. firms will decline either because they lose market share or because they are forced to meet lower market paces. Because private firms depend on internally generated capital, which would decline with reduced market share, low profits may mean that the capability of U.S. firms to launch new aircraft will be diminished and may even be eliminated. Lower expected profits may discourage U.S. firms from introducing new-technology aircraft. In addition, U.S. firms must overcome the fact that AI has recently introduced new-technology models in both the narrowbody and widebody markets. These markets may not support additional entries from both U.S. firms. The lower prospects for profits in the industry may cause U.S. firms to seek additional foreign investors. It is conceivable that these firms could eventually lose control of new programs and may even be asked to transfer valuable technologies overseas as a condition of foreign investment.

"In summary, then, the pressure of inefficient AI programs in the marketplace will cause the size of the U.S. civil aeronautics industry to be smaller than it would be otherwise. Resources will be reallocated to other investments where achievable rates of return are higher. However, it is possible that the greatest loss to the U.S. economy will come as a result of the loss of significant, beneficial spillover effects for sectors other than aviation as well as in the economy more generally. It is important to note that these losses are likely to be permanent because only a very small number of manufacturers are likely to survive in any given aircraft size category."

Though written in the unemotional language of economic analysis, the report sliced into Airbus with rare abandon. It was not an impartial piece of work — no consideration was given to the historical background of the industry, or to the fact that many of the damaging effects predicted for the U.S. economy had already been felt by the Europeans. But it went to the guts of what Americans felt about the issue: the Europeans were subsidizing a wild venture with no hope of an economic return, with the implicit aim of destroying the most profitable manufacturing sector the United States had left. It was economic pillage.

This was a battle fought with pens rather than swords, and if the Europeans were to strike back, it would need to be with numbers, charts and statistics. Airbus paved the way for the counterattack with a report on American subsidies to Boeing and McDonnell Douglas, prepared by their rival set of U.S. economists. It concluded that in the years between 1978 and 1988, the U.S. government contributed around $23 billion to the two companies in direct and indirect support. By far the greatest part of that — 45 percent — was in research and development grants from the Defense Department for aircraft and electronics equipment. Another 20 percent of the total came from what was described as profit subsidies on defense contracts, and the rest contributions by the U.S. government to general aeronautical research, funds released by NASA for research into aircraft and space technologies. The figures were less precise than those of Gellman, but indirect support is necessarily harder to trace than the direct support given in Europe. Its appraisal met with a ferocious response, including a ratty reply from Boeing which reminded the Europeans how military research and contracts had defended Europe from communism, not helped the company to dominate the commercial aircraft business.

The Airbus report was merely a first shot. In December 1991 the European Commission countered the specific findings of the Gellman report with a document prepared by the Washington law firm Arnold & Porter. The numbers had gone up considerably over the intervening three years: this report concluded that over the previous fifteen years the U.S. industry had benefited from massive and systematic government support to the tune of $22 billion. or $41 billion if interest costs were added over the lifetime of the loan or subsidy (as Gellman had done); the estimate for European subsidies had been neatly trumped.

The report pointed out that this was mostly indirect support, funnelled though defense contracts, but outlined what it perceived as the crossover benefits between military and civil work. It also noted, tellingly, that none of this aid had to be repaid, as had the aid to Airbus, at least in theory. Boeing conceded that it had received military contracts worth $40 billion in the past decade, but claimed that the three main Airbus partners had, over the same decade, been awarded military contracts worth $85 billion.

All of which goes to show that anything can be proved with statistics. Each side backed the other into a corner with the subsidies argument, although Airbus was always more vulnerable because its subsidies were direct rather than indirect. The Europeans cheerfully admitted that they subsidized their industry, but claimed that the U.S. did the same. But the Americans would not concede that their industry had benefited from the vast defense budget, or admit that both the major civil aircraft manufacturers being also major defense contractors had helped them in any way.

The second arena of conflict — the American claim that the Europeans used political influence to sell airplanes — provided a more vivid spectacle than the dry parade of statistics in the subsidies row. Allegations of high-pressure sales tactics have long been part of the aerospace industry, usually with justification. We have already seen examples of Giscard's diplomatic salesmanship in the Middle East, but plenty of other examples have cropped up over the years. A few are worth retelling.

One early example was a sales competition between Boeing and Airbus in Turkey in 1984, when the A310 was narrowly chosen over the 767. Boeing had been optimistic because France was not popular in Turkey that year; they had been reluctant to recognize its new government, and had ruffled Turkish sensibilities by allowing a monument to Armenian genocide to be unveiled in Paris. A few days before the airline was due to make a decision Franz-Josef Strauss turned up. He stressed that the A310 was practically a German plane; a Turkish plane even, if you counted the contribution of all the Turkish guest-workers in Germany. He hinted that buying a few Airbuses would help Turkey's cause if it applied for EC membership. It was a sentimental approach, pitched with considerable cheek, but it worked — the sale went to Airbus. Boeing persuaded the U.S. Trade Office to complain to the West German Economic Minister, Martin Bangemann, but he replied that there had been no official contact between the German government and the Turkish airline. Which was true up to a point. Strauss travelled in his private capacity.

More serious allegations cropped up in India, where charges of corruption are common. In March 1989, the Indian Central Bureau of Investigation filed some preliminary papers stating that in 1985 Airbus, together with International Aero Engines, had paid bribes to eight former Indian officials to scrap a letter of intent already signed to buy Boeing 757s for Air India; in its place the airline agreed to buy thirty-eight A320s for $1.47 billion. The document said that the contract had been placed with a full evaluation, and that after an A320 had crashed near Paris in 1988 warnings about its safety had been disregarded. Reports in the Indian media suggested that Rajiv Gandhi, Indian Prime Minister at the time, may have been involved; he had been an Indian Airlines pilot, and was pictured trying out the A320 at the 1985 Paris Airshow. The entire Indian Airlines fleet was grounded in 1989 after an A320 crashed in India, killing eighty-nine people.

Boeing people are adamant that Airbus plays tricks in the market-place. Chris Longridge, vice-president in charge of sales, claims the Europeans regularly trade aid for planes. "The Prime Minister of one country said to me, 'I know my national airline wants to buy Boeing. But I am powerless to do so. I must buy Airbus, simply because if I do not, the aid to my country will be cut off.' I argued with him, but he said, 'Unfortunately the decision on this is being taken by the French government.' So sure, we run up against that all the time. You know, it's a pity the United States never had an empire."[8]

The Europeans are totally unabashed by their ability to pull political strings to sell aircraft; indeed, they are quite proud of skills honed over the years. "We use some political influence, as would any country in the world," confirms Bernard Ziegler, with a shrug and a puff on another cigarette. Airbus officials meet Boeing's outrage and revelations with detailed descriptions of how smoothly their governmental back-up works. "French government support has been the most vocal because it encompasses a lot of politically orientated activities," says Michel Dechelotte. "When the Prime Minister or President of France goes to a foreign country where there is a running sales campaign, the Prime Minister — this applies to Mr. Balladur or any of his predecessors — will raise the Airbus issue. And it comes from every related department. When a French minister goes anywhere, the first question is 'Is there a running Airbus campaign?' And my job is simplified, because I don't even have to investigate where or when the visits are. I am informed. This political support. . .not measured by money, is wideranging, is traditional and is open. It is not a hidden thing. . .we have no qualms about the support."[9]

The Germans, too, have played their part. "The Germans want to catch up. [Their influence was] fairly limited, to places like Turkey or South Africa. Now there is a conviction that they must help, if only to counter the massive support which the U.S. is providing to Boeing," says Dechelotte. "In 1993 we had a problem with a sale of A340s in China which was being held back because of a row between France and China over arms sales to Taiwan. But we were quite happy to wear a German mask, and took the opportunity of a visit by Chancellor Kohl to complete the deal. Diversity can be an advantage, because we can play it to push Germany in China, Britain in India, France in the Middle East, and so on." Britain too has played a modest role. Under Thatcher, there was no prospect of political support from London. Her successor, John Major, is more willing. "There has been a big change. Before it was basically hands-off. The view was that British Aerospace was only a small subcontractor of a bizarre thing called Airbus, which was a second Concorde anyway. But there has been a growing awareness of the importance of Airbus for the U.K. economy and support has been more forthcoming."

The Europeans neatly deflect charges of political lobbying by making a virtue of them — a tactic which makes the Americans look priggish when Airbus retorts with its own claims of political interference in aircraft sales. Specific allegations have been laid on the table with the U.S. government when it has complained about Airbus behavior. In Thailand, in 1986, the Europeans say the U.S. Ambassador to that country threatened a 6 percent increase in duties on Thai textiles imported into the U.S. if its airline bought Airbus rather than Boeing planes. In South Korea, they say, the government was shoehorned into buying Boeing by threats of retaliation against the massive trade surplus Korea runs with the U.S..

Boeing's dealings in Japan display a similarly heavy-handed approach; the trade deficit with the U.S. would hardly be helped by a decision to buy Airbus, a point the Europeans say is raised by American trade negotiators. And Boeing's subcontracting work is presented as more than it is: "I was trying to sell A310s in Japan," recalls Adam Brown, head of planning at Airbus, "when the minister stood up and said, 'Ah, gentlemen, this has been a wonderful year for the Japanese aeronautical industry. This is the year in which the Japanese YX airplane entered service in the skies of Japan.' The Japanese YX is, I understand, also known in other parts of the world as the Boeing 767. That is tough to beat."[10] Airbus alleges that the situation is getting worse. "We have indications that the Americans are providing big bucks to Kazakhstan to destabilize a preliminary deal Airbus has signed there. They are preventing Japan Airlines from even allowing Airbus to submit a commercial offer, on the grounds that the Japanese industry has been invited to participate on the 7J7. In Russia they are saying to President Yeltsin that it is money for contracts," contends Michel Dechelotte.

Boeing does not agree that it indulges in anything so underhanded. At the suggestion that Washington has a bigger aid budget, and more political leverage than any of the European capitals, Longridge becomes coy: "We are terrible at that in this country. Those guys in Washington, do you think they could organize that? We have trouble countering what Airbus does. We are just simple folk out here. We just think, gosh, we make airplanes, they make airplanes, and we should both let people decide for themselves what they want to buy." Many Europeans find it hard to believe that Boeing became the dominant player in the world industry through being simple folk, even if the company does take cover behind its hayseed, country-boy image, contrasting it with the worldly cynicism of its European rivals. The act plays well to a home audience, suiting America's self-image as the purest of nations.

In terms of breaking the negotiating deadlock, the debate did not take either side much further. Every artillery round from one side was met each time with a return volley from the other. Yet the American allegations of waste and inefficiency at Airbus, plus the judgement that taxpayers' money was disappearing down a well, did create fissures in the European camp. In 1987, there were growing pressures for the consortium to find a surer commercial footing, and a committee was set up to investigate its management. Dubbed the Four Wise Men, the members were drawn from the partner countries: Jacques Benichou, from the French Aerospace Industry Association; Peter Pfeiffer, a former director of Bayerische Vereinsbank and former member of the supervisory board of Deutsche Airbus; Emilio Gonzalez García, deputy general manager of the Banco Español de Créditor and Lord Sterling, chairman of P&O and one of the coterie of businessmen close to Thatcher.

The four men trucked around the Airbus system before producing a brief seventeen-page report which ripped apart much of Airbus's management. It recognized that the consortium had achieved huge success in the marketplace, but questioned whether it was close to achieving commercial success. They conceded that Airbus had to push a low-price strategy to enter the market and win credibility with the airlines, but suggested, "What is required is an Airbus Industrie structure which would be more responsible for all parts of the programs, more concerned with profit and loss, and less dependent in its day-to-day operation on each industrial partner. The partners, on the other hand, need to control more closely Airbus Industrie's decisions since they bear all the risks."

Sweeping internal changes were recommended. The top priority was to turn Airbus from a GIE into a normal limited company, a change the report admitted would be complex and take many years. But if it were converted into a company with regular accounts, more orthodox decision-making would be possible, and financial viability open to outside inspection. The report also suggested making the supervisory board smaller and defining internal management more tightly, in particular appointing a senior finance director, and opening the books fully to the partners so that each would have a clear idea of what was happening inside Airbus. The informal system of reserving particular jobs for different nationalities should be ended. If the changes they recommended were made, the Four Wise Men concluded, "it should be possible to reach a break-even point in the next five years."

Within Airbus, there was some surprise at the recommendations. Pierson, who has a freewheeling view of his role, dabbling in all aspects of the consortium's affairs, told colleagues he was thinking of resigning if the reorganization did not work out to his satisfaction. In the event, a huge amount of steam was generated but little happened. More significantly, Franz-Josef Strauss died in 1988, prompting a reorganization anyway. Despite the strictures about ending the division of jobs by nationality, the new president was another German, Hans Friderichs, a former Free Democrat politician. The following year it was decided that there would be no change to Airbus Industrie's status as a GIE, at least for the time being. Pierson remained in charge, and a British finance director was appointed. Although the changes were minor, the structure had been rocked; the partners had been set against one another, and the viability of the consortium called into question. The Americans could perhaps chalk that up as some sort of a victory.

On the other side of the Atlantic, the Americans were not just relying on politics to weaken competition from the Europeans, or on fissures within the consortium to stifle its challenge. Shrontz, shaken by the success of the A330/A340 program and the progress being made by the three-engined MD-11 overcame his reluctance to launch a new aircraft program. On October 15, 1990, he unveiled his response. An order of thirty-four planes, with options on a further thirty-four, from United marked the formal launch of the 777, a giant twin jet to compete with the A330. About $4 billion would be sunk into building the new plane.

Shrontz had been reluctant to commit himself to so risky a venture. "We started out by looking at a stretched 767," says Phil Condit, president of Boeing, and the man slated to take over from Shrontz in due course, who headed up the 777 program. "But it would have not had enough capability. We looked at a 767 with a new wing, or a 767 with a partial double deck, but in the end we decided we needed a new plane. Stretching a plane is relatively economic, but the more you change the more it costs."[11]

Boeing had been planning the 777 for more than a year, and it was a late entrant in a crowded market. The A330 and the MD-11 had already racked up $30 billion in orders, the bulk going to Airbus. The 777 promised as great, if not greater, fuel efficiency, and offered greater range for a twin jet than the A330. Interestingly, for the designers in Toulouse who had listened to Boeing lectures on the recklessness of its technology, it would feature many of the fly-by-wire control systems Airbus had pioneered and which Boeing had scorned over the years. But it did not have much in the way of new attributes and would not be in production for several years. The one new feature was an option for a folding wing, suggested by American Airlines to allow the plane to fit into landing slots designed for older, smaller aircraft.

The 777 had been hawked around eight airlines, but only United showed real interest. Airbus was competing fiercely for the order, and during one long week Airbus and Boeing sales teams were cloistered in the airline's headquarters, in separate rooms. United officials wandered from camp to camp, turning the thumbscrews, hinting that the other side had offered better terms. Both sides were handed a list of fifty-four demands the airline wanted fulfilled before it would consider placing the business with either side. Boeing won, but it had been a close call.

Other orders were slow in coming, and they were expensive. British Airways, another faithful follower of Boeing, signed up but only after it had made Boeing extend the plane's range. Still, it was a significant victory, and one that sent Pierson into such a fit of pure rage that he banned all Airbus staff from travelling on British Airways flights, and wrote to the European Commission demanding an inquiry into the purchasing policies of the British airline; dark rumors about the relationship between BA's chairman, Lord King, and Boeing still circulate in Toulouse.

Boeing had its customers, but launching the 777 was going to impose a huge financial burden on the company. Boeing's initial thought was to turn once again to the Japanese as risk-sharing partners, and they proposed that Mitsubishi, Fuji and Kawasaki take a 25 percent equity stake, as well as supplying parts. But Boeing had spent the decade fuelling fears about subsidized European competition and was now bitten by its own rhetoric. The proposal was adamantly opposed by U.S. government officials and congressmen, who argued that it would provide the Japanese with the foothold they needed to establish themselves in the industry; a foothold they would develop to overcome the American industry. Tactfully, the Japanese decided to take on the subcontracting work only without any equity stake. (Ironically, had the deal gone ahead, Boeing would have benefited from the subsidies the Japanese government provides to its aerospace industry — subsidies which, to the puzzlement of Europeans, have not prompted complaints from Washington or Seattle.)

Whatever the difficulties, Shrontz had his new airplane, and his range was at least staying level with the family offered by Airbus. He would have preferred to knock Airbus out through government lobbying, but the 777 was needed, because it became increasingly clear that U.S. government efforts to end subsidies were not getting very far. As the U.S.-European talks dragged through their fifth year, the issue was referred to the GATT in two formal complaints by the U.S.: one over the broad subsidies issue, the other a more specific protest about additional subsidies the German government gave to Deutsche Airbus by protecting it from exchange rate fluctuations. Shrontz was getting impatient: "Boeing and McDonnell Douglas have a strong case for retaliatory action under U.S. law," he told the U.S. Council on Forcign Relations in January 1992. "We see such action as a last resort because it would be protectionist in nature and because we believe that GATT and other multinational mechanisms are more consistent with our goal of resolving the issue under international law. But Airbus and the EC should understand our position. This issue must be resolved. Twenty-one years of subsidy is far too much. Enough is enough."

The outburst was well-timed. That same month, Patrick Buchanan, the maverick far right-winger who was running against President George Bush for the Republican Party nomination, raised the issue during the New Hampshire primary. He called for immediate countervailing duties against Airbus, insisting that America should tell the Europeans it would "protect Boeing because they are the people who built the planes that kept you free." That populist message struck chords with Americans: they felt that their economy and standards of living were under siege, and resented that they had paid for the Cold War, while the Europeans and the Japanese had used the money they saved to attack American industries and American workers. It struck them, in a personal and bitter way, as unfair.

The populist theme was taken up by other candidates in the 1992 race. In the televised presidential debates, the computer billionaire Ross Perot raised it, picking up sympathetic support from Bill Clinton, who made a big play of his determination to do more to protect American industries, and Boeing in particular, than the Republicans had ever done. Yet for all the rhetoric spilled, and all the demonology woven around Airbus, American politicians preferred words to action. Complaints were made to the GATT. It is true that both the major American manufacturers and the U.S. government had lawyers and legal actions lined up to slap punitive, retaliatory tariffs on Airbus. As in the Cold War, the weaponry was there, the ammunition primed and the troops on alert, but the trigger was not pulled, and the order to fire never came. The reason was similar to the logic that prevented the Cold War turning hot: mutually assured destruction. Except, in this case, the Americans were worried that the damage they might do to themselves would be much worse than any they could inflict on the Europeans.

The American negotiating position was weaker than originally thought. They could wield a big stick, but the Europeans were never seriously concerned that they would use it. In Europe, there are 2100 aircraft, either in service or on order, made by Boeing or McDonnell Douglas, which includes the big fleets operated not just by British Airways but by Air France, Lufthansa and Iberia, all national airlines of the Airbus partner countries. Airbus has only 600 aircraft in service or on order in Europe. In the U.S., the disparity is even more marked. There are 5100 Boeing or McDonnell Douglas planes in service or on order with U.S. carriers, compared with just 400 for Airbus.12 It did not take long to assess who would benefit from a trade war. "Boeing always turned out to be the most conciliatory of the American factions because they cannot afford to have a trade war. It would hurt them more than it would hurt us in view of our respective amounts of business," says Dechelotte.

For Boeing, whether to turn nasty or not was a tough decision. "We looked at a lot of different possibilities," concedes Ray Waldman. "We did an analysis of the consequences of legal actions against Airbus, and the potential for retaliation in Europe. A hard line would have said that it would have caused us a lot of pain in the short run but in the long run we would have a much healthier environment. But we have a lot of important customers in Europe, and they are not anxious to become a captive market for Airbus. And it would just transfer the competition to the world outside Europe and the U.S. Airbus would still be subsidized in that competition, so we would end up sticking our U.S. customers with high prices in order to meet subsidized competition outside this country."

Crunching the numbers, Boeing concluded that it could not afford to act tough as well as talk tough; whatever the provocation, the self-destruction incurred in a trade war would be unbearable. In that jumpy atmosphere, a compromise was always inevitable, and in April 1992, a tentative bilateral agreement was reached between the European Commission and the U.S. Trade Representative. The two sides agreed that future direct subsidies for new aircraft programs would be limited to 30 percent of total development costs, and conditions would be imposed on the timing of repayments. The number was inevitably a compromise; the Europeans had been looking for more like 45 percent, while the Americans hoped to drive it below 20 percent. The agreement also limited indirect subsidies to no more than 5 percent of a manufacturer's civil turnover, and specified that governments would not put pressure on other governments to buy aircraft. Consultations would be held on the issue of transparency, and each side pledged not to launch unilateral trade actions against the other, although both could ask for a suspension of the agreement if a manufacturer's business was being badly hit by external factors, political or economic.

For seven years' work it was something of a damp squib. The Americans had conceded the principle that aircraft programs could be legitimately subsidized, and Airbus felt they could live with 30 percent from now on; the cash generated by the existing range was already reducing the need for subsidies. The issue dragged on for another eighteen months; the accord still needed to be incorporated into the GATT to apply to potential competitors outside Europe and the U.S., and to become seriously binding. When the Uruguay round was finally completed, Dechelotte and the Airbus team had secured the vital footnotes to preserve the European funding system; although aircraft would now fall within the GATT rules on subsidies, the footnotes specified that financing based on royalties would not count as subsidy, even if government money was never repaid because sales of the product never climbed high enough for the royalty to match the subsidy. In effect, the European system of funding Airbus through grants that might or might not be repaid depending on sales, built up through a quarter of a century, had been legitimized under the latest GATT agreement. Dechelotte and his colleagues could afford a sly smile — "I think the European interests have been preserved," he commented afterwards.[13] The American assault on Airbus had been deflected if not disarmed. Its guns would be quieter from now on.

For all the heat and smoke, not a great deal had been achieved by the American attempt to destabilize subsidized European competition. As a ploy, it had an impact on the market; in the most heated moments of the battle, Alan Boyd was telling Toulouse how Boeing salesmen were hinting to customers that it would be safer not to buy Airbus planes, since a trade war might erupt at any moment, disrupting the supply of spare parts, and perhaps even leaving them liable for punitive duties on their planes. The name of Airbus had also been blackened with the American public, creating unease among airlines about the impact on their customers of offering European rather than American machines. If it spiked some Airbus sales campaigns, it had been worthwhile; and there were plenty of people in Europe who suspected that had been Boeing's intention all along. But pulling the rug of subsidies from under the Airbus partners would have been a far greater achievement, particularly before the A330/A340 program had been completed.

That American objective failed. The most open geo-industrial conflict so far had ended in a muted victory for the Europeans. More worrying still, for Seattle, new Airbus strategies were looming on the horizon; it was clear that the Europeans were planning an assault on the highest ramparts of the Boeing fortress: the Jumbo. If that was to be averted, new ploys would be needed and new guns brought into play.

9

THE PINCER
MOVEMENT

A light drizzle fell that Sunday in early September, and grubby, gloomy clouds hung low. It was typically grey English weather in a typically grey part of England. At Farnborough, a small provincial town near London, the world's aerospace industry had gathered for the 1992 Airshow. It was a chance to proclaim their wares, boast about their latest products and, behind the scenes, in the tents and chalets where they sheltered from the rain, to plot the latest twists in the geo-industrial game.

Airbus was putting on quite a show: the new A340 was making its public debut, and crowds gathered along the runway as the four-engined plane drifted lazily out of the clouds and performed a quick turn for the spectators before coming in to land. The Russians were out in force, and providing one of the main themes of the show. With the Cold War now over, the old states of the Soviet Union were realizing that they too would have to play geo-industrial politics, and they wanted to get their chips on the table. Eighty-one senior Russian officials were at Farnborough, including the Industry Minister, and the Commander in Chief of the Russian Air Force, and they had brought with them more than twenty airplanes, including MIG fighters, and the first of the new Tupolev Tu-204s, commercial passenger planes fitted with Rolls-Royce engines, which the company was hoping to sell in the West. The whole caboodle — the product of fifty years of intensive effort to build an aerospace industry under communism — was up for sale to anyone with hard currency, but, as the salesmen lingering by the planes discovered, there were few takers. Their presence at the airshow, however, served to underline the changes of the past two years. Under cover of a geo-political struggle between two ideologies, a struggle between competing economies had been waged and had gathered in ferocity over the decades. With the ideological war ended, the economic struggle, pitting the three great trading blocs against one another, had emerged to become the war that counted. The Russians were no more than a sideshow in this struggle; the battlefields were different now, and the weapons were civilian rather than military.

The real action was taking place not among the MIG fighters, nor at the stand where a mock-up of the European Fighter Aircraft, the plane being built to shoot down MIGs, was on show for the first time. It was taking place in the chalets where the two dominant manufacturers of the civil industry were squaring off. In a press tent for the journalists who loiter around these events, the protagonists were only a few feet away from each other. On the right of the marquee, the Boeing team would put their case. On the left, separated from the enemy by a few sheets of canvas, the Airbus team would present theirs. Boeing had delivered Phil Condit, and he would join battle first. A tall, clean-cut, all-American figure, with square jaw and broad shoulders, he stood alone before his audience, delivering a standard exposition of the Boeing philosophy.

"The issue is not which manufacturer has the newest airplane," he said. "It is not which airplane has the most composite materials or the most aluminum alloys. Nor is it whether the pilots are looking at liquid crystal displays rather than CRTs. The question is: have we met customers' needs and added value?" It was a polished performance, bland but self-confident, and skillfully included some sly digs at Airbus amid the boosterism for his own company. But the interest focused on one small section of his speech. "Some airlines have expressed an interest in an airplane larger than the 747-400," he said, almost in passing, "for entry into service around the end of this decade. Boeing is meeting with interested customers to identify requirements and define possible configurations. These include both 747 derivatives and all-new airplanes, with seating capacities up to 750." This reference drew most interest when the questioning began. Did that mean Boeing was planning to build a Superjumbo? Condit hummed and hawed and shifted from foot to foot. "Everything is under consideration," he stonewalled.

The Airbus team was featuring three of their most prominent figures: Jean Pierson, Bernard Ziegler and Stuart Iddles, the English finance director. Pierson sat center-table, flanked by his two lieutenants. As Condit wound down his briefing, the journalists crossed into the Airbus section of the tent. As they sat down, Pierson began a long exposition uninterrupted by either of his colleagues. Indulging in his own form of boosterism, he talked about the A340, the largest civil aircraft built in Europe. He talked about the fast-rising revenues of the consortium: $4.6 billion in 1990, rising to $7.6 billion in 1991, an increase he expected to see repeated in 1992; and he pointed out that the first profits in 1990 doubled in 1991, although he did not give an actual figure. Its share of the market was healthy; 33 percent for all aircraft above one hundred seats in 1990 and 29 percent in 1991. He talked about new programs: the A321, a new 186-seat stretched version of the A320, was going into production, and the partners were looking for launch customers for the A319, a shortened, 124-seat version of the same plane. And so on and so on.

Trickles of sweat forming on his expansive brow, smoke curling around him, Pierson then began laying into Boeing. "We are setting the standards in the industry and the others are not," he said, with a gallic shrug, his thick French accent dripping with sarcasm. "But we must make sure we have the tools in Europe to stop indirect support of the industry," he continued before launching into a long, ironic attack on American export subsidies. With evident enjoyment, he spent ten minutes complaining about how the American industry enjoyed excessive government subsidies, hinting that the Europeans might have to consider retaliation.

But the real meat was in his update on what Airbus called the UCHA (ultra-high capacity aircraft) and what the journalists persisted in calling the Superjumbo. He said that Airbus plans for a 600-seat plane were well advanced, and that the consortium had been talking with ten airlines about putting together a program to be launched in the next couple of years: "We are in dialogue with airlines to finalize a project that will be a great success." A questioner pointed out that Boeing was doing the same thing. Pierson shook his head, throwing it forward in small head-butts, at the mention of the opposition. "We will be ahead and we will come up with fresh ideas,' he insisted. What ideas? "Humph," Pierson stonewalled, fixing his Pyrenees glare on his interrogators. He puffed on his cigarette, and let the answer drift away with the smoke.

Both Condit and Pierson were being less than honest that day. On the Wednesday following the press briefing, Pierson paid a rare visit to the Boeing chalet, a group of tents near the main exhibition hall. There, in enemy territory, he met John Hayhurst, the Boeing vice-president tapped by Shrontz and Condit to head the company's investigations into the Superjumbo. The two men had a brief discussion about a proposal that was to have profound consequences: that Airbus and Boeing should join forces to build the giant new plane. It was an explosive development, which, when it became public three months later, presented briefly the prospect of a grand reconciliation between the implacable foes of the industry. It would also provide a stage for the most deadly plotting and counter-plotting in the battle between Europe and America.

The idea of a Superjumbo had been around for a while, and Airbus had, until now, made all the running. The 747 was twenty-five years old, and was showing its age, even though the 747-400 had involved a major redesign. Although the 747 was a giant when it was built, with the growth in air travel in the intervening quarter of a century, it was starting to look small. Airlines were saying that they needed something bigger. Stephen Woolf, chairman of United Airlines, had publicly stated his desire for a bigger plane, as had British Airways, which already had a team working on the specifications it would like to see as a launch customer. Several of the Asian carriers, which operate between some of the most densely populated cities in the world, were also interested. The Japanese domestic routes, already flown by 747s, were crowded with planes and traffic. The only way to squeeze these huge numbers into limited airport and airspace was bigger planes. But there was no bigger plane on the market. The 747 was still the biggest you could buy.

For Airbus, the Superjumbo presented an intriguing commercial possibility. The consortium and its partners had labored under the disadvantage that they were not competing with Boeing in the very big jets. Indeed, nobody was. The 747 had provided Boeing with a lucrative monopoly, which it exploited ruthlessly. Costing up to $148 million (compared with about $80 million for an A340, depending on how hard you haggled), the prices of the Jumbos were non-negotiable; if you wanted one, you paid list price. The only way to shave a little off was to agree to buy a whole fleet of Boeing planes, parcelling up 747s with 737s, 757s and 767s. This gave the company a powerful marketing tool to sell its entire range; where that did not work, it used the profits from the 747 to subsidize the rest of its range — the Jumbo gave it headroom to fight dirty on price with Airbus on the smaller planes. "They enjoy a monopoly because they have fully amortized their investment, and they can dramatically cut the price of the aircraft if they need to, so it is very difficult to compete with them head to head," reflected Bernard Ziegler.[1] Something bold and different would have to be devised.

Adam Brown, head of planning at Airbus, who enjoys an unofficial role as the philosopher of the consortium, saw the Jumbo problem as the knottiest Airbus had faced. "Boeing took a heroic risk on the 747 and it almost broke them. But they are now a monopoly and good luck. . .when you try to negotiate on price. But we cannot hope to compete head to head with the 747. It was designed in the 1960s, using 1960s dollars. If we were to develop a new plane in the same class it would have to be with 1990s dollars, we would be right at the beginning of the learning curve for production, and it would be really tough for us. So. . .we thought of. . .dealing with the 747 in a pincer movement."[2]

The pincer movement was the riskiest and deadliest gambit Airbus had deployed in the war against Boeing: A tactic on the aeronautical chessboard which threatened to checkmate Airbus's American opponent in two sweeping moves. The first was already in place: the A340. It challenged the 747 on range, but had fewer seats. Although it was smaller, its advanced technology meant its running costs were comparable to the Jumbo on a seat-per-mile basis, and it had been designed for airlines to use on long-distance flights where there was not enough traffic to justify a 747 (known in the industry as "long-thin" routes). "We are only just becoming aware of the full potential of the A340," Brown says. "For a whole lot of routes it is a more profitable solution than the 747. If you put a 747 on a route then you can always make it a heavy route if you discount the fare enough to fill the plane. But on a lot of routes the A340 will allow the airlines to operate in the market a lot closer to the point of revenue maximisation than the 747. It is very undemocratic, and rather reactionary, but in purely economic terms the airlines might do better by leaving behind all the backpackers and the guys with the open-toed sandals and concentrating on the higher yield part of the market. That will generate more revenue at less cost. But it needs to break airline thinking. Classic airline thinking is to put a 747 on a route and instruct their people to fill it. Down the line, they don't know what to do, so they reduce the price and fill the plane. Everyone is happy. But they shouldn't be happy because even though the plane is full, the airline is losing money."

In the early 1990s, there was some sign that the marketing pitch for the A340 was having dramatic effect. Though it was a very bad time for all the airline manufacturers, with the airline industry still gripped by recession and clocking up huge losses, Airbus still sold fourteen A340s in 1993, while Boeing sold only two 747s, the worst year for the Jumbo since it was launched. "Judging by the 1993 results, the A340 has damn near killed the 747 all by itself," says Brown. But Airbus strategists were unconvinced that the A340 was enough competition for the 747 by itself. As the market showed upturn, airlines would be back for big planes. And it was here that the second half of the pincer movement would be deployed: an Airbus Superjumbo. "We have attacked them from below with the A340," says Bernard Ziegler. "Now the idea is to come from over the shoulder with a high capacity plane." With a Superjumbo, carrying 600 people or more, plus the A340, the 747 could be left floundering between the two. The monopoly would be broken, and so would the financial strength of Boeing.

It was an audacious strategy, and one that was always likely to be harder to implement than to describe. Building a plane with 600-plus seats is not easy. For a start there are some formidable technical issues. Building a Superjumbo is not quite like building a 747 but bigger. The landing gear would be so heavy, to give just one example, it would buckle the tarmac on most runways, so the whole wheel section would have to be radically redesigned. The air turbulence created by its mass could bring down smaller jets in its vicinity; mitigating technologies would have to be developed. A way would have to be found to squeeze the plane into existing landing slots. And so on.

Airbus designers came up with various options. One was to squash two A340 fuselages together, to make something looking like the two humps of a camel. The resulting machine would be curved at the side, but relatively flat at the top and the bottom, making the fuselage act like a wing to give the plane additional lift; a design concept which had already worked on the space shuttle. Another idea was a plane designed as a flying wing: a vast, single wing, with the passengers inside a machine rather like a flying saucer. A third was for a more conventional widebody tube on a grander scale, with two decks or even three. Size threw up other issues. For example, the difficulty of distributing meals to 700 or more people led to the idea of a canteen rather than passengers eating in their seats. And if a canteen, why not a cinema? To some designers, the plane was starting to resemble the old ocean liners, not the cattleship design and atmosphere of the venerable 747.

Designing it would be difficult; so too would building it. The brand new Airbus plant in Toulouse, opened in 1990 to build the A330 and A340, was already the largest building in Europe, and the 747 plant outside Seattle was still the largest in the world. A plant to build a Superjumbo would dwarf them both, throwing up logistical and engineering challenges so far unimagined. For starters, the Airbus system of ferrying bits of the plane around Europe in SuperGuppies would not work for a machine of these epic proportions. Then there was money. The investment would outscale any previous aircraft program; perhaps by as much as $14 billion. It was clear to Pierson that this was a project where the European consortium could not fly solo.

The most natural partners were in the East. They certainly had the money and they might also have the ambition. Early in February 1992 Brown flew to Tokyo to hold talks with Mitsubishi, Kawasaki and Fuji, the three players in the Japanese aerospace industry, all of whom were deeply involved with Boeing on the 767 and the 777. Brown was ready to offer them a deal: join up with Airbus to finance and build the new Superjumbo. "It's a strategic decision for the Japanese," he said at the time. "They are at a crossroads. Either they become real partners with Europe or they go on being subcontractors for the U.S."[3]

Brown was received cordially, and this time there was more to the discussions than standard Japanese politeness. Relations between Airbus and the Japanese had been improving; the Japanese had signed up as subcontracting partners on the A321, but nothing would be decided there and then. The Japanese gambit was smoothly executed. Since finance was one of the main obstacles, there was nowhere better to go than Japan. Also, Airbus analysts reckoned that of the nine airlines they could identify who would buy a Superjumbo, five were in Asia, and two were Japanese; Japan Air Lines, and All Nippon Airways (the others were Cathay Pacific,

Singapore Airlines and Korean Air in Asia; United and Northwest in the U.S.; and British Airways and Iberia in Europe). Having an Asian partner in the program, and preferably a network of subcontractors throughout Asia, would be crucial in winning orders in that part of the world. But the most significant part of the ploy was the geo-industrial angle. The Japanese are firmly in the Boeing camp, and Airbus sales in Japan are tiny (one A320 to All Nippon, and 25 A300s to Japan Air System). Yet despite twenty years of involvement with Boeing, for which they had delivered their airlines as loyal customers, the Japanese manufacturers had not progressed beyond subcontracting. Their ambitions were being effectively stifled by Seattle. They were still, in effect, industrial serfs, much as Boeing had wanted the British to be. But if Airbus could exploit their growing sense of disillusion, the consortium could open a rich vein of money and markets. There was no better tool for leverage than the new Superjumbo.

Airbus was letting its fingers walk through other parts of the atlas as well. Russia was one possibility: the Russian aerospace industry was not reckoned a serious competitor, but it might be one day, and it was worth keeping lines open, tying them into the European rather than the American camp. There were also more big empty factories and more idle or low-waged engineering workers in Russia than anywhere in the world. The former Soviet Union might well be the place to build the new Superjumbo; it would certainly be a lot cheaper than in Toulouse or Hamburg or Bristol.

Then there were the Chinese. With an economy emerging from rigid communism, China was already a fast-growing market for both Airbus and Boeing (complete with angry shouting about the Americans trading planes for market access), and was unlikely to be satisfied for long to be just a customer for Western goods. It would want to be a supplier as well, and it too would have to be fitted into the global web of alliances. It was also likely to be an important market for Superjumbos. As the population grows richer, routes such as Shanghai-Guangzhou will be among the most densely travelled in the world.

The most significant response to Airbus plans, however, was not in Tokyo, Beijing or Moscow, but in Seattle. Boeing could not be expected to sit on the sidelines while the strategists in Toulouse deployed their pincer movement. The aircraft business has few secrets, and Boeing quickly had a good idea of what Airbus was up to: they could work out what a combination of the A340 and a Superjumbo could do to their range as quickly as anyone. As Pierson moved his pieces up the board, Boeing had to think about a blocking formation. Shrontz's first move was to appoint John Hayhurst as head of a task force to study the options. Hayhurst began by briefing the design team, instructing them to look at what would satisfy the demands of the airlines for a bigger plane.

Plans were put together for a stretched 747, with a longer fuselage; for a 747 with a double deck running its whole length. Another idea was to add a doughnut-shaped, circular section to the fuselage in the middle of the plane. All three would be relatively cheap, involving only modifications to the existing design, but it would be difficult to house more than 550 seats or so, and the changed design might reduce both its range and fuel efficiency. Any of these options would work as a temporary solution and, in the absence of alternatives, the airlines would no doubt buy them. But none would be an answer to the Airbus Superjumbo. To counter it, the company would have to consider an all-new aircraft; an expensive alternative when it was still engaged in design and development work on the 777. Particularly when the development costs on a plane bigger than the 747 would be massive. After all, the last time Boeing had tried anything on that scale, the company was nearly bankrupted. This time the finances would be even worse.

Hayhurst began discussions with the airlines, and quickly discovered that at least a handful were seriously interested in a Superjumbo. There was a real demand, and a real risk that Airbus might move in to fill it. Boeing needed to respond quickly. Hayhurst and Shrontz began plotting a gambit of their own to counter the European moves.

Some lines of communication had already been opened up between the U.S. and Europe. McDonnell Douglas had been trying to squeeze its way into the act, making more noise, with less substance, than the other two contenders. It had proposed a doubledecker, four-engine aircraft called the MD-12 — which looked rather like a bigger MD-11 — carrying about 600 people, and had started hawking pictures, sketches and wooden models around the airlines, although none showed any interest in signing up as a launch customer. But the company had reached a preliminary agreement to sell a stake to Taiwan, which raised the possibility that the Taiwanese might come up with the funds to bankroll the scheme. Shrontz was sufficiently edgy about the combination to start lobbying against it in

Washington, raising the spectre of an "Asian Airbus," subsidized by government money and competing as fiercely with the Americans as the Europeans. The Taiwanese eventually backed out of the deal, but not before talks had been held with British Aerospace about building the wings for the new plane. The British were interested, but decided they could not proceed without their European partners. Even so, the McDonnell Douglas maneuvers raised beguiling possibilities for Boeing. If they could talk to the Europeans, so could Hayhurst and Shrontz. The British had always been the loose cannons on the Airbus ship, and were always ready to talk. Boeing had tried to gull them before, without success. Perhaps they should try one of the other partners.

The rising power within Airbus was a German called Jurgen Schrempp, a man regarded with some fear and much suspicion by the staffers in Toulouse and the other partners in the consortium. Schrempp's rise to power was rapid, riding the charge into the aerospace industry made in the late 1980s and early nineties by Germany's (and Europe's) largest industrial company, Daimler-Benz. In 1988, Edzard Reuter, the tall, thin, waspish chairman of the motor manufacturer best known for its luxury Mercedes cars, was keen to diversify away from the automobile industry. His vision was of an integrated transport and engineering conglomerate. The West German government was keen to bolster the country's involvement in the aerospace industry but wanted to staunch the huge flow of subsidies and losses which had made the Federal Republic the largest net contributor to Airbus over the years. The solution it settled on was to sell both Deutsche Airbus and Messerschmitt-Bolkow-Blohm, the main military aircraft contractor in Germany, to Daimler-Benz; it had previously talked to BMW, Bosch, and Siemens, but none of them had been interested.

The sale was controversial, since it involved massive write-offs for past losses, and included promises that subsidies would continue. It also raised fears of fascist revivalism, always a potent symbol in Germany; the Social Democrats talked of a military-industrial complex, and German papers pointed to the reunification of Daimler and Messerschmitt, which together had built the engines and airframes for the most effective fighters of the Nazi war machine. These were painful allusions for Reuter; as a boy he fled to Turkey with his family to escape the Nazi regime, and he has been a lifelong Social Democrat. He is also a sensitive soul to find at the head of a motor industry conglomerate, and has been known to try the patience of prospective industrial partners by reading them poetry and playing the piano. Nonetheless, convinced of the combination of motor cars and aircraft, he pushed ahead with transforming Daimler into a broadly based transport group, and completed the deal.

The takeover took Daimler into the center of power at Airbus. Traditionally, Aérospatiale had taken the lead among the four partners in setting the direction for the consortium. The Germans had an equal shareholding, but the relative weakness of their industry made the French the natural leaders. Now, the industrial might and muscle of Daimler-Benz would make the Germans more of a force to be reckoned with. Reuter appointed Schrempp to head his aerospace division. One of the most ambitious young executives in the company, a workaholic who sleeps only three hours a night, Schrempp made his name sorting out the Mercedes truck divisions in South Africa and in the U.S., and was tipped as a possible successor to Reuter (who, in 1994, became chairman of the supervisory board at Airbus). Schrempp set the new division on an aggressive path, forging deals right, left and center; he took over Fokker, the Dutch manufacturer of regional jets; he forged an alliance between Daimler's aircraft engine unit, MTU, and Pratt & Whitney to build new engines; he set up a consortium to develop a European space shuttle, and established alliances to build European helicopters and fighter aircraft. At the same time, he trimmed ruthlessly the layers of management that had built up in the state-owned German aircraft industry, which struck outsiders as one of the most inefficient in the world.

If Boeing wanted to prise away one of the Europeans, Schrempp looked like its man. Informal lines of communication were set up between Hayhurst and Schrempp, with British Aerospace also invited to the table. At the meeting with Pierson at Farnborough Hayhurst was updated on what was happening, but nothing about the proposed deal pleased him. What Hayhurst had to offer was simple: the Airbus partners would join Boeing in a study to examine whether there was a demand for a Super-jumbo, and what sort of plane might meet it; then they would see if the two sides could collaborate on building the plane.

For the Airbus partners there would be some obvious advantages. They would not have to shoulder the huge financial burden of building the Superjumbo by themselves, a burden which would push significant prof-itability even further into the future. They would not have to build a

Superjumbo in competition with the Americans, which would be crippling for both sides. With a joint Boeing/Airbus plane they could be guaranteed a market and a financial return — and the pincer strategy would be more or less intact. The 747 would be left floundering between the A340 and the Superjumbo, and the monopoly profits Boeing earned on the biggest jets would have to be shared with the Europeans. It was not everything they had been looking for, but it went a long way, and the risks were much less. The outline of a deal seemed to be in the making: "It is like playing chess," commented Schrempp later. "It is good to get in close to the enemy."

The concept of a joint study was approved in principle, but Boeing could not resist capping its move with some mischief at the expense of Airbus. On January 5, 1993, the company put out a press release saying that Boeing had agreed to form a joint study to examine building a Superjumbo with Deutsche Airbus, the new subsidiary of Daimler-Benz, and with British Aerospace. No mention was made of Aérospatiale or Airbus. The next morning the papers were full of the deal, portrayed as a venture between the Germans and the Americans. To most outsiders it seemed that Boeing had succeeded in one of its great long-term goals: splitting the Airbus partners and tempting one or more into its camp. "The future of Europe's most successful cross-border industrial partnership is under threat," the *Financial Times* reported solemnly.

Schrempp was on holiday, sunning himself on the beaches of South Africa and unavailable to clarify the situation. In Toulouse, Pierson was spitting blood, furious at what he regarded as the treachery of the Germans and the British. He regrouped his forces and a statement was released saying that Aérospatiale and CASA were also part of the joint study. Pierson insisted that Schrempp had been mandated to talk to Boeing by the Airbus board and that he was nothing more than a representative in a discussion between the consortium and Boeing; a supervisory board meeting on December 15 had agreed to open up exploratory talks between Boeing and Airbus and named Schrempp to lead the discussions. Indeed, when Schrempp had come back to the supervisory board with a draft agreement, he was told during a bruising session that it was not good enough and to go away and renegotiate with Boeing. Schrempp later conceded that much, but claimed the joint study had been his idea, a claim also made privately by British Aerospace executives.

Boeing meanwhile was having great fun. Its spokesman was instructed to tell reporters that it could not strike a deal with Airbus, because Airbus did not really exist; it was just a marketing cover for the partners. "How can we have a study with something that doesn't exist?" they reasoned gleefully. That line had the effect of making Pierson crosser still. He revealed that he was going to Japan for further discussions with the Japanese about joining an Airbus consortium to build a Superjumbo. His rage now almost out of control, he weighed into Boeing. He commented acidly, "Either Hayhurst does not remember meeting me [at the Farnborurgh Airshow], which would be impolite, or he has a short memory, which would be embarrassing for a project manager, or Boeing has hidden thoughts, in which case we have been warned." To rub salt into the open wounds, he added that the third possibility was the most likely.

Pierson had indeed been warned — both about the strategies Boeing would use to stir dissent in the Airbus camp and about the probability that some of the partners would be strung along by Seattle. The story quietened down, and Boeing admitted they were dealing with all four partners, whether you referred to them as Airbus or not. Its spokesman explained away the confusion by saying it had been unable to contact representatives of Aérospatiale, British Aerospace or Airbus when American journalists first asked about the story, so the company had just said it was negotiating with DASA. Amid the confusion one thing was clear: for what was meant to be a joint venture, the row over who was in and who wasn't was hardly a great start. Peace was clearly still some way off.

The idea of the study was for both sides to put up small amounts of money and a few people to look at the technical and industrial issues involved, and, more importantly, how to structure a deal so that the two sides could work together. Boeing, not surprisingly, shot down the idea that it should join a GIE with Airbus, a proposal mischievously floated by the French. The study was meant to last for a year. As its first twelve months came towards an end in January 1994, with only limited progress made, the two sides began to think about extending it. Aérospatiale insisted that if it were to go any further, it would have to include Airbus as part of the formal structure; the French were still wary about the scope given to Boeing to drive wedges into the consortium. Boeing refused. It did not want the enemy camping on its doorstep. It also knew that Airbus staffers would prefer to go ahead with their own Superjumbo. The issue came to a head at a meeting between the consortium companies and Boeing in London in March 1994, where the French threatened to scrap the whole deal. Boeing backed down a little, agreeing to allow Airbus an advisory role, and on those terms the talks about collaboration went into a second year. But most of those involved thought they would go on for a long, long time.

Which would suit Boeing just fine. Just as delay had suited the Europeans when the Americans were attacking them over subsidies, so delay suited Boeing now that Airbus was attacking its monopoly on the big jets. So long as the 747 remained the biggest available, Boeing's grip was intact, as were the monopoly profits on the plane. The best outcome would be no outcome at all: they would not have to invest in a new program or share profits with the Europeans. Seattle could keep talking for a few years yet. They might not be able to hold off the Superjumbo for ever, but if they could keep it in limbo until the development of the 777 was out of the way, their ploy would have been a great success.

In Toulouse, Airbus staffers were always doubtful that the two sides could ever get beyond talking. "Personally, I have a bad feeling about this because I do not see how we can cooperate with Boeing, and I do not see the necessity," said Bernard Ziegler. Others within the consortium believed that a joint venture would never survive scrutiny by anti-trust regulators in either Washington or Brussels. In the meantime, Airbus was still designing its own plane, talking to the airlines, pondering who the collaborators should be, and waiting for its partners to give it the green light to put the second sting of the pincer in place. And Boeing was still designing its own Superjumbo, separately from the joint study. By the middle of 1995, the joint project was quietly scrapped. A brief statement said the study of the market had not found sufficient demand for the giant plane. A lot of smoke had been raised by the initiative; the fires, meanwhile, had been burning elsewhere.

Those disagreements, coupled with the downturn in the travel industry, had dampened demand for the new plane. The pincer strategy was still in place, but until the Superjumbo front was opened up, the most vital battlefield would be between the A330/A340 and the new 777, which went into service in 1995. "I think the contest will be crucial," says Phil Condit, "but it is an important competition over a long time period. There won't be an answer this year or next. I'm sure the A330 will still be there in ten years, and the competition will still be real."[4] Airbus strategists are inclined to agree. After Boeing decided not to replace the 737 with a new plane, simply making another derivative instead, the staffers at Toulouse concluded that the company was ceding eventual leadership of that sector to the Europeans.

"The decision to go with the revamped 737 rather than the 7J7 will. . .mark the end of the dominance of that once great company," Adam Brown says. "Everything they have done for the last twenty years has been purely reactive. The 767 was a response to the A300. The 777 is a response to the A330/A340 and this [the revamped 737] is their response to the A320. History is full of examples of companies that took a huge lead in the marketplace and then lost it through complacency. History will show that this decision marks the first step in their decline."

There is an implication here that Boeing has lost its nerve, a view for which there is some evidence, though much of it is circumstantial. The willingness of the men in Seattle to follow the paths laid down by Airbus is but one indication of the somersaults since Allen had departed. Where once it had led the industry, breaking new ground, inspiring new departures, it was now content to leave the ground-breaking to others and give chase where necessary. Boeing executives deflect the criticism, claiming that the company has often been the second or third player into a market segment, and that it has not done them any harm in the past. "I have never found it a disadvantage coming from behind," Phil Condit says. "If anything, it's an advantage, because the other planes are fixed in design. We were fourth into the market with the 737, but the sales are exactly the reverse of those positions."

There is truth in that — for the dominant player it can often be an advantage to come from behind; so long as the brand is strong enough to ensure sales, you don't have to take risks discovering what the customers will buy. But there is falsehood as well. Each time the trick is played the dominant player gets weaker and the challenger stronger. Then one day, the dominant player is no longer dominant, and the trick stops working. As a strategy it makes sense for a while; and it certainly maximizes profits in the short term. Yet to many of the veterans of the industry, both inside and outside Boeing, it seems that the company was so badly rattled by the traumas of the early 1970s that it permanently lost its nerve. It had travelled the distance between boldness and timidity, and now preferred the calm of the bunker to the noise of the field. Certainly, to many it appeared as if only embers remained of the fire that had once driven it.

By the time the world aerospace industry reconvened at Farnborough in the fall of 1996, the indications were that Boeing would come up with a relatively timid response to the demand for a new, large plane. Before the airshow opened, the industry was alive with rumors that the men from Seattle would use it as a platform for the launch of two new aircraft, the 747-500 and the 747-600. Instead of designing a whole new aircraft, as Bill Allen and Juan Trippe had done, the more cautious planners now running Boeing preferred to upgrade an existing machine. They had forgotten, presumably, that had Allen chosen only to upgrade the 707, rather than create the Jumbo, it would have probably been the DC-10 that captured the skies. And Boeing would never have risen to dominance in the aerospace industry.

The new planes would be bigger than the existing 747; in a normal three-class configuration, they would be able to carry up to 550 passengers. Boeing was telling airlines they would launch the plane by the end of 1996, and that it could be in their hands by the turn of the decade so long as they were willing to sign up as launch customers. The new planes would have a brand new wing, and would also have fly-by-wire control systems; the same systems Boeing had been so scornful of when first introduced by Airbus, by now established in the 777 and about to be installed in the 747. It would also have a slightly longer upper deck. But those changes aside, it would still look like the plane that had been designed by Joe Sutter some thirty years earlier.

If the 747 upgrades were to be launched at Farnborough, Boeing hoped to have three launch airlines: Malaysia, Singapore and United were the front-runners to take the new plane. In the event, however, the launch did not take place during the week of the airshow; according to rumor, that was because the Malaysians were not prepared to sign on the dotted line right away.

Prevarication among the airlines was understandable. While Boeing was attempting to sign up launch orders for the new 747, Airbus was fighting a fierce rearguard action. Its fear, and Boeing's desire, was that all the airlines in the market for a large plane would take the new Jumbo, thus crushing the demand for the Airbus alternative. To stymie the launch of the new 747, Pierson had whisked away the world's airline buyers for a luxury weekend in the French countryside near Toulouse. His aim was to spend two days explaining the marvels of the planned 3XX. If he could not actually sell them the new plane, then at least he could persuade them to delay their decision until they could choose between rival planes. The airlines could see the wisdom in that. As far as they were concerned, Boeing had held a monopoly on the top end of the market. And they knew from long experience that whenever Boeing and Airbus were competing for the same orders, prices from both manufacturers fell dramatically. Even if they did want the 747, once the 3XX was flying it would be a lot cheaper.

So far as Airbus was concerned there was now no doubt the 3XX would be launched, and it would be sometime in 1997; the plane, it reckoned, could be with the airlines by 2002. Some of the wackier designs had been dropped, and the plane had now taken on a fairly conventional shape. It would be a long, wide metal tube that just happened to be a lot longer and wider than anything else in the sky. Its first version would carry about 550 passengers, the same number as the stretched 747. But later versions, and a 3XX-200 was already being discussed with the airlines, would be able to carry almost 1,000 passengers. That plane would certainly be the king of the skies.

The key difference between the 747-500/600 and the 3XX would be the position in the lifecycle of the planes. Even Boeing officials acknowledged reluctantly that their new planes would be the last in the line of the Jumbos. If they wanted to make it any bigger they would have to come up with a completely new plane. The 3XX, by contrast, would be the first of a range; future upgrades over the next quarter of a century or so would see it gradually increasing in size.

That would, Airbus hoped, be the trump card. Though strategically vital, the 3XX would be vastly expensive. Airbus was estimating it would cost at least $8 billion, and many independent analysts figured the true figure could be closer to $10 billion. Financing it would stretch Airbus to the limit. Already the consortium had conceded it would have to reformulate itself as a limited company. Now the talk was of an eventual stockmarket listing; already a report from the American investment bank Lehman Brothers had pinned a putative value of $18 billion on the enterprise. Yet a listing would be only one way of raising the money. Some would inevitably come from the governments in the four partner countries.

And the rest would come from outside the consortium. Before finally pushing the button on the 3XX, Airbus was holding talks about bringing a range of outside partners into the project; plenty of Far Eastern candidates were still being touted, but so were American companies such as McDonnell Douglas and Northrop. Bringing in an American partner, the strategists in Toulouse were well aware, would blunt any protectionist attacks on the plane in the U.S.

The result of the battle between the new Jumbo and the 3XX will not be known for several years. But the boldness of the moves made by Airbus were yet another indication that the flames in the industry had moved elsewhere.

If there is a coda to this story, it came on January 3, 1994. Jean Pierson had called his top officials together in the executive offices of the consortium's headquarters. It was the start of a new year, the twenty-fourth of the consortium's existence, and Pierson wanted to make clear that it was also the start of a new chapter in its grand adventure. He reminded his staff of how the supervisory board had agreed a strategy for Airbus in 1975. The strategy was to create a family of aircraft, competing with the Boeing family, and the objective was to take 30 percent of the world's civil aerospace industry. "That strategy has now been largely achieved," he said. It was time for a new strategy to be put in place.

The new direction was to center primarily on costs. It has long been an axiom that Airbus, for all its marketing and design achievements, is not the most efficient manufacturer. A quick tour of its production plants illustrates why. Airbus has become byzantine, complicated even by the standards of European cooperation. Freight doors are made in Donauwoerth, in Germany; tail parts in Seville, in Spain; forward fuselages in St. Nazaire, in France, and Naples, in Italy; wing parts in Chester, England. Parts are made in one country, then flown to another for more work to be done, then back to the first for yet more work. It is a maze few can comprehend, and although the planes do get built on schedule it seems a strange way to build anything, least of all a huge capital-intensive product to be sold in a market characterized by tough price competition. The four partners cream off the revenues by being subcontractors rather than shareholders, but none of them has any idea how much profit their co-investors are booking because they do not see the profit margins on each part supplied. The system provides no incentive to drive costs down, because it is in the interests of the partners to bid high for subcontracting and draw their profits that way. If they bid low the consortium would take the profits, which would have to be shared four ways. If they bid high, they keep the subcontracting profits for themselves. Harmony has not yet persuaded any partner to bid low.

Driving costs down is the way the consortium now sees of moving forward. Shrontz had launched an initiative in the early 1990s to push down costs at Boeing by 25 percent. The strategic implication was clear: cheaper planes that would enable the company to settle into a long and bloody price war with Airbus, and Airbus would have to drive down its own costs and prices. At the same time, the European strategists were beginning to believe that a significant change had taken place in the industry. Airlines were no longer interested in technology, because passengers were not. The limits of subsonic flight had been reached, and a new experiment in supersonic flight was still a long way off. Airlines now competed on taking people from point to point with the minimum of delay and unpleasantness and at the lowest possible price. To help them drive down prices, they would be looking for cheaper planes; cheaper, not just to fly but to buy.

In such an era, Airbus had to be a cheaper manufacturer. And it could not be that until it changed the system built up over the last twenty-five years. The preference of the staffers gathered at the Toulouse headquarters in January 1994 was to see Airbus transformed into a limited company, which would permit a major assault on costs. The British were in favor, the French opposed, but could perhaps be won round, and the Germans were sitting on the fence. It was time for Airbus to become less of a political entity, symbolizing the Old World's attempts to remain an industrial power, and more of a normal commercial entity.

That was just the background. It was time for Pierson to outline a new objective. With the 30 percent market share now achieved, Airbus had to set itself a new target. This time, the target would be more explicit: "Beat Boeing," said Pierson, with an expansive gesture. An objective of no less than 50 percent of the civil aerospace market had been adopted at a formal meeting of the supervisory board. The Americans would be pushed into second place; nothing less than dominance of the industry would do.

"It is clear that we have reached a new platform and the objectives that have driven us will no longer serve," Adam Brown said later. "They have to be replaced, and this is what replaces them. The implications of it are fundamental, on things like cost, efficiency, right across the board. The adoption of the 30 percent market share objective. . .did carry with it the assumption that Boeing was always going to be number one, the dominant player in the business, and what we are now saying is that we no longer accept that as a given. And why should we accept it as a given? Why should we accept that in any area of our activities we should do less well than those guys. Why?" It was a question that found no answer among the staffers listening to Pierson's declaration; few people answer back in his presence even on less grand occasions.

To commemorate the occasion, lapel badges were distributed among the staff; against a white background, the familiar blue Boeing logo ran across the middle; stamped above it, in black lettering, was the word "Beat." Management by lapel badge and bumper sticker is very much in keeping with Pierson's style; he is a man who loves the megaphone. It is also in keeping with the style of the consortium, which has always shouted about its achievements, making a lot of noise and raising a lot of smoke.

That the consortium could set the objective and distribute the badges was a small reminder of the distance travelled. So too were the figures released early in 1995 which showed that in the past year Airbus had, for the first time, sold more planes than Boeing. Since the days of the Comet and the Caravelle, since the disasters with the Concorde, the Europeans had watched their industry decline into a sink of defeatism. They had watched as Boeing had carved out mastery of the American and then of the world industry. When Beteille and Ziegler sat in their office in Paris plotting their assault on the masters, their vision had seemed too crazy even to be publicly stated. Now, the enterprise those two had planned could talk openly about taking control of the industry, and nobody would laugh. The new objective would be accepted with deadly determination. That, in itself, was a mark of the transformation wrought as old national identities had been submerged, public money had been poured in, political forces mobilized. The European industry had re-established itself as one of the most powerful in world aerospace. The journey had been long, difficult and, at times, incredible. But it had met its goal.

CONCLUSION

WAR WITHOUT END

In early February 1993, during the second month of his presidency, Bill Clinton paid a visit to the Boeing 747 plant in Washington State. With the revival of U.S. economic power a theme of his campaign, there was no more appropriate place to start because nowhere is more symbolic of America's industrial might, or of the economic siege it now feels itself to be under.

Clinton was at Boeing to host what he termed a summit meeting of the aerospace and airline industries; eleven airlines sent their top officials, and all the main American airframe and engine manufacturers were in attendance. It was a listening session, called by the President to learn more about the difficulties of the industry and to show that he was doing something, even if it was only talking. A tub-thumping populist by every instinct, Clinton also talked to the workers directly. In the afternoon, the 3000 or so workers on the line downed tools, gathering within the vast empty spaces of the plant to listen to the President. The mood was sour. There was an air of bitterness in the plant, an atmosphere Clinton quickly sensed. Boeing had just sent out letters to many of the workforce warning that they might be among the 28,000 the company would lay off in 1993 — its response to the downturn in the industry.

Clinton ripped into the forces which, to many there, seemed responsible for depriving them of their jobs and their security. "A lot of these layoffs would not have been announced if it had not been for the $26 billion the United States sat by and allowed the Europeans to plough into Airbus." he said. "My trade ambassador, Mickey Kantor, will be closely monitoring the agreement which was made finally last year with regard to limiting European subsidies for Airbus. We'll be seeking tough new disciplines on those subsidies. You know, I've seen these agreements made for years. I've seen people promise us they'll do this, that and the other thing and then nothing ever happens. This time we will change the rules of the game."

It was a tough and unsubtle pitch against foreigners who played by different, un-American, and unfair rules. The President was happy to play on his listeners' darkest fears and remind them that though other politicians had deserted them, he would not.

Airbus was used to being roasted by Boeing and senators and congressmen, but this was different: a president of the United States had attacked them directly and by name. A response was called for. The attacks would hurt them in the American market, if nothing else. It was decided that John Major should go to bat for the Europeans. Kohl and Mitterrand were too marked by past trade conflicts, and the British were supposed to have a "special relationship" with the Americans. The Prime Minister was due to have a meeting with Clinton in Washington later that month, and the Airbus issue was added to the agenda. If Clinton wanted to pick fights, the Europeans were waiting.

Major had some success. After he had restated the arguments, and reminded the President that the two sides had just reached bilateral agreement on the subsidies issue, Clinton's statement modified the views expressed so trenchantly in Seattle. At a press conference, he put a different emphasis on the battle. "It costs a great deal of money to develop an aircraft, to break into new markets and to go forward," he explained. "The argument I was trying to make to Boeing workers is, and I will restate it here, that the adversity they have suffered in the past is through no fault of their own. That is, they have not failed by being unproductive, lazy or asking too much. But Europe was able to penetrate this market because of the Airbus policy. And the blame was on our own government for not responding, not Europe's for trying to get in. That was their right. It was legal under international law and they did it."

For Pierson and his people there were important nuances in that statement — in some ways it was a vindication of all they had done. Clinton had acknowledged that theirs was a legitimate enterprise, and that Europeans had a right to make airplanes. There had been a reluctance in the U.S. to allow that point in the past: both manufacturers and government officials had been known to remark that Europeans made good cheeses, and other products — why were they trying to make planes as well? Recognizing their right to be in the market was progress of a sort, but it contained a threat as well. Clinton was criticizing his predecessors for not having done enough to help the U.S. aerospace industry. And he was promising to do more.

As the mid-point of the decade approached and Airbus prepared to celebrate the first twenty-five years of its incursion into the aerospace business, the nature of this conflict was subtly changing shape. There was now grudging recognition that the U.S. market would have to be shared with the Europeans; that this was a war of attrition, where there would be no knock-out blows. That change was in part a reflection of a shift in the political climate. With Clinton's election, the tacticians and strategists who had pioneered the Airbus experiment now had admirers in the White House. Laura D'Andrea Tyson, Chairman of the Council of Economic Advisers and therefore a senior adviser on economic and industrial matters, had written admiringly about Airbus in her work on state promotion of high-technology industry. The notion of using the state, in partnership with private enterprise, to promote the prosperity of the nation was no longer anathema in U.S. government circles. Beneath the charged rhetoric, a form of convergence between the two camps seemed to be underway.

Clinton quickly fulfilled his promise to help the industry. In Congress a bill went forward in 1993 to create a consortium, called Aerotech, funded with up to $10 billion of government money, to subsidize the industry; opinion varied on what precisely should be done with the money, but some at least thought it should be an American Airbus — a small plane to compete with the A320. The bill did not become law, but it picked up backing and chimed with the policy of a White House known to be looking to save McDonnell Douglas's civil aerospace business if the expected collapse came. Clinton also authorized an extra $1 billion a year in NASA spending on research on civil aerospace, money specifically aimed at helping the American industry to regain its technological edge, which NASA conceded had been surrendered to the Europeans.

In the end, it was Boeing, rather than the U.S. government, that came to the aid of McDonnell Douglas. In December 1996, the Seattle company surprised the rest of the world, but few people within the industry, when it announced it was buying McDonnell for $13 billion, and that the name of its long-time competitor, perhaps the most celebrated in American aviation, would disappear. With sales of $48 billion, and 200,000 employees, the entire civilian aerospace industry — plus a large chunk of the military production — of the U.S. would now come under Boeing's control.

By the end of 1996, McDonnell Douglas badly needed to do something. In civilian aerospace, the MD-11 had failed to kickstart the company, and plans to build a new Jumbo in collaboration with Asian partners had come to nothing. By now, the company was down to just 5 percent of the world market. It has also lost some key military contracts, putting the financial future of the company in danger. It had, earlier in the year, held merger talks with Boeing, which had initially come to nothing. It had also held talks with Airbus, partly about collaborating on the 3XX, partly about subcontracting some of its manufacturing (building planes on American soil, the strategists in Toulouse figured, would defuse much of the criticism of the consortium in the U.S.). It had also looked at the possibility of taking over an electronics company to diversify its activities. But in the end it was only Boeing that was making a credible offer for the company, one that Wall Street shareholders would not allow it to ignore.

The deal strengthened Boeing, removing a competitor that could still be an occasional thorn in its side, and bolstered its position in military aerospace, where it had never been so dominant. In private, Boeing officials would probably concede the deal gave a point or two to Airbus. The objective of the consortium had always been to take out McDonnell Douglas before going after Boeing, and the airlines would now be determined to make sure Airbus stayed in business, since they could never tolerate handing a monopoly of the market to Boeing. But, for the Seattle company, the advantages of the deal outweighed those drawbacks.

The merger certainly had the backing of the White House. Putting together Boeing and McDonnell Douglas would create the kind of national champion the Clinton Administration had wanted to encourage. And now, instead of having to juggle its attention between two very different companies, it could devote its energies to supporting the enlarged Boeing.

The most dramatic demonstration of that commitment had come in Saudi Arabia. As we saw, Clinton mobilized his entire administration to swing the order to Boeing and McDonnell Douglas. As Mitterrand had described himself as the top Airbus salesmen, so Clinton was happy to act for Boeing. This was the first time Mitterrand had competed with another head of state, and the clash was a dramatic illustration of how economic and trade competition had risen to the top of the political agenda. American sources said the President would not be involved in day-to-day sales campaigns, but would be the big gun on huge orders or in tricky political situations. The competition was changing shape.

In a way it was a tribute to Airbus; imitation is the sincerest form of flattery, and the techniques being deployed by the Americans looked remarkably like those the Europeans had used for more than two decades. Perhaps the main difference was that the Americans felt less comfortable with the role than the Europeans had been. Clinton's overt salesmanship drew some sharp rebukes from Americans who felt the presidency was created for something better than flogging aircraft. A columnist in the *Washington Post* wrote of "crass mercantilism" and concluded, "It demeans the Presidency."

Which perhaps it does; selling aircraft is a less noble task than creating peace, promoting equality and so on. But if you live in a world of crass mercantilism, you have to be realistic; ignoring the reality may cost the jobs of thousands of people. Which brings us neatly to a question that has so far been evaded — who is right and who is wrong? and for all its achievements, has the Airbus adventure been worthwhile?

The case against Airbus usually starts prosaically: it is subsidized, and subsidies are wrong. Subsidies pour taxpayers' money into industrial ventures they would not endorse privately, and distort the market because they allow some inefficient producers to drive out more efficient producers. To which the defense has two answers. One is to say that Airbus has not been subsidized at all. It has received government loans, which are being repaid; Airbus maintains that $600 million was repaid in 1991 and $700 million in 1992. Repayments of $1 billion are scheduled for each year from 1993 to 1996, then $600 million each year to 2006 (a total of roughly $10 billion over fifteen years). Certainly the European governments believe that the A320 program will be profitable, and the A330/A340 too, but it is acknowledged that the A300 will never show a profit. To argue that it is wrong simply because it has not made money from day one is to impose ridiculous demands; few businesses make money from day one, nor is manufacturing at a loss to gain presence in a market a tactic restricted to Airbus. This is little more than standard commercial practice. The second line of defense is that the American industry has been subsidized as well, and the European subsidies, though more explicit, are nothing more than a counter-balance to the advantages enjoyed by U.S. manufacturers. Whichever line of defense is chosen, the charge can be deflected.

A more sophisticated allegation invokes the notions of comparative advantage and opportunity cost: the American industry has a comparative advantage in producing airplanes, largely because of the historical weight and dominance of its industry. It will therefore always be able to produce planes more efficiently than the Europeans. Although Airbus may be able to make up with subsidies the difference in relative efficiency and so compete effectively, the opportunity cost is ignored. The money spent on Airbus could be used for industries which already do have comparative advantage, and where the returns would be higher. The point is that the money consumed by the consortium might be better used elsewhere.

This comes closer to the nub of the issue, but there is still a defense. Comparative advantage in producing planes, like most high-technology products, is not natural. It is created over time. If the U.S. has an advantage, it is the result of historical circumstances, not of geography, resources or other natural factors. By spending money on Airbus the Europeans can create comparative advantage in making aircraft. Once that has been done, skilled, well-paid jobs and valuable exports will follow, earning unanticipated wealth for Europe. For the protagonists, that is what industrial policy should be about; nurturing industries, making advantages, and thus creating sustainable wealth. For them, Airbus represents all that is best about policies of industrial renewal, and is an example that should be followed elsewhere. In Europe, and in Brussels in particular, there is constant discussion about "creating Airbuses" for other industries, ranging from computing to films.

In truth, the answer to who is right and who is wrong is unlikely to be settled in the dry arena of academic theories; the answer is more likely to turn on which side of the Atlantic it is posed. For Americans, Boeing will always be in the right. Europeans, with the exception of those devotees of Americana sometimes found in Britain, will support Airbus. In a clash between continents, people root for the home team; the blinkers of nationalism come down, blinding the spectators to anything but the virtue of their own side. They recognize that their own prosperity and security is dependent on the strength of the economies of their country or continent, and that prosperity is dependent on the success of their industrial champions.

More than pride is at stake here; the economic fate of continents hangs in the balance, with all that implies. Which is why compromise is impossible. And why the war continues without end and the battle rages without redemption. Too much is at stake for either side to abandon the field now.

NOTES

Chapter 1

1. *Sky Fever: The Autobiography of Sir Geoffrey Dc Havilland* (Airlife Publications, 1979).
2. *Audit of War* by Correlli Barnett (Macmillan, London, 1986).
3. *Sky Fever.*
4. *DH: A History of De Havilland* by C. Martin Sharp (1982).
5. *Sky Fever.*

Chapter 2

1. *Vision: A Saga of the Sky* by Harold Mansfield (Madison Publishing Associates, New York, 1986).
2. *Barons of the Sky* by Wayne Biddle (Simon & Schuster, 1991).
3. ibid.
4. *Boeing in Peace and War,* by E.E. Bauer (TABA Publishing, 1990).

Chapter 3

1. *Concorde: The Inside Story* by Geoffrey Knight (Weidenfeld Nicolson, 1976).
2. ibid.
3. *British Aircraft Corporation: A History* by Charles Gardner (Batsford, London, 1981).
4. *An American Saga* by Robert Daley (Random House, 1980).
5. *Clipped Wings* by Mel Horwitch (Cambridge, Mass., 1982).
6. *Concorde: The Inside Story.*
7. ibid.
8. ibid.

Chapter 4

1. *Boeing in Peace and War.*
2. Author interview, April 1992.
3. *Widebody: The Making of the 747* by Clifford Irving (Hodder and Stoughton, 1993).
4. Author interview, April 1992.
5. *Widebody.*
6. *Boeing in Peace and War.*

Chapter 5

1. *The American Challenge* by Jean-Jacques Servan-Schreiber (Penguin Books, Harmondsworth, 1969).
2. *The Crossman Diaries* by Richard Crossman (Hamish Hamilton, 1977).
3. Quoted in *The Sporty Game* by Jonathan Newhouse (Knopf, 1982).
4. ibid.
5. *Dogfight* by Ian McIntyre (Praeger 1992).
6. Quoted in *Business Week,* January 1982.

Chapter 6

1. Seattle *Post Intelligencer,* 1980.
2. Quoted in *Empires of the Sky* by Anthony Sampson (Hodder and Stoughton, 1984).
3. *Widebody.*
4. Author interview, 1992.
5. Quoted in *Fortune,* 1978.
6. Quoted in *The Sporty Game.*

Chapter 7

1. *The Sporty Game.*
2. *International Collaboration in Civil Aerospace* by Keith Heywood (Francis Pinter, 1986).
3. ibid.
4. Author interview, April 1992.
5. Author interview, 1993.
6. Quoted in *Dogfight.*
7. Author interview, 1993.
8. *Dogfight.*
9. Author interview, 1993.

Chapter 8

1. Author interview, 1993.
2. Author interview, 1993.
3. Quoted in *Boeing in Peace and War.*
4. Airbus has had to deal with several crashes of A320s, but the consortium has not yet had to shoulder the blame, which investigators have attributed to pilot error. It has also been hit by strikes, particularly at British Aerospace, where the supply of wings was held up by industrial action, creating tensions within the partnership.
5. Quoted in *Dogfight.*
6. Author interview, 1993.
7. The report excluded contributions from Spain as being too small to be worth worrying about, but noted that money from that country, plus money from the two associate members, the Netherlands and Belgium, made the total even higher.
8. Author interview, 1993.
9. Author interview, 1993.
10. Author interview, 1993. It is worth noting that Japan Air Lines operates the largest fleet of 767s outside the U.S.
11. Author interview, 1993.
12. Quoted in Airbus Industrie booklet, *Competition in Commercial Aircraft Manufacturing.*
13. Author interview, 1993.

Chapter 9

1. Author interview, 1993.
2. Author interview, 1993.
3. Quoted in the *International Herald Tribune,* 1992.
4. Author interview, 1993.

INDEX